P9-CCZ-683

Ford, Jack S.

GV
885.3
.F67
1989

The fundamental five

DATE DUE

GV
885.3
.F67
1989

LIBRARY/LRC
OUACHITA TECHNICAL COLLEGE
P.O. BOX 816
MALVERN, ARKANSAS 72104

OUACHITA TECHNICAL COLLEGE
LIBRARY/LRC

3 9005 00003 4029

The Fundamental Five

About the Author

Jack Ford has coached at all levels of basketball. He may be the only coach in Indiana to have both an NCAA championship ring and an IHSAA ring. In 1986, he was an assistant for the NCAA National Champions, the University of Louisville. In 1980, he guided the New Albany Bulldogs to the state championship game of Indiana High School basketball.

In 26 years of head coaching at the high school level, he has enjoyed a degree of success. He has been selected coach of the year eleven times, won over 300 games, won twenty-one league and tournament championships, seen over 100 of his players continue to play college basketball in almost every state of the union. He is now the dean of coaches on the prestigious UPI Board of Coaches, going into 12 years. The International Sports Exchange selected Coach Ford to coach the first team of Indiana players to play overseas.

Coach Ford has had the best season in the schools history at five different high schools. At each of these schools his teams broke about every record, team and individual, in the school's history. The teams won more games, more tournaments, and more conference games than any other time period. This was done while competing against some of the finest teams in Indiana, the hot bed of high school basketball in the world.

Turning basketball programs around has been a trait of Coach Ford. The first year at Boonville, the team had the first winning season in eight years and made it to the championship game of the Sectional, also first in eight years. The second year capped off the best season in the school's history, making it to the Sweet Sixteen by winning not only the Sectional but the Evansville Regional. At Leesburg, they had not had a winning season in over ten years and had only won four games in the previous three years. They not only had the best season in the school's history, but won the most games in a row, most points in a game (120), highest single season scoring average, and won the first tourney Leesburg had won in 42 years. It was also the first time the Blue Blazers had ever been ranked in any poll. Madison–Grant had never won a sectional or county championship before Coach Ford came. The Argylls topped off the best season in the school's history with both championships. Lowell had lost 64 games in a row just prior to Coach Ford's arrival. They had never won a sectional. The Red Devil's won two sectionals while having the best years ever in basketball during Coach Ford's stay there. At New Albany, the state's oldest high school, Coach Ford had the only undefeated season in the school's history. He also had the best record in the Hoosier Hills Conference including 3 conference championships, and 4 sectional championships in a 6 year period. They had won only 1 conference championship in 20 years. His teams were state ranked every year, including 1980 when they were ranked number one.

Coach Ford has written several articles for various publications. He has a weekly newsletter that is sent to various media throughout the state of Indiana. He has spoken at many clinics but this is his first attempt at a book on basketball.

The Fundamental Five

Jack S. Ford
Washington High School

WM.C.BROWN
DIRECT

wcb

Chairman of the Board *Wm. C. Brown*
President and Chief Executive Officer *Mark C. Falb*
Wm. C. Brown Direct
A Division of Wm. C. Brown Publishers
Championship Series
President *G. Franklin Lewis*
Vice President, Editor-in-Chief *George Wm. Bergquist*
Vice President, Director of Production *Beverly Kolz*
Director, Championship Series *Thomas E. Doran*
Editor *Edward Bartell*
Editor, Academic Athlete Series *Chris Rogers*
Project Editor *Beth Kundert*
Production Editorial Manager *Colleen A. Yonda*
Production Editorial Manager *Julie A. Kennedy*
Publishing Services Manager *Karen J. Slaght*
Manager of Visuals and Design *Faye M. Schilling*

Copyright © 1989 by Wm. C. Brown Publishers. All rights reserved

Library of Congress Catalog Card Number: 88–63267

ISBN 0–697–06371–2

No part of this publication may be reproduced, stored in a retrieval
system, or transmitted, in any form or by any means, electronic,
mechanical, photocopying, recording, or otherwise, without the
prior written permission of the publisher.

Printed in the United States of America by Wm. C. Brown Publishers
2460 Kerper Boulevard, Dubuque, IA 52001

10 9 8 7 6 5 4 3 2 1

Dedication

To Nancy, a true coach's wife, daughter Jill, and to the outstanding players, including my son Ric, who have made ``The Fun of Basketball is Winning''.

Contents

Foreword

In the spring of 1985, Jack Ford, no stranger to us at the University of Louisville, had an appointment with me to interview for the volunteer assistant position previously held by Scott Davenport. Jack had had a fine high school coaching record — the previous seven years had been spent at New Albany High School, Indiana, just across the river from Louisville. His 1980 team played in the Indiana High School Final Four in Market Square Arena just a week after we were winning the NCAA Championship there. There were as many spectators for those games as there were at the NCAA Finals. The Louisville media, always realizing the intensity of Indiana high school basketball, had given it great publicity. We had followed many of Jack's teams and recruited some of his players. Jack had brought his teams to our practices and games several times; therefore, when Jack was interested in joining us, I knew it was not just a matter of casual interest.

Jerry Jones, my long-time assistant at Louisville, encouraged considering Jack for the position. Jerry grew up in Indiana, played at Merrillville High School, and had coached at Crown Point. These two Indiana high schools are rivals of Lowell High School, where Jack had coached for six years. Jerry first met Jack in the mid-sixties in Lake County, Indiana and remembered him as an enthusiastic coach who turned around a losing program. (Lowell had lost 64 games in a row prior to Jack's arrival. Jack is still the winningest coach they have ever had.) Jerry now lives in Jeffersonville, Indiana which had dominated southern Indiana basketball until Jack arrived and brought back the tradition and glory to New Albany basketball.

Jack Ford always believed that high school coaches should associate themselves with their local universities. Since his players often attended practices and saw our team play, they employed many of our techniques. Jack used our program to help promote his own and was so well informed on Louisville basketball that the transition to our program was an easy one for him.

I believe personality is a factor of a coaching staff — that the staff should reflect the personality of the head coach. Jack told me that was one of the reasons University of Louisville appealed to him. He felt his personality could relate to ours and liked our approach to the teaching of basketball. A lot of my ideas are techniques from *my* mentor, John Wooden, who Jack had admired before I came to Louisville.

During the course of our 1986 championship season, it was clear that Jack wanted to work and be involved. Though he had always been a head coach he wanted to be the best assistant he could possibly be. Beyond his job requirements he gave me notes on scrimmages, scouting reports, and developed a chart for covering our offenses and defenses that Jerry Jones used in evaluating our games.

Jack also accepts challenges. At one of our first practices, players were asked to make 8 of 10 free throws before they could leave. Avery Marshall, a freshman from Myrtle Beach, South Carolina, was at Jack's basket during the drill. Jack came into the dressing room long after the rest of the staff had left. He wouldn't let Avery leave until he had met the task. I told him that if he wanted a challenge, make Avery a free-throw shooter. Avery did make 10 in a row several times in practice late in the season.

Jack's experiences have given him a good basketball mind. At halftime, coaches would always meet in my office in Freedom Hall. More than once Coach Ford had noticed something that could help us in the second half.

He has always tried to be active in practice. At one practice we were isolating Pervis Ellison on a roll to the basket. Jack was guarding Pervis, really denying Pervis the ball. I stopped the drill and reminded Pervis that he was "letting a 47-year-old man beat him." The next play Pervis stepped over Coach Ford, got the ball, and slammed it home. Pervis had "hooked" Jack, who lost his balance and landed on his behind. I grinned. Jack said later, "I wish you hadn't said that!" However, he knew it helped Pervis work harder.

Jack Ford has a Christian background and has always started each game with the Lord's Prayer as we have at the University of Louisville.

Coach Ford also started a favorite "coaching ritual." After I had finished talking to the team after the first win, Jack quietly came up and wrote on the blackboard, "The Fun of Basketball Is Winning." Subsequently and automatically the players would say as I walked out, "Write it up, Coach Ford." Jack Ford truly loves the game and his enthusiasm spreads.

In reviewing his book, I found Jack Ford's philosophy to have players fundamentally sound very evident. At Louisville, we always try to recruit fundamentally strong players; nonetheless we still work a great deal on fundamentals. If all of our players with their natural talent had all the fundamentals listed in this book, our job at the university would certainly be easier. Jack's teams at New Albany were always fundamentally strong.

In reading this book, it is obvious that Louisville basketball has had an influence on the text. The sideline break (fly fast break), the high post offense, guard cuts (2-cut) are all part of the Louisville basketball program. Jack's numbering approach is different than ours, but the fundamentals taught certainly would help any player entering our program.

Denny Crum
University of Louisville,
Kentucky

Acknowledgments

The list of people who have contributed to this book either directly or indirectly are numerous. I am sure I will leave someone out. However, my wife, Nancy, provided the majority of the clerical and grammatical help for this text.

There were many coaches who have had an influence on basketball in my life. High school coaches Don Reichert (Fort Wayne South Side), By Hey (Fort Wayne North Side) and Virgil Sweet (Valparaiso High School) were the most influential on the prep level. My college coaches at Indiana University, Gene Ring, Lou Watson, and Branch McCracken gave me an opportunity to play and learn. Present college coaches Bob Knight (Indiana) and Gene Keady (Purdue) have influenced my style and many others style in this great state of basketball.

I want to especially thank Denny Crum and Louisville's number one assistant, Jerry Jones, for the opportunity to be on the staff of the 1986 National Champions. It is obvious that this influence is shown in this book.

My assistant coaches not only helped develop many fine players, but contributed to my knowledge of the game. The following list includes not only the high school assistants, but many fine elementary and junior high coaches have also contributed. The coaches are Roger Parks (Brook); Scott Hosler, Carel Prater, Charles Lentz (Leesburg); Bill Weiand, Armand Reyes (Lowell); Jim Miller, Dave Strasemeier, Jeff Summers (Madison-Grant); Mike Huey, Tom Miller, Keith McKinney (Boonville); Steve Johnson (Elkhart Memorial); Charlie Vass, Louis Jensen, Doug Bierman (New Albany); and Steve Brothers, Bill Thompson, Charlie Goddard, Rob McCormick, and Mike Hankins (Washington).

Special thanks should be given to the players, especially the many All-State ones that include my son Ric, All-Americans Richie Johnson, Dave Bennett, and Bubby Mukes.

Introduction

This text was developed after years of experience. I have been fortunate to coach on all levels of basketball — elementary, junior high, high school, and NCAA Division one.

Why purchase a coaching book?

1. To find an offense or defense that will fit your personnel
2. To find a new offense to replace your old one
3. To perfect your ideas of offense and defense
4. To find drills and "little things" that will make your ideas work better

When I decided to write this text, I kept the above in mind. Most of the ideas are not new. Basketball is a relatively simple game — you don't want to complicate it — yet, there are a lot of little things you may have time to perfect, if your talent is sufficient. Also, the "little things" may make average talent into championship teams.

Fundamentally strong teams are usually the winners. Great athletes can overcome fundamental mistakes and win. However, with athletic ability being nearly equal, fundamentals will come out on top.

The Fundamental Five takes the five most basic plays in basketball and deals with them individually and within an entire offensive and defensive concept. Individually each of these plays can be developed into an entire offense. If a player can perform these five offensive maneuvers, he can perform *any* offense. In the same manner, if he can defend these five plays, he can defend any offense.

The plays have been called by various names; however, the pick and roll, pass and cut (sometimes called give and go), cut through, pick opposite, and shuffle cut are the most popular names for these five plays. The text will show how these have been used as offenses as well as parts of offenses. The fundamentals of these five basic plays, both offensively and defensively, will be outlined.

The offensive concepts are multiple, applicable to both man and zone defenses. The concepts are carried into special situations, out-of-bounds plays, press offenses, delay offenses, etc. and are easy to teach and install. The concepts are expandable; they can be run directly from the fast break. All levels of play can adapt to this material.

This book can be used at any level. The elementary and junior high coach can definitely use the basic fundamentals and even use each play as an offense. These fundamentals eventually will fit into any high school program. The freshman and junior varsity programs can continue the development of fundamentals and preparation of the varsity offense. The varsity coach can use the fundamentals to sharpen his offense or even use the fly fast break with the ruled offense.

College-level coaches recruit talent and sometimes raw talent isn't fundamentally sound. The fundamentals, especially in defense, need to be developed — the Fundamental Five may provide some insight. Both the high school varsity and the college coach may discover in this book some ideas of toning up his offense or defense. These ideas, tested over a period of 25 years on all levels of basketball from the third grade elementary to Division One collegiate level, are sound, no-frills, basic basketball ideas.

The chapter on the coding system will help coaches and players communicate offenses and defenses. It shows a simplified way of explaining and communicating various offensive patterns so that everyone understands what is going on in the offense.

The chapter on the zone offense simply gives some fundamental ideas of attacking various zones, including the match-up. The five fundamental offensive plays can be used to attack zones.

The fast break chapter deals with the use of the sideline break. The traditional three-man break is still an outstanding way to run the break; however, the ideas of the sideline break may give some different aspects of getting into offense from the break. The offense could be set or a ruled offense.

The ruled offense chapter concerns itself with a passing motion type of offense involving all of the Fundamental Five. Philosophies may differ here. This may give some coaches ideas how to add to their present offenses by adding some of these ruled options.

At the end of the chapter, there are some specific drills that have been tested by championship teams on their way to tournament titles. Drills that relate to the offense and defense are important. Some of these drills can be used for pre-game warm-ups.

This book is not a cure-all. It doesn't cover every phase of the game. However, if every player you coached had mastery of the Fundamental Five, both offensively and defensively, the game would certainly be easier to coach.

I hope you enjoy this material as much as I have in developing it. Most of it is "borrowed" from excellent coaches in the game. However, all of it is fundamentally sound and successful — it has provided twenty-one league and tournament championships and has awarded me with 11 Coach of the Year honors. Five different high schools employing these fundamentals each had the best basketball season in their school's history. The Fundamental Five has helped me develop a motto in one of the most competitive basketball states in the union: "The Fun of Basketball Is Winning!!"

The Fundamental Five Coding System

Development of the Fundamental Five

One of the most demanding problems in education today is deciding what to teach — the same problem extends into coaching. The offense or defense you choose may determine success or failure. Any coach (or teacher) will tell you that he wants a fundamentally strong team. This is why the Fundamental Five was developed.

I was searching for the ultimate offense: the one I would never want to change during my coaching career, no matter what my personnel was like; the offense that could be used in the elementary and junior high systems; one that was simple enough to relate to the young player, yet complicated enough to compete with the better defense of today's basketball.

One of the biggest problems for the high school coach is the constant turnover of personnel. Unlike the college or pro coach, he cannot recruit a big pivot man or quick, slick guard to run a specific offense. He must do with whomever turns out, and he must have the right offense for them. Even so, the offense must fit the personnel.

When I began looking for the "just right" offense, I had several things in mind. First, it had to be adjustable to the various defenses, such as man-to-man, zones, match-ups, etc. Second, it had to be adjustable to the various levels of our basketball program — you cannot always run a complicated offense on the elementary and junior high levels. There had to be developmental phases.

In analyzing the trends in offense, I kept coming across five specific movements. Every offense I studied possessed at least one of these moves. I thought, why not adopt all of them? And that is what I did. I started with the alignment best suited to our personnel and then slotted in the five fundamental movements or plays. I determined which of the plays were best suited to the talent at hand.

However, all of the fundamental moves were worked upon. This is still the basic premise today, even though we use a ruled passing game offense as well as pattern offense.

It did not make much difference what our initial alignment was (2-1-2, 1-3-1, etc.). The plays remained the same. In short, the five fundamental plays, with individual options, made up our offense. My original alignment was a one-guard offensive set because originally I only had two boys over six feet tall to play forwards and was fortunate to have the good ball handler to play the point. It really didn't matter what alignment was used.

This enabled me to educate everyone in the school system on the offensive fundamentals they would be using on the high school varsity. The Fundamental Five were simple enough to be taught in the elementary grades, yet they gave us a great deal of flexibility. If any coach in the system needed a different alignment, because of personnel, he could use it and switch emphasis on the plays. The fundamentals of the varsity offenses were still being worked upon.

The teams I coached early in my career were not very patient. I had been through the era of the "Hurrying Hoosiers" as a player at Indiana University. I was influenced, as most young coaches are, by my college experience. Therefore, the fast break was the thing we concentrated upon. I still believe the break is the most potent offensive weapon in the game. Some of the things Branch McCracken taught at Indiana University are still valuable in the concept of the fast break.

If we didn't get a good shot off the break, we always seemed to get one off the first option of whatever play option of the Fundamental Five we ran. More often than not, we probably forced the shot. We won, at least our share. There didn't appear to be any need for changing.

However, as scouting got better, as defenses, coaching, and competition improved, my philosophy changed somewhat. A few losses took care of that; good defensive teams were controlling the break. My teams may not have been as overpowering. We needed more than the fast break and one or two good play options at the end.

Development of the Coding System

At this period of time, I felt we had five different offenses, run from various sets. The plays were basically mirrored. If we didn't get a shot from the right side, we ran it to the left.

However, I found that instead of running continuous pick and rolls or pass and cuts, we could develop patterns using more than one of our plays. I didn't want to complicate things, just execute well; I didn't want to go to any particular pattern offense but instead have a multiple-option offense.

Before any multiple-option offense can be performed, the fundamental moves described in the subsequent chapters must be learned. I have had high school teams who had trouble handling anything beyond the first move. The

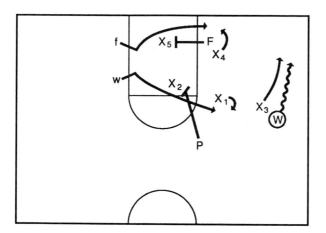

Diagram 1.1   41 Play (4 Option)

problem with most offenses is execution, no matter what level of play it is. However, as one progresses up the ladder of basketball ability, the need for second and third options is necessary.

The five basic plays make up the basis of the code system. A 23 "two three" play is simply a 2 play followed by a 3 play. It is easier to say run a "23" than to say "run a pass and cut followed by a clear out cut through off the baseline screen." Of course, the more digits involved, the more complicated the offense. Obviously, it is going to take longer to explain using words. The options are usually pre-set or told during a time-out.

RULE: If we are going to run any multiple play, we have pre-organized the second and/or third options. We only call the first number of the play during the game; e.g., if we are running 3 as a second option of a 23 play, we call out "2."

This is where I feel the ingenuity and individuality of coaching takes place. In our system of play, the offensive options used by the varsity may not be the ones best suited to the reserve squad. However, we are teaching the same fundamentals and if players are asked to change, the change is not as difficult.

Concentration and scoring on the beginning play option is important. Proper execution should result in a good shot. However, good defensive execution is going to try to stop a good shot from being attempted. You cannot just keep saying, "If you execute properly, you will score." Sometimes defensive execution on a certain play will be much better than the offense. However, in doing so the defense may give up something on the next option. They may overextend themselves in defending the first play so that the second option is easier to execute.

Suppose the offense is running 41. Diagram 1.1 shows the 4 play with the defense sagging and switching. The 4 play, a pick opposite, is difficult to execute because of switching and sagging of both the defensive forwards and guards.

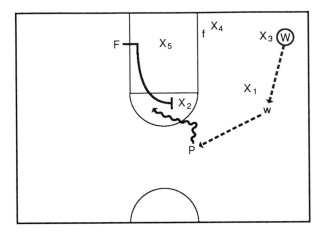

Diagram 1.2   41 Play (1 Option)

Note that X_1 and X_2 have sagged so deep that W must pass back to w. If w is a good shooter from where he receives the ball, you will have your good shot. If not, or if X_1 recovers to w before his shot, the defense may have won this phase of execution.

The defense is now "set up" for the 1 option if P is a good shooter. The 1, pick and roll, play is a two-man play and the offense should be better able to execute the play as shown in diagram 1.2. X_2 and X_5 must recover to defend P and F on the 1 play.

Other options may be good in this situation. Scouting, game conditions, etc. may determine the options. Coaching determines which options and the Fundamental Five prepares the players for changes.

Since there are 25 plays or play patterns by using the two-number system, it is obvious that a team would not use them all. But the teaching of the Fundamental Five can lead to such diversity. A set play type of team could theoretically run a different two-option play each time down the floor and not repeat during the game. This obviously would take extremely intelligent players, but change certainly can be communicated on an easier basis.

Methods of Orally "Calling Plays"

The lead guard or point guard calls out a play each time down the floor. This is why many teams have gone to a point guard or floor general. The oral command could come from the coach and then be relayed to the players. Since all players might not be able to hear from one local call, it is certainly recommended that the call is "relayed" orally to the other players. Coach Denny Crum of the University of Louisville feels his voice is recognized by the players on the floor. His play calling is relayed by the players.

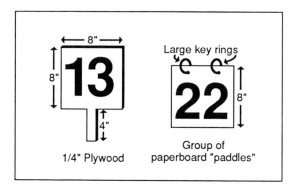

Diagram 1.3 Diagram of Paddles

"Finger Signals"

For years teams have been calling signals by the use of the number of held-up fingers. The pros use this method. The Fundamental Five easily relates to this because of the number of fingers. Again the use of a single guard helps, although any guard with the ball could signal the play after a corresponding signal from the coach.

"Huddle" at Free Throw

Many teams huddle both offensively and defensively when a free throw is being shot. This is certainly a golden opportunity to get a play(s) called. Obviously, unless you are going to stay with a certain play pattern until the next free throw, a series of plays must be called. This is an excellent time to change the offensive set-up and run the plays from a high post rather than a low, etc. It is also an excellent time to set up a press. Your opponents know this too and it could keep them off guard.

Paddle or Card System

Indiana high school basketball is exciting. It has the only million-dollar high school tourney in the world. Needless to say, avid fans are noisy, making verbal contact with your players on the floor sometimes impossible. The method of holding up fingers (especially with multiple offense) is obviously confusing.

Defensive and offensive paddles about the size of table tennis paddles were constructed to give our players better knowledge of when we are changing defenses or offenses. (Diagram 1.3) Usually one coach is designated to handle the offensive paddles and another to handle the defensive ones. A player needs to just glance over to the bench to determine which offense or defense we are in.

The advantages created by the use of these paddles are unlimited. We eliminate the time-out for a change of offense or defense. Many times during a game, precious time is gained by a player not conversing with the coach. The ball is not stolen because of confusion of what offense the team is playing. Out-of-bounds plays are read from the bench.

Other methods similar to the paddle system could be used, such as large cards or even a large blackboard. We use the large cards to designate the player alignment, such as high post, stack, etc. or to get other information across to the players quickly, without confusion; after all, coaches are "supposed" to stay on the bench.

Some coaches are concerned that opposing coaches and players will know what they are doing on offense and defense. To a degree this can happen. However, our philosophy has always been that what is most important is that our players know what we are doing. They are trained to look at the paddles and signs and follow up with automatic reactions. The opposition has only one week or less to prepare their players to "look" and often, in fact, make more mistakes looking for our play changes and trying to remember what the numbers and signs stand for than if they would just play the game.

As with everything else in this book, the paddle system is something we like and have had success with. I have seen a lot of coaches try this in the 20-plus years I have used it. Though it is not essential to the Fundamental Five, it has been a successful aid to communication.

I do not care that the opposition knows some of our changes. I *do* want our players to know what offense or defense *we* are in. If it is affecting the outcome of the game, I can always change the numbers and let 2 be 3, but I have never felt this to be necessary. In fact, if the opponents become so interested in looking at our paddles, we may have broken their concentration to the point where it can backfire on them.

Our players are taught to glance at the paddles, not "study" them. The Indianapolis 500 has been signaling to its fast-moving cars with signs for years. In fast-moving basketball, players can be trained to do the same thing.

Innovation has its drawbacks and humor. One year in the Sectional Tourney, our Madison-Grant team was playing Mississinewa, a local rival. The paddles had become one of the trademarks. Since we were the defending champions, the opposition was high for an upset. They had planned to hold up paper paddles with various numbers anytime our staff did it. We did not make any changes until nearly halftime. When we finally held up a sign, I thought our ten-point lead had vanished and they had scored an eleven-point play. Those paper paddles were flying and the cheering was deafening. I will admit it fired up the Indians, but we still won the game.

You take a lot of kidding when you try anything new or out of the ordinary. At one officials' banquet, I was presented a paddle with a whistle on it. I was supposed to hold it up when I wanted a good call. At the Sectional Championship game, I got that paddle out and called one of the officials over. For any championship game, there is bound to be tension, not only from the players and coaches, but the officials. When I told him that when I held this paddle up I expected a good call, he cracked up with laughter. Later during the game, after a controversial call I held up the paddle. He broke into a wide grin. I can't say we got better calls from it, but it certainly did not hurt his attitude toward us. Incidentally, we won the game.

If you use the paddle system or any other innovative system, you have to be ready for these kinds of criticism. However, if the end results are positive for your team's success, who cares. If you are winning, you will receive the most attention for this. If you are losing, nobody cares.

Three-Digit Offense and More

The majority of pattern plays or continuity offenses fall into the three-digit category. Since most coaches are forced to change their offense because of personnel changes, the Fundamental Five lends itself well to these changes. It mainly makes it easier for the coach to identify and communicate the offense to his staff and players.

Even the coach who picks out his offense early in his career makes some changes in options (or at least he should consider it). The college coach and pro coach who pick their personnel to fit their offense, still make changes in options. Any offense can be coded by the Fundamental Five. Therefore, the coding system is an aide in communication, not only in the basic offense, but in any changes that occur.

The Butler Offense, designed by Tony Hinkle, former great Butler University coach, is a 542 or 541 offense (see diagrams 1.4–1.7). Hinkle really likes to get to an isolated two-man play. This offense is still used by many teams in Indiana today. There are many more options than what I have shown, but the basic is a

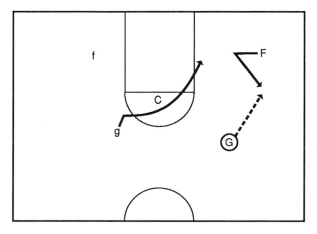

Diagram 1.4 Butler 542 (5 Option)

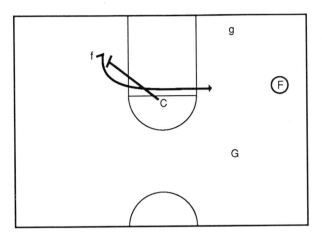

Diagram 1.5 Butler 542 (4 Option)

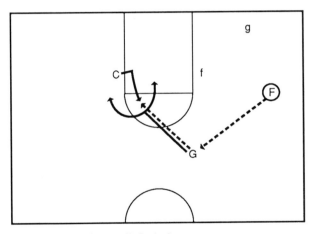

Diagram 1.6 Butler 542 (2 Option)

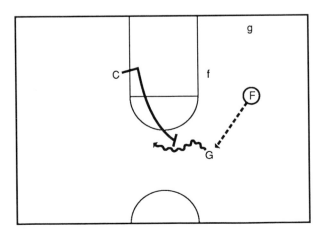

Diagram 1.7 Butler 541 (1 Option)

542 or 541. It is easier to understand and remember what a 541 is than a Butler or Oklahoma, both teaching offense and defense, and it is easier to communicate than saying "shuffle cut, pick opposite, pass and cut offense."

The Wheel Offense is another popular offense that could be called a 545 offense (see diagrams 1.8–1.10). The 5 play is a basic guard shuffle cut. The 4 play is guard picking opposite. The second 5 play is a double shuffle cut in some versions of the "wheel" as shown in diagram 1.10.

These are just a couple examples of three-digit offenses. I know there are multiple options to these, but directing your team to them may be easier with the Fundamental Five and its coding system. Even if you have established your

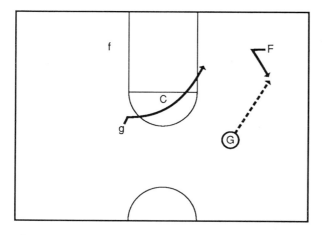

Diagram 1.8 Wheel 545 (First 5 Option)

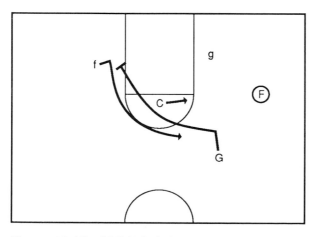

Diagram 1.9 Wheel 545 (4 Option)

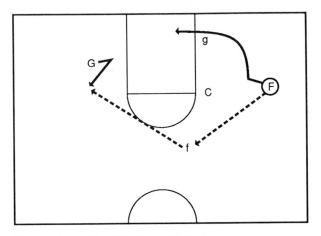

Diagram 1.10 Wheel 545 (Second 5 Option)

offense, certain options may be better than others for certain players; some options may be better than others for some opponents. It is easier to change or add the description of the option with a single-digit number whose execution has already been taught.

If you really want to get to multiple-digit offenses properly, it takes time. You usually do not get to multiple offenses executed properly in one season; in fact, it is difficult to get offenses executed properly until after Christmas each season. Even though we teach the fundamentals as early as the third grade, they still have to be reviewed and retaught. I generally start the season pressing and running the fast break (see Chapter 7, "Fast Breaking with the Fundamental Five"). It is not that I do not run our half-court offense, but I feel that pressing and running gets the team into shape and we seem able to control the tempo of early season games with this method. My players have run the break all summer on the outdoor courts and do not have to adjust as much. I have had teams come in and stall the first game of the season because they know I like to run early in the season, but this is unusual. If they lose, their fans are not very happy with that style of basketball the first game. When we do not get the shot off the break we want, we go into offense from the "fly" (see Chapter 7, "Fast Breaking with the Fundamental Five").

Half-court execution takes time and you must add options as you progress. I feel that too many coaches spend too much time working on their half-court offense too early in the season, instead of getting their teams fundamentally prepared. Working on the Fundamental Five first options both offensively and defensively helps prepare your team for the season. These options also help you see what your personnel is good at. Most coaches make changes as the season goes on anyway; the multiple offense will develop as your season progresses. The fundamentally strong team will be a winner in the long run. If you let your half-court offense develop as your execution develops, you will "find" your offense easier and it will be there when tourney time comes. I cannot really say what my offenses will exactly be for next season, but they will develop out of the Fundamental Five.

Defining Opponent's Offense

Look at diagrams 1.11–1.14 concerning an old but still very effective offense. The Drake or Auburn Shuffle, depending on your variations, was very popular in the early fifties and still is seen today. On paper it looks extremely complicated, but it is simply a 54 continuity. The 5 play is always started with the pass to a "forward." The second option really is the strong-side forward F, or whoever is in the strong-side position, coming across the lane to the ball. Since there is not a screen, it is not designated as a play with the coding system. Then the 4 option is performed with g and C. The offense is a continuity because f then dribbles the ball out to the G position to start the offense over, as shown in diagram 1.14.

   When your players are trained in the Fundamental Five, it is certainly easier to explain a somewhat complicated continuity like the shuffle. After every 5, there will be 4. Whether you are teaching the offense to use or to defend against, players should find it simpler, maybe not as easy as eating ice cream, but it surely aids in communication.

   After a huddle, some players will leave with the information you have given them; others are more confused then before the time-out. Diagramming the other team's offense is helpful but the oral communication of the 54, or whatever, stays with some longer. Mentally I try to have them go back thinking, "After the 5 cut, go to 4, pick away." Maybe I could have easily said "shuffle pick offense," but I have found that the numbers are easier to communicate with the majority of players.

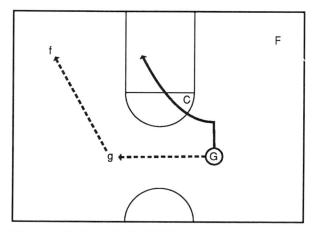

Diagram 1.11 Drake Shuffle 54 (5 Option)

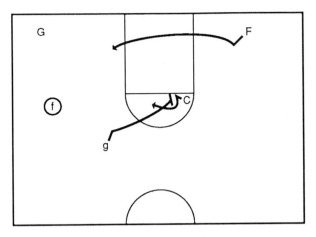

Diagram 1.12 Drake Shuffle 54 (4 Option)

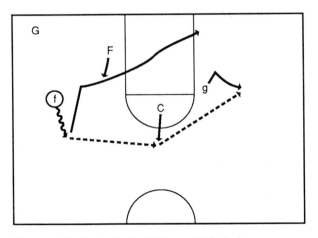

Diagram 1.13 Drake Shuffle 54 (Second 5 Option)

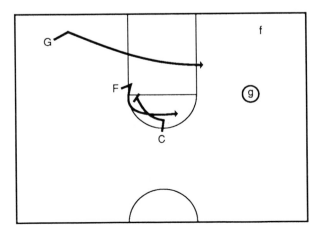

Diagram 1.14 Drake Shuffle 54 (Second 4 Option)

I want my players to understand what the opponent is doing. Isn't it easier to say the opponents are running a 531 offense than to say that the opponent will shuffle cut, clear the side by an offside screen after the pass back to the point, then pick and roll with the point and remaining forward! This may be what goes through the mind, but simplicity is obvious.

Even if the opponents run one series from the right side and one to the left, it is easier for the players and coaches to recall 43 from the right and 25 from the left. The digit should stimulate the defense to the option.

Our scouting reports are easier to understand. The scout writes a 54 continuity or 531 offense for the high post. Sure I want it diagrammed — I have better communication with it diagrammed and coded with the Fundamental Five. I want the part of the offense designated with what they are most effective with, the 5 or 4. Do they get the 1 isolated well on 531? I am sure in scouting it is evident what we are doing with the coding.

Step-by-Step Teaching

It is obvious that any offense is broken down by the play option. If a coach is interested in developing a system from elementary to senior high, he can determine when as well as what to teach. However, it is not assumed that the players are fundamentally perfect at any level. The step-by-step teaching of any offense can be done with the Fundamental Five. Use of the Fundamental Five certainly will make a coach take a better look at each individual option of his offense and the perfection of each option. Even if the coach does not believe entirely in the exact execution of the play option as was described previously, the breakdown is there. Modifications to suit individual coaches or even individual player's philosophy of execution can be made, however, it should be outlined and detailed. Instead of just showing the offense to the players, it can be broken down and presented in part.

Change of Offense, Not a Mental Detriment

The radical change of offense during a season sometimes has a tremendous emotional effect on a team: players may lose respect for the coach because he has not prepared them for the change that may be necessary; the invincible offense has been destroyed; execution of certain options may not be within the limit of the personnel; the offense is not being successful and the coach has gone to the drawing board.

A coach may never change his offense all year; however, if it becomes necessary, he can make the mental change easier. Maybe just a change of player placement or setting is needed. The coach who used the Fundamental Five has prepared his players for change. The approach to the team that a change is necessary does not have to be radical: "We are simply changing from a 53 to a 41 offense this week."

Changing Offense for Specific Opponents

If your team is prepared in the Fundamental Five, you may want to add specific options for specific opponents. New options are easily put in by changing a digit. If you feel that an upcoming opponent may be weak against the pick and roll, add the 1 option. You can present this to the team without changing your entire offense and without being mentally detrimental to the team. This is done by any coach in planning his attack against an opponent, but the Fundamental Five may explain it somewhat easier. This change may be done at halftime as well.

I look at the opponent's offense and if he does not use a particular option, I like to use it that week. The philosophy behind this being that if you do not have it in your offense, then you probably do not practice it that much. Again I may not use an option as much if that is the opponent's basic offense.

By using different options, we are harder to scout. I have certain "bread and butter" options that fit my personnel best, yet I do add or delete according to my opponent's strengths and weaknesses. These may end up being the "gravy" of the night.

Number 1: Pick and Roll

2

If you go out on the playgrounds, alleys, or barnyards, and watch the pick-up games, you will see one of the best two-man plays in basketball, the pick and roll. When the pros or colleges play the all-star games, you will see the pick and roll and the coach who does not include this in his offensive and defensive preparation is missing out. He is not using or preparing for one of the plays the players know and use. If it is not a major part of his offense, it certainly should be included, if for optional purposes only. Certainly it should be included in preparation, if for defensive purposes only.

However, just as with any offensive maneuver, execution can spell success or failure. Even though commonly used on the playgrounds does not mean it is done right. A good coach will be certain that any play is executed fundamentally correct. This is what the Fundamental Five is all about. Whether it is an option or your offense, the good coach teaches the proper execution of any phase of the game. Again, even if not a part of the offense, players need to know proper offensive execution in order to properly defend this maneuver.

The pick and roll can be a complete offense. One of the best season records I ever had was compiled with only the pick and roll as the man-to-man offense. When we did not get the fast break, we used the pick and roll as a close to our break. Needless to say, we put the ball up a great deal and averaged over 90 points a game from the time this was employed. Our scoring placed us among the top teams in the state even though we were one of the smallest schools. We scored over 100 points several times, peaked by a 120-point performance. Because of excellent execution of the break and the pick and roll, we seemed to make fewer errors and take an excellent choice of shots. The team was composed of excellent shooters. We did use Number 3 for our zone offense with Number 1 as an option. The team was not composed of good pattern players and the gyms were small with no room for movement. The pick-and-roll offense was right for this team — the Leesburg Blue Blazers had the best record in the school's history in their closing year.

I am not certain today whether this offense would be sufficient even for that particular team; however, it did show that a single fundamental offensive process, executed well, will win for a coach.

Obviously, the team that executes well fundamentally on any phase is going to be successful until the defense can adjust. The fast-breaking, good-shooting team should have this maneuver as part of this overall offensive plan because of the ease of going from the break to this option. It also opens the good outside shooter when the ball is reversed.

BASICS OF NUMBER 1

Since the basic principle of ruled play (see Chapter 8 "The Ruled Fundamental Five Offense") is to give individuals a chance to "do their best thing," the pick and roll fits right in. The forward *or* guard can call the screen. I have used both the verbal or the hand signal for this. How you signal is irrelevant, but you want your players to know. Signaling is important *unless* a forward is never to receive a pass, which is unlikely. This eliminates one of the faults in unstructured play: the forward coming up to pick for a guard and a guard passing to the same forward.

The result is usually a turnover.

RULE: If you desire a pick, call for it. If you are picking for a man, signal your intention, either by raising one finger or calling number "1."

One of the other concerns in "ruled" basketball is the play of the men without the ball. Number 1 works best when there is less congestion on the side it is being executed on. Also, if the shot is taken, statistics show that more rebounds are taken on the opposite side of the boards than any other position on the rebounding triangle. Therefore, rebound position away from the ball is desired. A down screen or back screen away from the ball not only opens a player for a pass, it opens up the rebounding position as the defense tries to adjust to the screen.

RULE: If Number 1 is being executed, do not bring your man into the area. However, he should be kept occupied so he cannot sag and congest the play area. Look for the shot to be taken and try to be in good rebounding position. Either perform a down screen 4 or a back screen 5 to open yourself for a pass or rebound position.

USE AT END OF BREAK

If the defense is back on the break, they generally jam the middle of the floor. The perimeter shot off the pick and roll can easily be taken, since the defense has a natural tendency to protect the basket. This is true of any perimeter play. The advantage of the fast break is to beat the defense down the floor. The small, good-shooting team can use the break with Number 1 to its advantage, because they will not have to shoot over the taller opponents because of the natural sagging techniques.

The placement of players in an offensive set-up naturally depends upon the talent. This is where some real coaching takes place. Deciding whether your players are inside players or outside players will determine your offense. If you believe in one leader, a one-guard offense may be the thing. However, even with one leader, a two-guard set-up may be used. Generally speaking, the player with the ball calls the set play. However, the other guard or a forward could call the play or the coach, using a card or paddle system, could call the plays. The details of a paddle system will be explained later.

GUARD-GUARD PICK

Generally, we do not permit the guard-guard pick and roll. If a guard picks for another guard, it is generally a "set-up" for a forward pick to follow. This is especially true if the guards are trying to beat the picks. We essentially are using a second screen for this maneuver.

RULE: Only forwards roll to the basket after picks. The only exception would be when we have a definite height advantage in the guards and nowhere else.

RULE: The guard pick is usually verbalized by the number "1" and the picking guard's first name: "1, Ralph."

Diagrams 2.1 to 2.4 show examples of the second screen for this maneuver. Since the offensive positions on the floor can vary as to personnel and coaching philosophy, I have attempted to show some of the set-ups possible in these diagrams. Throughout the text, I will show other set-ups; some set-ups may depend on how you come out of the fast break. As a coach reading this material, you may have to decide on the set-up. This is one of the assets of the Fundamental Five — flexibility. If a one-guard front is being employed, I will use P as the point guard with w and W as wings. The wings could be guards or forwards, depending on your personnel. The forwards will be f and F. If a center or single post man is used, he will be designated as C. The beginning coach may want to decide on one specific set-up and work from there. In diagrams 2.1 and 2.4, the

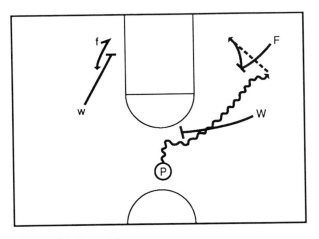

Diagram 2.1 Second Screen

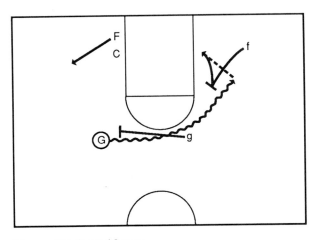

Diagram 2.2 Second Screen

wings are considered guards because they are not rolling to the basket. If defensive players are to be used in the diagrams, they may be designated by X_1, X_2, X_3, X_4, and X_5.

I have found that if the defense is aggressive enough to go "over the top" and beat our screens, there is a need for the second screen. Usually the defense will relax after beating the screen or be enough out of position from working "over the top" that the second screen by the forward will accomplish the guard to be open or force a switch.

Some defensive coaches have guards switch on all crosses, whether it be by dribble or movement. The guard switches on the first pick and if the defense is not ready, the second guard is picked by the second screen and a switch is forced.

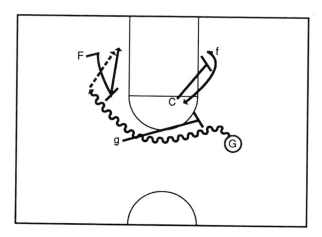

Diagram 2.3 Second Screen

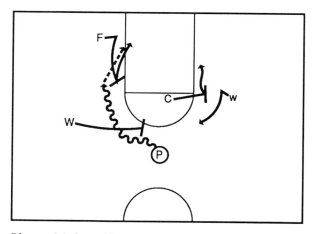

Diagram 2.4 Second Screen

GUARD FORWARD OR GUARD CENTER NUMBER 1

The lead guard (with the ball) calls this play. He may continue with the ball and use the screen himself or pass to another guard or wing for their pick and roll on their specific side. Various offensive set-ups can use Number 1 as a part of their offense. However, in each set-up, it should be noted that basically a two-man play develops.

Diagrams 2.5 to 2.9 show the guard with the ball in various set-ups in position to call Number 1. However, he may simply pass the ball to another player, as in diagrams 2.5, 2.6, and 2.7, and they may signal for the play. Diagrams 2.8 and 2.9 show the guard starting the play himself.

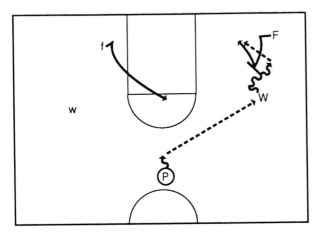

Diagram 2.5   Three-Guard Set — Number 1

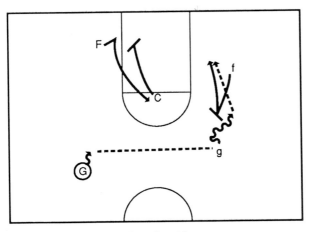

Diagram 2.6   High Post — Two-Guard Set

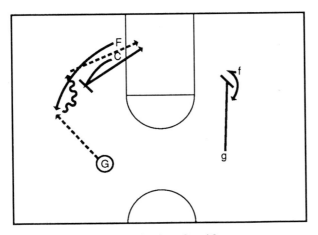

Diagram 2.7   Low-Post Stack — Two-Guard Set

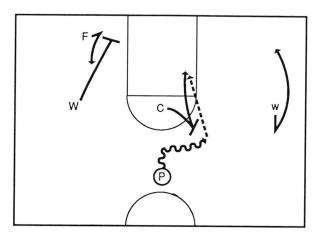

Diagram 2.8 High-Post — One-Guard Set

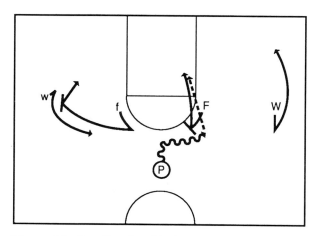

Diagram 2.9 One - Four Set — Number 1

NATURAL OPTIONS OFF NUMBER 1

Using strictly Number 1 as the single play offense, certain natural passing lanes may open even if the play is defended. Overplay of the one side of the floor is going to make the opposite side open if the ball is passed back. In diagrams 2.10 and 2.11, note that X_3 and X_5, although recovered, are somewhat out of position to defend hard. If w and f screen for each other, more work is necessary by the defense to recover.

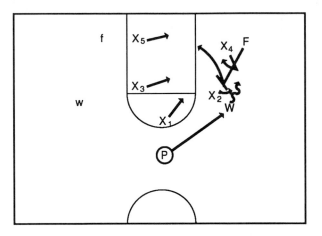

Diagram 2.10 Sagging by X_3 and X_5 — Jam Roll by F

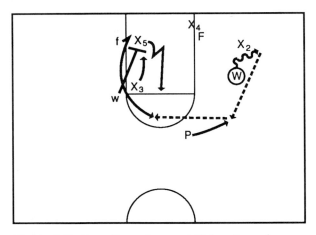

Diagram 2.11 Down Screen by w and f Before Reversal

Sometimes another option develops if there is a switch on the center guard pick or if the center passing lane is closed. If the defense has clogged the middle passing lane, even if a switch is made, the pass could be intercepted, if forced. Diagrams 2.12 and 2.13 show that when the defense collapses, the offense must go outside and then to the post. The center must post if there is a big man, little man switch. Again, it must be pointed out that if W and F would perform a screen away from the ball, congestion could be alleviated.

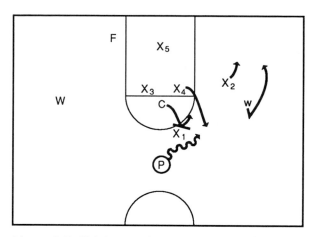

Diagram 2.12 High-Post Number 1 — Defense Sags

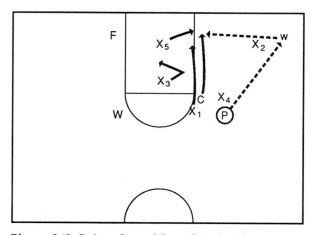

Diagram 2.13 Defense Sags — Offense Goes Outside

FUNDAMENTALS OF PICK AND ROLL

Before you can execute any one of the Fundamental Five you must understand ALL the fundamentals of the play. I have seen many teams use the pick and roll and fail to get good shots. This was not always because the defense was as effective as the offensive execution was poor. With today's explosive jump shooters, it is more often poor offensive execution rather than defensive prowess that the play fails. Naturally the better the defensive execution, the better the offense will have to be. Because of the effectiveness of the good, quick, jump shot, offense should beat defense.

Reasons Play Fails

1.   An improper screen is set.
2.   The guard fails to maneuver his man into the screen.
3.   The screen is not set on the proper spot on the floor.
4.   The screen is not wide enough to take out the defense.
5.   The screen is not held long enough to promote an open shot or switch.
6.   The roll is incorrect.
7.   The pass is intercepted or deflected.
8.   The defense overshifts and the guard fails to take advantage of the situation.

Setting a Good Screen

A good pick or screen is a primary requirement for Number 1. The sooner a player learns how to pick properly, the sooner a team can execute screen plays, which are a fundamental part of any offense.

The front pick, or screen, is the most basic and the one we encourage you to teach first. In this maneuver, the player faces his opponent to be screened. The rules permit him to set the screen as close as possible to the defense as long as the opponent can "see" him. In other words, the screen should be to the peripheral side.

The legs of the screener should be wide. He should split the offensive players side. In teaching this, I usually have a player stand with his legs close together and give him a slight push. He will fall backward. Then I tell him to spread his legs, bend his knees slightly, and get solid. This time I increase the push and he is much steadier. This usually gets the point across. Not only will the screen be more solid, but the roll will be easier.

The arms should be bent and the hands should be shoulder high across the chest. This serves not only to widen the screen, but to protect against defenders who run over the screens.

Making a Good Roll

If the legs are wide in the screen, it is easier to make a wide roll. A wide roll also helps to screen out the defender on the switch. The pivot should be made on the inside foot, or foot closest to the basket. It is a reverse pivot. The outside elbow should be thrown toward the basket and the outside hand put in the air as a target for the roll pass. The outside hand is now the inside hand, closest to the basket.

The buttocks should make contact with the defender being screened. This is the same as if a block-out for a rebound is being made. This puts the defense at the roller's back if a switch occurs. Care must be taken not to "hold" the opponent, but a certain amount of contact is necessary for the best results. Even if the guard with the ball shoots, the roller has excellent rebounding position because his man is at his back.

Guard Maneuvers to Run Defense into Screen

The guard assumes much of the responsibility for the success and failure of Number 1. There must be an inside maneuver to set up the execution of Number 1. Five fundamental maneuvers: the cross-over step, cross-over dribble, behind-the-back dribble, reverse dribble, or between-the-legs dribble will help the guard execute the play. Actually, all of these are not necessary, but the strong fundamental player will be able to execute more than one well.

RULE: The guard, player with the ball, is responsible to run his man into the pick once the screen has been set.

Cross-Over Step

If the screen is set close to the defense and the defense is tight to the offense, only a cross-over step is needed to run the defense into the screen. The offensive guard takes a stride step to the inside, getting the defense to shift inside, then crosses over with the same foot, running the defense into the screen. The guard should step as close to the pick as possible. Diagrams 2.14 and 2.15 show the

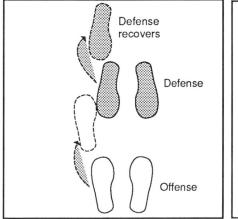

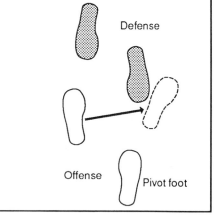

Diagram 2.14 Cross-over Step (to Outside of Defense)

Diagram 2.15 Cross-over Step (to Drive Right)

basic footwork going to the right. It is just the opposite with a screen to the left. The first step is with the left foot to the outside of the defensive player's right foot. This causes the defense to shift inside. As the defense moves to his right to adjust for this step, the offensive player crosses over with the same foot to outside the defense's left foot. The defense is set up to be screened easier. The pivot foot, right foot, must remain planted.

WARNING: Care must be taken so that traveling does not occur. Some players develop a bad habit of changing pivot feet instead of stepping across with the same foot.

Cross-Over Dribble

If the guard is dribbling when the screen is called, the guard is even more responsible to see that his man is "run into the screen." The cross-over dribble is one of the easiest, quickest ways to accomplish this. The dribbler moves hard away from the pick with the outside hand, changes hands and direction, and moves his defender into the pick. Remember, in a free-lance situation, the forward can be calling the pick so the guard can start maneuvering his man as soon as this is known. If you have decided to run Number 1 exclusively, the guard and forward will know that the pick is coming from the break.

Behind-the-Back Dribble

Since the days of Bob Cousy, the behind-the-back dribble has been developed into an effective method of changing direction. It is no longer a showboat move. It is better than the cross-over dribble because the ball does not come in front of the defender. If it can be executed as quickly as the cross-over dribble, it should be used. Diagrams 2.16 to 2.18 show the hand and ball position for a behind-the-back dribble change from left to right.

WARNING: Some players palm the ball when attempting this move. Players should be encouraged to keep the ball to the inside and back just before execution, then as the inside foot comes forward, push the ball behind the back to the opposite hand. The outside foot is now back in a natural stride position. This must be drilled in order to be perfected.

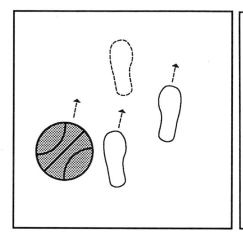

Diagram 2.16 Behind-the-Back Dribble (Ball in Left Hand)

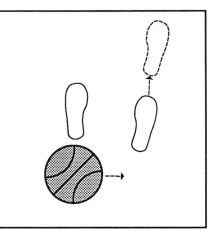

Diagram 2.17 Behind-the-Back Dribble (Ball Pushed Right)

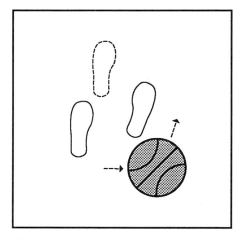

Diagram 2.18 Behind-the-Back Dribble (Ball Now in Right Hand)

Reverse Dribble

Another method to change direction and run a man into a screen is the reverse dribble. We teach the "Earl the Pearl" reverse dribble. This is because of the quickness of the move in comparison to the old reverse dribble. Instead of stopping and making a reverse pivot while dribbling, the pivot is made in continuous motion without an actual stop. The change of dribble is started with the same hand. If the player is dribbling with the right hand and starts to reverse direction, he should actually pull the ball back around himself with the right hand. The left hand then continues the dribble toward the basket.

Between-the-Legs Dribble

The between-the-legs dribble is exactly like the behind-the-back dribble, only the ball passes between legs. The legs give the dribbler protection from the reach-in. It is a difficult, yet effective, move but must be practiced to be perfected. The movement is like diagrams 2.16 to 2.18, except in diagram 2.17, the ball is positioned between the legs to the opposite hand.

Improper Placement of the Screen

If the screen is not set on the floor in the proper place, the defense can adjust too easily or does not have to adjust at all. When the pick is set in the middle of the floor, the roll is into congestion. The defense can "help" too much and still recover so the offense does not have an advantage.

In diagram 2.19, X_2 helps until X_1 gets over the top. X_5 also can check and recover while the middle is being "protected" by sagging forwards X_3 and X_4 until X_5 recovers.

In diagram 2.20, X_1 helps and can even steal the ball on the screen set inside. If the screen is set inside, the shot might be gotten off, but the roll pass is dangerous. Also, the danger of a double-up is more present because the drive off the pick is into congestion. Defensive player X_1 is in excellent position to double-up.

When the pick is set outside or on a clear side, the defense must make more adjustments or give up a shot. In diagram 2.21, if X_5 helps on the roll, then X_2 must help on C. X_5 can help, but if the pass is to the outside, F has the ball in a good position for a shot. Also, if C and f screen for each other, X_5 and X_4 must be aware of this and are not able to concentrate on helping.

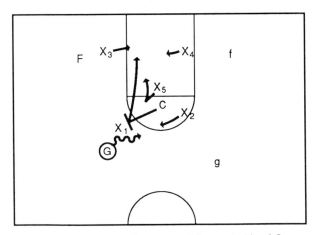

Diagram 2.19 Improper Placement – C Screens Inside of G

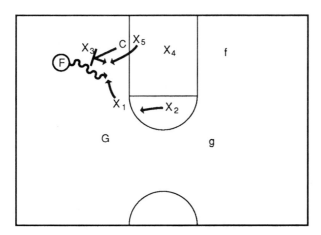

Diagram 2.20 Improper Placement — C Screens Inside of F

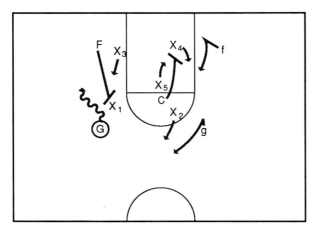

Diagram 2.21 More Effective than Diagram 2.19 — Outside

Diagram 2.22 also shows a more effective outside screen than diagram 2.20. X_4 can help, but X_1's effectiveness has been lost, especially on a double-up. Also, the screening of g and f will effect the help of X_2 and X_4.

If G clears after the pass, as in diagram 2.23, then there is more room and the screen on either side can be used more effectively. However, G must screen X_2 to be most effective. Therefore, X_1 must switch on g and does not double up on F in the corner. If X_1 clears with him, the room for movement is there. Since the pick and roll is basically a two-man move, the more room for the play, the better — g is a natural relief pass for the double-up.

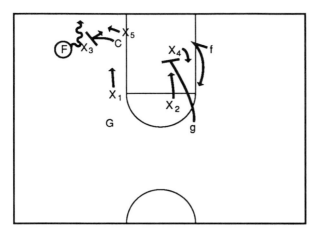

Diagram 2.22 More Effective than Diagram 2.20 — Outside

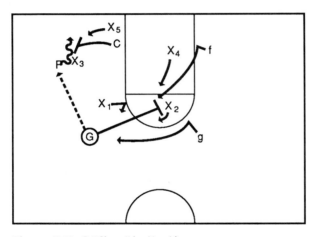

Diagram 2.23 G "Clears" by X₄ with g

If the screen is set too far outside, the guard has too long a shot for the play to be effective — then no switch will be necessary. If, as in diagram 2.24, G went straight off the screen, X₁ can "beat" the screen late because G is out of range for a good shot. Either the guard will let the offense take the shot unmolested or slide easily through the third man.

Diagram 2.25 shows the defense going third man. G again goes straight off the screen and X₁ slides through easily between X₂ and F to pick up G. In most cases, the guard has not taken his man inside enough for the pick. Sometimes the forward sets the screen before the guard takes his man inside and comes out before the guard has an opportunity to maneuver.

RULE: If the guard is dribbling, let the guard make an inside move first, before setting the screen. Then let the guard drive his man into the screen.

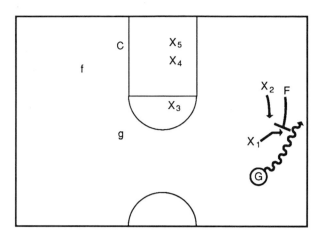

Diagram 2.24 Screen Too Far Outside — X_1 Can ''Beat It Late''

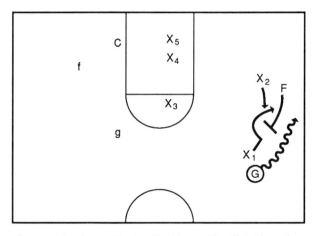

Diagram 2.25 Screen Too Far Outside — X_1 Can Slide Through

Setting a Wide Screen

Another reason the pick and roll fails is because the screen is not wide enough. The screen, whether it be front or back screen, should be set wide. The feet should be wider than the shoulders, yet the knees should be flexed to take the contact. If the screen is not wide enough, the defense can work ''over the top'' or slide through too easily.

If the screen is wide, the screener will take his first step wide to the basket. This also prohibits the defense from switching well enough to cover the roll. The long step produced by the wide screen keeps the defensive guard at the offensive forward's back. With the short step, the defense can front the roller with

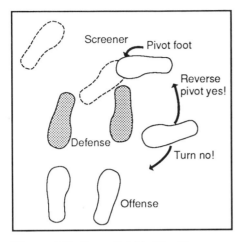

Diagram 2.26 Proper Roll (No "Turn")

less difficulty. The offensive forward more naturally seems to throw his lead arm up for a target with a long step. The move is made with the inside heel up and a pivot on the ball of the foot.

Diagram 2.26 shows that a pivot is made on the inside foot. The movement is toward the basket. The step made by the outside foot is of equal distance. Therefore, the wide screen provides longer distance. If the "pivot" is not a reverse, then a "turn" toward the basket is made. The turn will provide less screen as well as less vision on the ball.

Hold the Screen Long Enough

The screen must be held long enough so the defensive guard is screened out of the play. Too many times the forward rolls before the guard is screened and no switch by the forward is necessary.

RULE: The screen should be held until the offensive guard is past the screen. The guard is out of the peripheral vision of the forward before the roll is executed.

If the screen is released too early, the play fails. However, if the screen is wide and the switch is made, it really does not make any difference when the roll is made. The offense should have an advantage with the guard defending a forward. Even if the shot is taken outside, the offense has a definite advantage on the rebound. If not, the guard can take the ball away to the corner and the forward can post low.

RULE: If the switch is made, especially a jump switch, the guard should try to take the defensive forward to the corner and the offensive forward should post his "smaller" opponent.

The Incorrect Roll

The pick and roll can be a failure if the roll is incorrect. For some reason, many players turn rather than roll to the basket. The "turn" is a front pivot rather than a reverse pivot. The "turn" turns the offense into the defensive guard causing a moving pick (diagram 2.26). Also, the forward takes his eyes off of his teammate with the ball. The roll gets you to the basket quicker because the first step is toward the basket. The roll causes the defensive guard to be behind the forward rolling to the basket. Players must be drilled early in the teaching of Number 1 so the roll is a natural habit rather than a movement that has to be thought out.

The Incorrect Pass

Whenever a player passes through a defensive man on any offensive situation, either of two passes should be thrown: the bounce pass or the high pass. The push pass obviously is the quickest pass from one player to another (the shortest distance between two points is a straight line); however, it is the easiest pass to intercept by a player recovering on defense. The defensive man that is falling back to pick up his man or switching to pick up a man will move his arms between his shoulders and his knees the vast majority of the time. This is where the push pass goes.

RULE: Use only the high pass or the bounce pass on the pick and roll.

Failing to Compensate on the Overshift

Any good defensive forward is going to call out screens and a good defensive guard may try to overshift and beat the screen. Therefore, no screen, no switch, and the failure of the pick and roll occurs as in diagram 2.27. The offensive guard must be ready to cross-over, reverse, or behind-the-back dribble and change direction when the defense is in the obvious overplay. He must make the defense honest. The same moves that take his man into the screen can take him away if the defense overplays, as shown in diagram 2.28. Also, if the opponent has more than one player overshifting on the roll, the guard must find the open man to pass to.

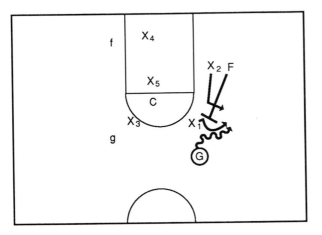

Diagram 2.27 X₁ Shifts "Early" and "Beats" Screen

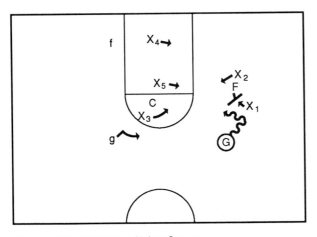

Diagram 2.28 G Reverses X₁ into Screen

DEFENDING NUMBER 1

There are fundamentally four basic ways to defend the pick and roll:

1. No switch
2. Jump switch
3. Slide through
4. Help and recover

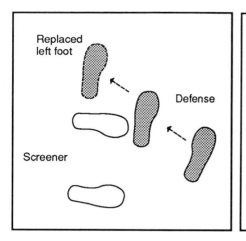

Diagram 2.29 "Step-Up"

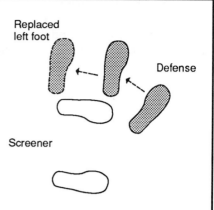

Diagram 2.30 "Belly-Up"

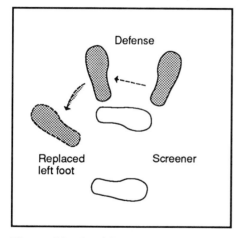

Diagram 2.31 "And Over"

No Switch

Whether this method is used or not, it should be practiced, especially early in the season. Aggressive players are needed; the forwards must be talking constantly; the guards must be quick and have ability to change direction. It is definitely the best way to play the game defensively because the defense never has to be involved in a mismatch.

The defensive guard must learn how to beat the screen. To go over the top, we call it the "step-up, belly-up and over." Diagrams 2.29 to 2.31 show the footwork on a screen to the offensive players' left. The feet are reversed for a screen on the right.

When the defensive forward sees his man going to set a screen on our guard's left, instead of calling out "screen left," we like to use the term "step-up left." This helps to remind the guard to step up with his left foot in order to beat the screen. It generally takes a couple of short quick steps to be in front of the screen. Then the defending guard throws his hip and stomach forward ("belly-up") and slides over the top of the screen.

The use of the hand nearest the screen also helps as a warning device of the screen. It also finds the screen to help with the step-up.

RULE: Call out screens when your man is setting a screen. Use "step-up right" when the screen is on the right and vice versa.

If the offense is not strong, generally you can beat many screens this way, especially if the defense is talking. Talking on defense is one of the most important factors in any good defensive team.

Encouragement of talking on both offense and defense are "sounds of beauty" to a coach's ears. Players must be drilled on this. Penalties should be assessed to players not conforming, especially early in the season. The aggressiveness during a game depends upon the officials. Smart teams adjust to the officiating. Some coaches teach only one way to defend against the pick and roll. If the officials are not letting you "do your thing," you must adjust to another way of defending the play. You could zone or use another method. It is certainly better to have practiced another method.

Jump Switch

If we switch, I certainly prefer the jump switch. If done properly, a charging foul can be drawn, a ball fumbled, or a trap developed. If you have been going over the top, the offense is also trying to adjust. Sometimes a change to jump switch will catch even a good offensive player off guard enough to cause an error.

The jump switch is just that. The defensive forward (or guard) makes a quick sideways jump in front of the dribbler. The most common mistake of most switches is that the offense never has to change its movement. In fact, the offense accomplishes what they wanted — a mismatch or a defensive player out of position. If a switch is hard enough, the offensive guard must stop, change direction, or charge.

RULE: If you make a jump switch, jump completely to the outside of the dribbler.

Most dribblers do not come close enough to the screen as they are driving hard to the outside. If a switch is made, they continue hard, but may have to move a little more outside. Very few dribblers come back to the pick side when a screen is set for them. If the jump switch is hard and far enough, an error

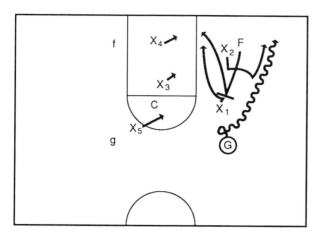

Diagram 2.32 Normal Switch

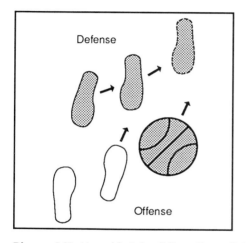

Diagram 2.33 Normal Switch — Offense Keeps Going Right

generally will occur the first time. In a normal switch, shown in diagrams 2.32 and 2.33, the outside defensive foot must slide backward to compensate for the drive; therefore, the defense is susceptible to an inside cross-over drive off his forward inside foot.

This defensive maneuver, of course, works better if the ball handler is weak. Even good ball handlers are usually stronger with one hand. We instruct our players guarding a dribbler to stay on the strong side. "Stay right," is part of our vocabulary. When the jump switch takes place on the dribbler's strong side, he must stop, charge or go with his weak hand. The jump switch should force the ball to the inside where you can get defensive help. This also prohibits the guard from going to the corner and letting the forward roll with the guard on him and

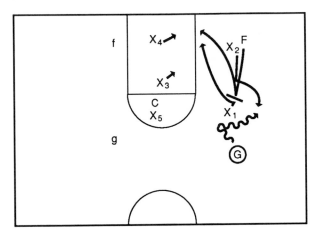

Diagram 2.34 Jump Switch

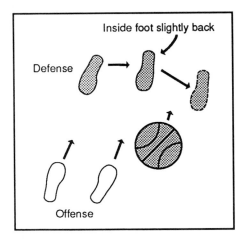

Diagram 2.35 Jump Switch — Defense Forces Offense to Change Direction

post. A natural double team has developed because a dribbler has gone toward the sideline and has been forced to stop. The experienced offensive guard will try to not panic under this situation, gain his composure, and take the forward to the corner. The defense must make this a quick, aggressive switch with hands up and moving to deflect the pass and prohibit good vision. The jump switch, as shown in diagrams 2.34 and 2.35, is made with the inside foot slightly angled inside so if the offense reverses inside, he will be better able to make the defensive adjustment. He is ready to slide back to the inside on a change-of-direction dribble.

RULE: If a jump switch is made, the switch should be made so that if the dribbler continues outside, a charge occurs.

If the dribbler makes a quick move to the inside and the defense has some-what angled himself for this maneuver, he does not have to drop-step to make the defensive adjustment. One of the common mistakes of the jump switch is to switch and let the offensive guard continue his maneuver. The defensive for-ward must get his body directly in front of the ball as the dribbler comes off the pick. He must be ready to take the charge. Practice taking the charge so the player knows it won't "hurt." Also, care must be taken so that the knee of the defensive player is not used to stop the dribbler.

RULE: If it is a guard-guard pick, we always want to jump switch.

The Slide Through

Some coaches believe that sliding through third man is a good way to defend against the pick and roll. When the screen is set, the defensive forward steps back and helps the defensive guard through. This is similar to the defense of the Number 2 play. However, since there is no handoff, the guard is in a much quicker and better position to shoot. Unless the guards are to be encouraged to shoot from the outside, this is not the best defensive option for Number 1 (diagram 2.36).

Help and Recover

This is really a combination of the no switch and jump switch. There is no real switch involved. The "belly-up and over" defensive move is used by the guard and a "helping" move is used by the forward. This method should be taught after the no switch and jump switch have been taught.

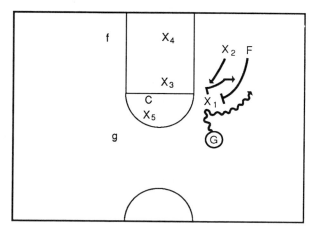

Diagram 2.36 Slide Through "Third Man"

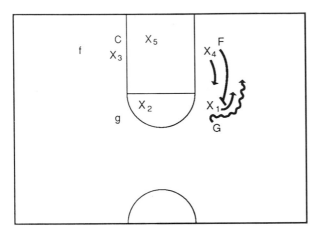

Diagram 2.37 G Still Has Good Drive Angle

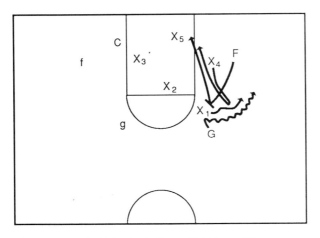

Diagram 2.38 G's Drive Angle Poor — X_4 Helps and Recovers

The defensive forward should be to the outside as if ready to jump switch. This forces the offensive guard to go outside a little farther off the screen and helps the defensive guard to "belly-up and over." Diagram 2.37 shows that even though X_1 has fought over the pick, G has a better angle to drive than in diagram 2.38 where the forward X_4 has forced G outside and given the defensive guard X_1 more time to recover.

The defensive forward X_4 must recover to his man with his defensive hand (outside hand toward the ball) constantly up and protecting against a pass from the guard. He is now slightly fronting his man F as he recovers to good defensive position.

Help-side (or weak-side) forwards, center, and guards are sagging to the ball to jam the area. The pick and roll is most effective, as in most maneuvers, when there is sufficient room to operate. The help-side forward should look for any high-low pass coming on the roll. He also should be prepared to take the charge on a hard roll by the offensive forward by establishing his position before the forward receives the ball and turns for the hoop. As soon as the defensive forward has recovered, the weak-side forward, center, and guard also recover to their respective men.

Even if a jump switch or slide through is done, the help and recovery principle of the help-side should be followed. Practice on recovering must be done in order to make the defense work.

You will probably find that you sometimes end up with two men on the shooter occasionally. This is not all bad. First of all, they would not be screening for the man if he could not shoot, and two men should discourage the shot even more. Secondly, you have a natural double-up situation occurring. This is why many coaches do not like to screen for the ball.

DRILLS FOR NUMBER 1

Drills in this book help to break down the Fundamental Five. There are certainly more than shown here. Some are strictly instructional. Most can be put on a competitive basis.

Competitive drills can be run in various ways. "Make it — take it" is a good method. If the offense makes the basket, he or the team remains on offense. If the offense fouls, it is a turnover. If the defense fouls, the ball remains with the offense. A specific number of "turnovers" can be set up for the offense with score kept. Losers may do a penalty (push-ups, laps, etc.). Usually, just keeping the ball is enough.

Sometimes negative reinforcement is necessary. This should be kept at a minimum. However, if you as a coach believe in this, there are some ways to accomplish this. Take a certain phase of the drill that you really want to emphasize and require they do five push-ups, laps, etc., if this phase is not done correctly.

However, drills can be made with positive reinforcement: if they do them right, they will not run laps at the end of practice. Personally, I prefer drills to be fun.

Shooting drills should not be competitive at first. Form should be concentrated upon; speed and quickness should come after form is developed. This is basically true of all drills.

Drill 1: Chair Drill for Forwards

The forwards line up along the baseline, facing chairs near the free-throw line. A coach, C, or manager, M, signals for the forward to come up and set a screen. The forward must wait for the coach to drive before he rolls. The coach alternates the timing and checks for faults. These must be eliminated before using

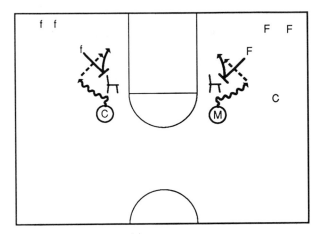

Diagram 2.39: Drill 1 Chair Drill for Forwards

defense. The screen should be set close to the chair so the "turn" is prohibited and a good pivot is produced. In the very beginning no ball is used, just the pivot on the chair.

1. Manager, coach, or player dribbles off chair.
2. Forwards come up, set screen, and roll off.

Drill 2: Chair Drills for Guards

The guards line up out front. Each of the specific guard moves are worked on: Cross-over step, cross-over dribble, reverse or "Earl the Pearl," behind-the-back or between-the-legs dribble. After these are executed satisfactorily, the coach can add a reaction to the chair drill by calling the move or shot he wants as the guard reaches the chair.

1. Guards use move off chair.
2. Coach observes.
3. Guard rebounds own shot and returns to line.

Drill 3: Chair Drill for Guards and Forwards

The process is the same as for the previous two drills. The pass to the rolling forward can always be thrown. Care must be given to the type of pass, high or bounce, that is thrown. It could be signaled by the coach. The type of guard move can also be designated (cross-over, behind-the-back, etc.).

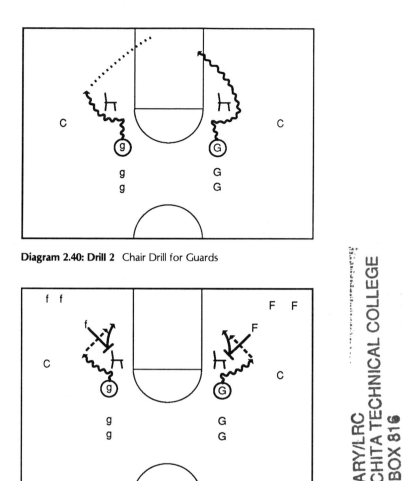

Diagram 2.40: Drill 2 Chair Drill for Guards

Diagram 2.41: Drill 3 Chair Drill for Guards and Forwards

LIBRARY/LRC
OUACHITA TECHNICAL COLLEGE
P.O. BOX 816
MALVERN, ARKANSAS 72104

This drill can also be a reaction drill with the coach calling for a pass, drive, or shot. In all cases, player position should be checked, along with the proper foot movement.

1. f comes up and sets screen on chair.
2. g dribbles off screen.
3. g can shoot or pass.
4. f rebounds and returns ball out to line of guards.
5. Use both sides of floor.
6. Coach observes.

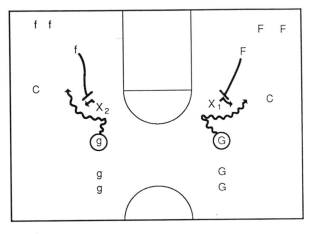

Diagram 2.42: Drill 4   Two-on-One Guard Drill

Drill 4: Two-on-One Guard Drill

Only one defensive guard is used. The offensive guard can be permitted or prohibited from the overshift drive. The coach can designate one offensive move
only (shot, drive, cross-over, etc.). The coach can designate the defense to go
over the top or slide through behind. This could be designated a defensive drill.
However, our philosophy of drills is that drill concentration be offensive or defensive. The roll pass can also be thrown in this drill.

Drill 5: Two-on-One Forward Drill

This is a chair drill with the forward being defended. The defensive forward can
be designated to switch, help and recover, or either. Concentration is made on
the pass, either high or bounce, to the rolling forward.

1. F comes up and sets screen on chair for G.
2. X_2 switches, or helps and recovers to F.
3. F and/or X_2 rebounds and returns ball to guard line.

Drill 6: Two-on-Two Drill

This should not be attempted until the first five drills are acceptable. The coach
can designate moves both offensively and defensively, such as: guard must pass,
defense must switch, no switch, help and recover, no inside drive, guard must
shoot, etc.

1. F sets screen on X_1.
2. G comes off screen.
3. F rolls.
4. X_2 and X_1 switch, help, and recover.

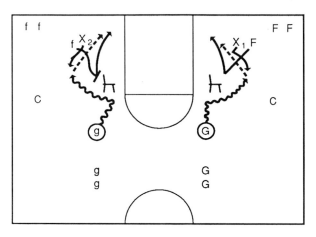

Diagram 2.43: Drill 5   Two-on-One Forward Drill

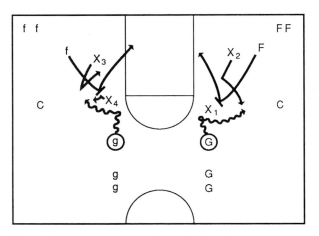

Diagram 2.44: Drill 6   Two-on-Two – Number 1

Drill 7: One-Man Shooting Drill

This drill is like one-man chair drill only the shots are concentrated upon as well as the moves. These can be done from guard and forward. Coach can call for a shot or drive for reaction. A manager can be used for the nonshooter.

1. F sets a screen for G; G dribbles off screen.
2. Either F or G is practicing shots.

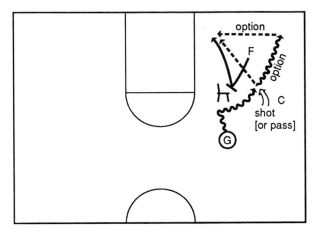

Diagram 2.45: Drill 7   One-Man Shooting (F or G)

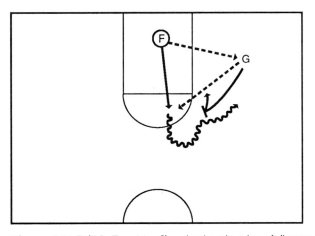

Diagram 2.46: Drill 8   Two-Man Shooting (continuation of diagram 2.45)

Drill 8: Two-Man Shooting Drill

This is simply a continuation of Drill 7.

1.   F sets screen for G.
2.   G cross-over dribbles (or other move) and shoots over screen.
3.   F rolls for rebound.
4.   G breaks to either corner, yells "outlet" and receives pass from F.
5.   F is out-of-bounds if ball is scored.
6.   F breaks up the middle and receives pass from G.
7.   F is now in guard spot and drill continues as G screens for F.
8.   Managers could be added as dummy defense.
9.   F could also receive pass from G and do the shooting.

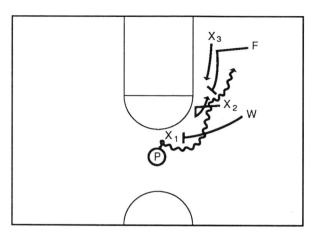

Diagram 2.47: Drill 9 Three-on-Three

Drill 9: Three-on-Three Drill

This drill is used to practice the guard-guard-forward-one play. It is almost the same as two-on-two except the first pick is by a guard and there is no roll by him. It can be done from any three-man offensive set-up. This drill can be offensive or defensive as the coach can designate both offensive (shot, pass, drive, or type of move) and defensive (no switch, switch, etc.) options.

1. W sets screen on X_1 for P.
2. P dribbles off screen.
3. X_2 switches on P.
4. F sets screen on X_2 for P.
5. X_2 and X_3 switch or help and recover.
6. F rolls to basket.

Drill 10: Four-on-Four Drill

We do a lot of four-on-four drills. Since we generally carry about 24 players and have three coaches, we divide the squad into three groups of eight. The play is basically the same as two-on-two. However, if the play is defended on one side of the court, the ball is reversed quickly to the opposite side for a Number 1 there. Help-side team defense can be practiced as well as offensive ball reversal.

1. G goes off screen set by F.
2. X_3 jump shifts.
3. G passes to g.
4. g and f perform Number 1.

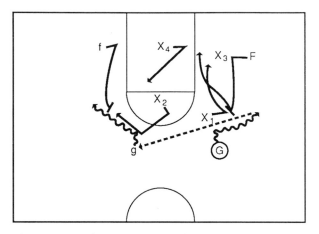

Diagram 2.48: Drill 10   Four-on-Four (G Reverses to g)

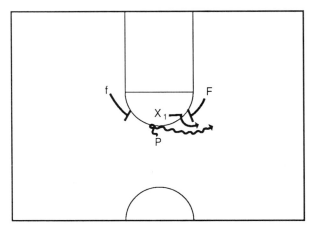

Diagram 2.49: Drill 11   Over the Top

Drill 11: Over-the-Top Defensive Drill for Guard

It is like the two-on-one guard drill. It should be practiced after the guard has had proficiency in that drill. The guard can take the defense to the right or left. The defense must go over the top and beat the screen, using the "belly-up and over" method. The offense is usually instructed to shoot after taking one dribble past the screen. This drill can be used in preparation for a high double-post point guard offense.

1. X_1 is guarding P.
2. F or f sets screen on X_1 for P.
3. X_1 tries to beat screen.

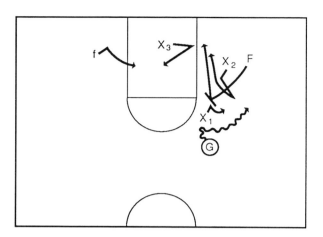

Diagram 2.50: Drill 12 Weak-side Forward Help and Recover (Three-on-Three)

Drill 12: Weak-Side Forward Help Drill

It is the same as two-on-two drill only a weak-side forward is added. The help-side defense can be practiced for help and recover on the Number 1. G can be instructed to hit either F or f. Player X_3 can practice taking charge on F when he rolls. Again, the coach decides the emphasis of the drill.

1. F sets screen on X_1 for F.
2. X_2 and X_1 switch, jump switch, or help and recover.
3. X_3 helps then recovers to f.

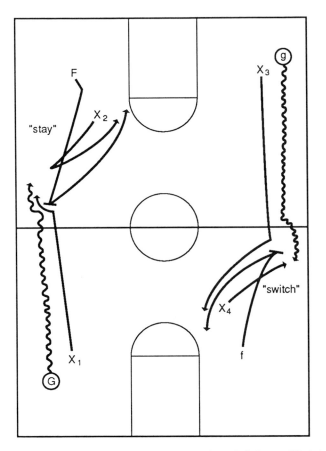

Diagram 2.51: Drill 13 Two-on-Two Number 1 Full Court — "Switch," "Stay," or "Fire"

Drill 13: Number 1 Full Court (Two-on-Two)

It is the same as two-on-two except the full court is used. The help and recover or the jump switch can be used. The offense should start to beat the defense more often after this drill has been used because of the added space. The same options (switch, no switch, pass, no pass, etc.) that were used in the half-court drill are applied. The defensive forward could call for switch, stay, or "fire," de-pending on what he sees as a possibility for a charge, forced bad pass, etc. as the dribbler advances. "Fire" means he wants the guard to double-up with him.

1. G (or g) starts dribbling up floor with X_1 guarding him.
2. F comes up to set screen on X_1 for G.
3. X_2 switches, helps and recovers (stays), or "fires" (doubles up).

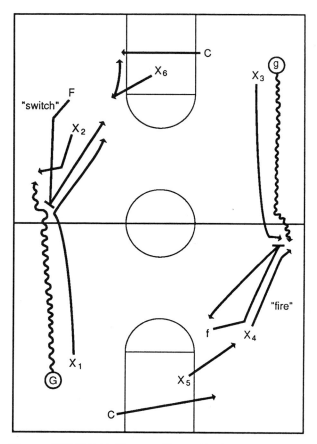

Diagram 2.52: Drill 14 Three-on-Three — Number 1

Drill 14: Number 1 Full Court (Three-on-Three)

This is Drill 12 (weak-side forward help drill) except it is on a full-court basis and there is more help on the roll play from the help-side forward X_3. If X_2 and X_1 "fire" (double up), X_3 must try to intercept the pass to either F or f. Drills 13 and 14 are good introductory drills for full-court pressure defense or offense.

Both sides of the floor can be used with G and F going down left-side of court, while another pair of players, g and f, are using the right side. This utilizes space well. This is shown in Drill 13 as well.

1. G and F perform full-court Number 1.
2. X_2 "switches," "stays," or "fires."
3. X_6 helps and recovers on C.

3

Number 2: Pass and Cut

The second fundamental play in basketball is passing the ball to a forward and cutting. This play is almost as old as basketball itself. Again, players should be fundamentally strong in this move. Diagrams 3.1 to 3.5 show this play in five different set-ups.

The Biggest Misuse in Basketball

When scouting an opponent, one of the first things I look for in their offense is what the guard does after he passes to the forward. I know many coaches key their offense this way. In doing this, they sometimes misuse one of the easiest

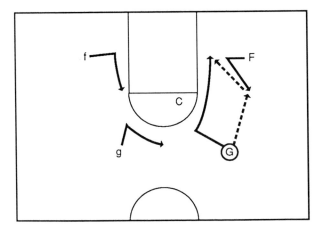

Diagram 3.1 Number 2 from High Post

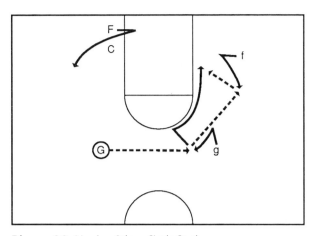

Diagram 3.2 Number 2 from Single Stack

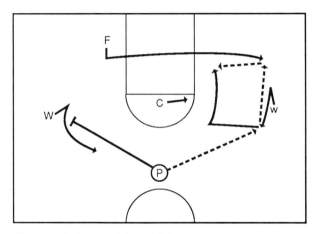

Diagram 3.3 Number 2 from 1-3-1

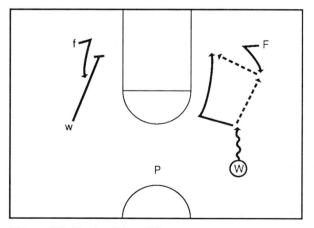

Diagram 3.4 Number 2 from 3-2

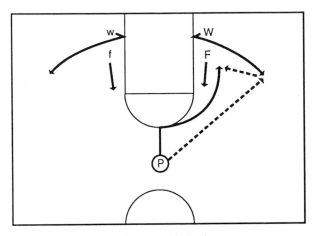

Diagram 3.5 Number 2 from Double Stack

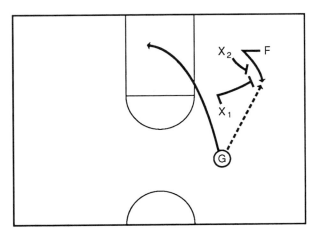

Diagram 3.6 Double-Up on F

ways to score in basketball. The guard brings the ball down, passes to the forward and cuts to the opposite side. However, the guard doesn't even look for the return pass, because he is just getting the offense started. What a waste! The coach who lets his players do this is passing up a scoring opportunity. After all, isn't the name of the game putting it in the hoop?

Not only is there a scoring opportunity misused, but there is a good chance of a trap on defense if the offensive guard isn't looking for the return pass. The defensive guard X_1 knows that player G in diagram 3.6 isn't looking for a return pass, and he can double up on F any time. If the offensive guard is getting the ball from the forward, the defensive guard has to be careful in doubling up.

If the play is to see that the center C, as in diagram 3.7, gets the second pass and G is simply a cutter with no offensive threat, we tell X_1 to sag all the way and help the middle (forget about G until F passes back out). The statistics

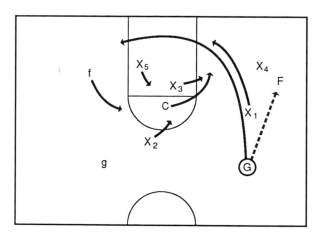

Diagram 3.7 Help on C by X₁

I've kept show that more than half of the guard-forward passes and cuts are susceptible to this kind of defensive pressure. I'm sure many coaches call this their first option, but the ball seldom ends up in the cutter's hands. With the first cutter as a definite threat, defensive help on other options is lessened. Complete defense will be discussed later in this chapter.

The Two-Step Move

We try to do every cutting movement *two* steps from the ball, then break to the ball. The forward should take *two* steps in toward the basket, then break toward the ball to receive a pass from a guard. The guard then takes two steps away from the ball before making his cut toward the basketball. This has been called a V-cut; we call it the two-step move for obvious reasons.

RULE: When making a cut without the ball, take *two* steps away from the direction you are planning to travel, and come back to the ball.

The idea of the two steps is twofold. First, you don't get a lazy cut. Modern defensive philosophy promotes using the sag toward the ball. Some coaches do not permit the defensive player to change their defensive stance the first step. They teach the defensive forward to "open to the ball" on the second step toward the basket. They feel that most players will only head-fake a step to the basket first or at the most take only one step. In my opinion, this is true because the defense usually "goes" for this. In turn, the offensive player can become lazy in his effort to get the ball; however, when this lazy offensive player runs into good defense, he becomes frustrated because he can't get the ball. The two steps will give him a chance to leave his defense and cut sharply for the ball. If the defense

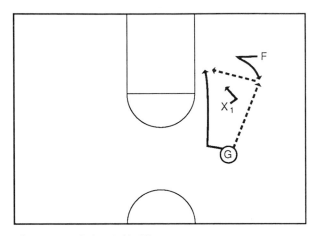

Diagram 3.8 G Cuts Behind X₁

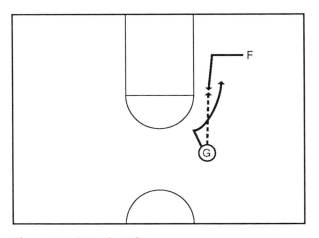

Diagram 3.9 F Up After 2-Step

doesn't go in with the two-step move, the offense simply cuts behind the defense. Diagram 3.8 shows the offensive guard G cutting behind his defender, X_1. Diagram 3.9 shows forward F coming up to the ball after his two-step.

The second reason for two steps is the position at which the man receives the pass. If a player makes only a head fake or takes one step, he will receive the ball farther from the basket with an equal factor of defense applied. The closer you get the ball to the basket, the easier it is to score — the receiver is in better position to score and the forward isn't flirting with the out-of-bounds line when he receives the pass. Look at diagrams 3.10 and 3.11. In position A (where a two-step is used) the player receives the pass in a much better position than B.

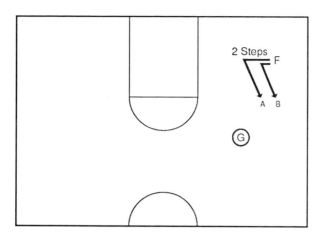

Diagram 3.10 A — With Two Steps

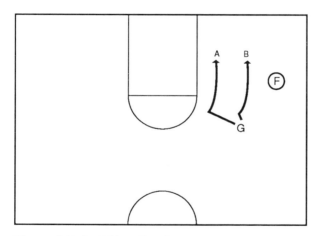

Diagram 3.11 B — Without Two Steps

"Pinning" the Forward

When taking the two steps, the offensive forward should make sure the second step is above the defensive player's front foot. Therefore, the two steps must be slightly forward if the defensive man is playing any type of denial. This helps ''pin'' the defense before breaking out to the forward position.

There is a defensive philosophy (and it is a good one) that contends if you can get the offense to do what it doesn't want to (start from farther out on the court, use the left side, go to the center rather than a forward, etc.), you will completely upset their offensive pattern. This is basically true, especially against a pattern or set offensive team. The two-step helps the offense to get the ball closer to the same spot every time because of the area the defensive player has to defend.

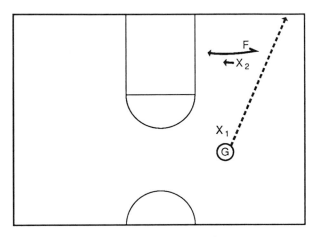

Diagram 3.12 No Two-Step – G Throws Ball Away

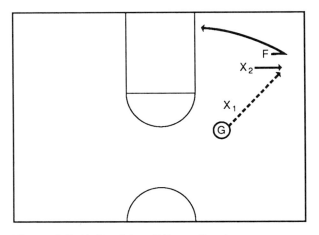

Diagram 3.13 No Pass Fake – G Throws Pass Away

Backdoor Two-Step

There is a time when the defense definitely is trying to prevent the pass from going to the forward. He is strictly overplaying the forward. The defense is now susceptible to the backdoor cut. Instead of two steps toward the basket, the forward takes two steps away and cuts backdoor for the pass from the guard. This helps the timing of the guard because he knows that the forward isn't coming to get a pass in the first two steps and won't throw the ball away. I have seen the pass thrown out-of-bounds without anyone touching the ball, as in diagram 3.12; or the defense intercepting the pass, as in diagram 3.13, when an easy basket should have been scored.

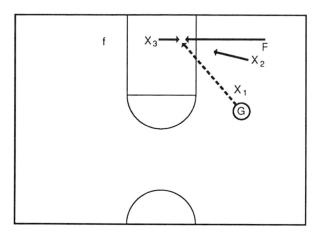

Diagram 3.14 No Two-Step – F Gets Pass Too Late

RULE: If a forward takes two steps away from the basket, he backdoor cuts to the basket.

RULE: If a forward is backdooring, the guard "freezes" the defense by a pass fake on the first two steps.

By starting away from the basket the guard knows that the forward is going to backdoor. He has been drilled on this. The pass may not be completed, but not because the guard didn't know he was making a backdoor cut. By freezing the defense with a fake, he makes the defense more susceptible to the backdoor. This is simply a pass fake when F takes his two steps outside. The area for receiving the pass is greater if the forward takes two steps away first. Even if the forward makes a good direct backdoor move, he has to receive the ball inside the lane. The help-side forward should be in position to intercept, as in diagram 3.14.

If the forward takes two steps outside first, he receives the ball sooner and help must come after he has received the ball in a good scoring area, as in diagram 3.15. It would help, also, if f would recognize the defensive pressure and flash to the post area.

If a team is in a tight man-to-man pressure situation, the guard can use the backdoor two-step when a guard-to-guard pass is being thrown. In the same way the forward has more area to pass, so does the guard. The guard takes his man toward the 10-second line and breaks to the ball, as in diagram 3.16. He won't get the ball for a lay-up like the forward, but he will be in a good position for a jumper or a penetrating move. The passing guard should "freeze" the defense with a pass fake. This move should help to lessen pressure defense from the guards. Obviously, in this pressure situation, it helps if the offense spreads out the defense.

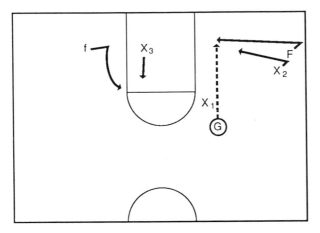

Diagram 3.15 Proper Backdoor Two-Step by F

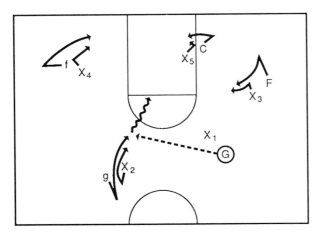

Diagram 3.16 Backdoor Guard Two-Step

Forward Receiving Ball

Another item I look for in scouting an opponent is to see what the forward does upon receiving the ball. Does he face the basket? A player who is still parallel to the baseline isn't going to be much of an offensive threat unless he can hit 30-foot hook shots. If a coach has forwards who can do that consistently, he is in great shape and doesn't need this or any book. Any forward receiving the ball must be drilled into facing the basket immediately upon receiving the ball. He is now a threat to score, either on the shot or on the drive.

The forward should come to a jump stop with a hand out to give the guard a target. This is especially true when there is pressure. However, a player should do this, like the two-step, every time so that it becomes a habit; then, when pressure is applied, it will make no difference. The forward then uses a reverse power pivot or front pivot.

Reverse Power Pivot

If the player pivots on the outside foot (foot nearest the sideline), he should reverse power pivot. This is a reverse pivot by pulling the inside foot toward the sideline without taking the player's eyes off the cutting guard. The ball should be powerfully pulled through the chest area to avoid the defense stealing the ball. This makes the pivot foot the outside foot. It does improve the passing lane to the basket. A player should *not* front pivot on the outside foot, because it puts him farther from the basket.

Since the pivot foot is the outside one, the drive to the baseline is direct. Care must be taken *not* to cross over to the baseline, since it will involve changing pivot feet. The cross-over move will be to the inside. Whichever way the player pivots, care will need to be taken to prevent traveling.

Front Pivot

The most common pivot is on the inside foot and a front pivot. The player doesn't take his eyes off the cutting guard. The player is as close as the reverse power pivot on the outside foot. The player can now make a cross-over step to the baseline and a direct move inside.

Cross-Over Step and Drive

The forward should pivot on the foot he likes to drive off of. The forward should *never* pivot so his back is away from the offensive cutting guard, unless he is going to reverse drop-step pivot and drive. The cross-over step to either the baseline or middle needs to be practiced. This, of course, depends on what pivot they use. We drill the players early in the season to be sure that this is a habit. Most of the players have been drilled in elementary, junior high, etc. on this principle so a little reinforcement is all that is necessary. This is the same move used in Number 1. This cross-over must be practiced and drilled properly so that one of the most common traveling mistakes is avoided — the changing of pivot feet before the drive.

The very simple drill of a manager passing the ball to the forward, pivot (front or reverse power), face basket, cross-over, and drive should be worked on. This should be done first without defense from both sides of the floor as well as to the middle and baseline. When defense is added, it should not, at first, be pressured to the point of overplay. The cross-over step is again analyzed and the travel is looked for. Good defense is stressed on protection of the baseline before trapping defenses are introduced to the offensive player.

RULE: Forwards should never pivot away from an offensive cutting guard, unless they are going to reverse drop-step pivot and drive. They should either reverse power pivot on the outside foot or front pivot on the inside foot.

The Reverse Drop-Step Pivot and Drive

Many times a fine scoring opportunity is missed when the defense is putting on pressure. In fact, the offense helps the defense to keep applying more pressure unless the backdoor cut on the reverse pivot and drive is used to alleviate the pressure.

The reverse drop-step pivot can be used effectively when the pressure is such that the backdoor cut isn't effective, but the defensive forward is out of position when the ball is received. If the defensive man is reaching for the pass, he can be scored upon.

The forward should always put a hand out for a target for the guard. On receiving the pass with the defensive man leaning to the outside, the forward should reverse drop-step pivot, and drive to the basket. The power lay-up is then used to score. Usually only one dribble (at the most two) is necessary if the pivot is made *before* the drive. Too many players start to dribble before they pivot. This slows them down so the defense can recover. By pivoting first, the defense is usually held to the back of the offensive player.

RULE: If reversing to drive to the basket, *always drop-step pivot first,* then drive.

Guard Receiving the Ball

As was stated previously, we shouldn't waste a scoring opportunity on the first guard cutter. However, if we can return the pass to the guard, he must have some moves to score. We try to teach three moves to our first cutting guard: the power lay-up, the turn-around jump shot, and the step-under move.

The Power Lay-Up

Upon receiving the ball, the guard goes directly to the basket with his shoulders parallel to the basket and powers his way directly to the basket. Sometimes, a head and ball fake will help some players to score more, especially against an aggressive defensive man. Power and aggressiveness is important especially if the defensive is beaten and is behind or at the side of the shooter. Many three-point plays develop from this maneuver and is the same one we teach our low-post men to use when they have their man beat on the baseline.

The Turn-Around Jump Shot

If the defense is quick to recover and has the baseline cut off for the power lay-up, the first thought is for the turn-around jump shot. As the player tries to drive parallel for the power shot, he finds himself cut off. He reverse pivots on his *outside* foot (foot away from defensive man) and shoots his turn-around jump shot.

OPTION: We do permit, in fact, *encourage,* an optional *jump* hook shot when the offense is found in this same position. The offensive man can help hold off his opponent with his nonshooting hand, much like a regular hook shot. However, it has the advantage of the added height of the jump. The shot is taken at the peak of the jump with a flick of the wrist. It is not a long-distance shot, but very effective in close, especially against taller, opponents.

The Step-Under

When the defense is aggressive, they might not only stop the power lay-up, but try to stop the turn-around by quickly recovering in order to block the shot. When this occurs, we encourage the use of the step-under. As the pivot for the turn-around occurs, the offense sees the defense adjusting quickly. Now, he crosses over and steps under his defensive man's arms and powers to the basket. This move is also used by our baseline men in the low-post position. The key is getting the defense to commit himself for the block, then step under his arm that he is trying to block the shot with. It becomes a natural move. The pivot foot shouldn't move until the shot is attempted.

By having our guards learn these under-the-basket moves, they are prepared to play under the basket, if we need them, at any time. If when younger, a player was used at guard and has grown tall enough now to be a post man, we have "been developing" some skills for him around the basket. Every player should learn post moves to take advantage of the situation when he can post his man.

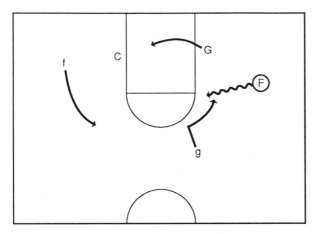

Diagram 3.17   Second Guard, or Dribble-Back

The Second Guard, or Dribble-Back Option

If the forward doesn't shoot, drive, or return the pass to the first cutting guard, we are ready for the second guard, or dribble-back, option of Number 2. The forward drives to the foul line extended and returns the ball to the second guard, as in diagram 3.17.

RULE: The second guard should move *out* from the top of the key directly in line with the near foul *lane* extended before the forward dribbles to the foul-line area. (diagram 3.17)

This rules gives the second guard a better cutting angle for a lay-up. If the guard stays on the opposite side of the floor, he is moving away from the basket and only has jump-shot potential, as in diagram 3.18. By moving directly in line with the free-throw line extended, he has a good angle for a drive or at least a closer jump shot. The second guard is also in a position to go inside if his man overplays the outside move as shown in diagram 3.19.

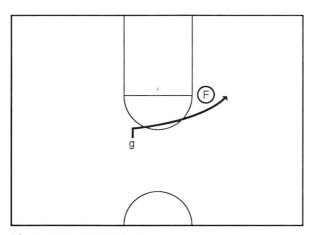

Diagram 3.18 "Bad Angle" for g

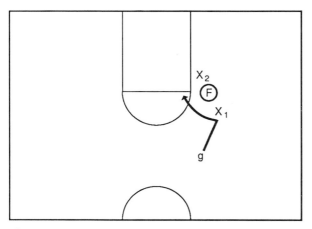

Diagram 3.19 Inside Cut by g

Close-Out Pivot

RULE: When a forward hands off to a cutter, he steps up with the inside foot and tries to close out the defensive guard who is going over the top.

The close-out pivot by the forward handing off is designed to "take out" the defending guard. When the forward hands off with the inside pivot foot, the defense has even more room to go over the top (diagram 3.20). This is especially true if he drops his nonpivot foot when he hands off the ball. By stepping up

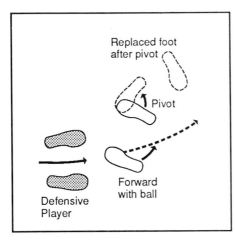

Diagram 3.20 Reverse Pivot "Opens" for Defense

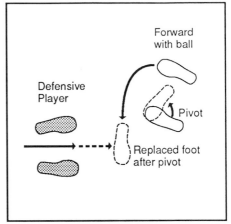

Diagram 3.21 Close-Out Pivot "Screens" Defense

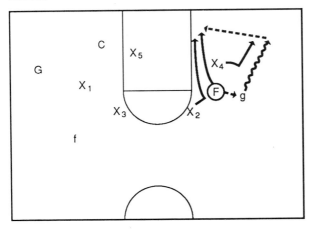

Diagram 3.22 Switch — Drive to the Corner

with the inside foot, the defense is "closed out" (diagram 3.21). The ball must be protected by the forward during this option; he must not be standing up. The forward doesn't pivot until his teammate is there. If the guard is "bellying up" to get by the natural screen, he can be closed out by the step-up. The forward must dribble up and make a jump stop, so he can use either foot as the pivot foot, in case he must close out to an inside cut.

Second Guard Rules and Option

RULE: When the opposing forward switches, the guard should, if he still has his dribble, drive to corner so forward can take small defensive guard to low post. (diagram 3.22)

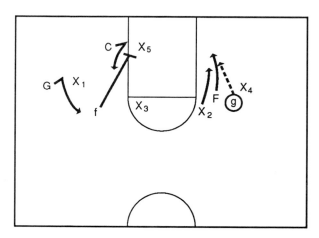

Diagram 3.23 Jump Switch — "Roll" to Basket

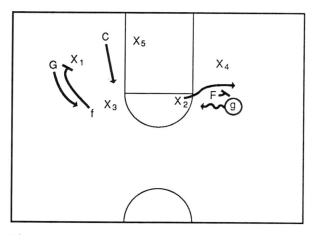

Diagram 3.24 Third Man Slide Through — Reverse with Screen by F

RULE: If the guard has no dribble because of a strong jump switch, the guard should maneuver as on a pick-and-roll switch and pass to the rolling forward. (diagram 3.23)

RULE: If the defense goes third man, the forward should try to provide a screen for the guard, as a Number 1, to reverse and shoot over. (diagram 3.24)

RULE: The second guard *never* cuts until the forward has dribbled up to the free-throw area.

As the forward dribbles to the free-throw line, the defense may get lazy or even try to overplay the middle. When this happens, the forward can use the "Earl the Pearl" move, named after the great Earl Monroe of the New York Knicks.

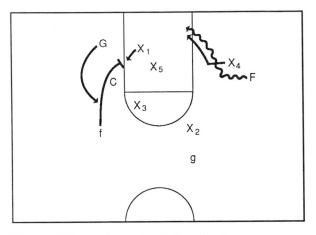

Diagram 3.25 "Earl the Pearl" — X_4 Overplays F

We like this method of reverse dribble the best, because it is so much quicker and thus more difficult to defend. The reverse dribble should be made with the dribbling hand. It is a backward push with the outside hand and reverse pivot with the same motion, changing hands *after* the pivot to the basket has been made. Diagram 3.25 shows this move. If the guard was cutting before the forward gets to the free-throw area, he should not bring his man into the area and hinder the reverse dribble drive.

RULE: If the forward with the ball starts to dribble, no cuts across the lane should be made.

This rules gives the forward an opportunity to have a one-on-one situation. If the offensive weak-side players cut into the lane, not only will the one-on-one situation be jammed, but the second guard option will also be harder to execute. Down screens 4s or cross-screen 4s, with players interchanging positions, are encouraged to keep the defense active away from the ball. Diagrams 3.23, 3.24, and 3.25 show examples of this screening off the ball.

Fake Handoff

The forward has another option, especially if he anticipates the jump switch of his man to the second guard. Remember, if he uses the close-out pivot properly, he has taken out the opposing guard. When the second guard gets to the hand-off spot, the forward fakes the handoff, causing his man to switch. Then he pivots inside for the jump shot with the opposing guard trying to pick him up as shown in diagram 3.26.

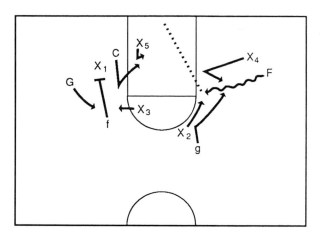

Diagram 3.26 Fake handoff by F, Then Shot

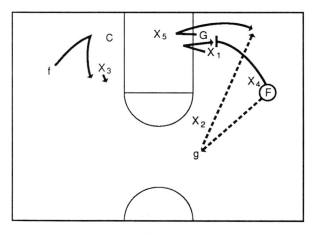

Diagram 3.27 Pass-Back "5" Option

Pass-Back "5" Option

If the defensive second guard sags to prevent the drive or dribble-back option, the forward can pass back to the second guard. This is also true if the forward has lost his dribble for some reason. I use this option when the forward isn't a good ball handler. Diagram 3.27 shows the pass-back from F to g. Then F screens for G in the low post. G takes two steps inside before coming off F's screen. A good shot may occur in the corner for G. Also, if G's man switches onto F, a mismatch may occur with F being open in the low post.

　　I call this the pass-back "5" option because it is similar to our 5 end line out-of-bounds play. It is not really a shuffle cut 5 play, but a 4 play. However, we had developed the "5" out-of-bounds play before we started using this option.

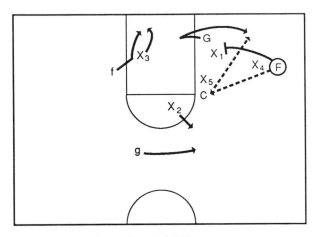

Diagram 3.28 High-Post Pass-Back "5"

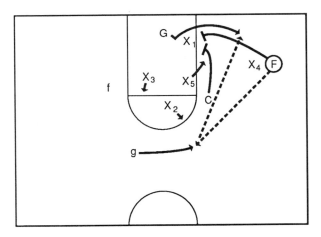

Diagram 3.29 Double-Screen Pass-Back "5"

Since this is a baseline screen, I suppose I could have called this a "3" as well. The baseline option of Number 3 can be used after the pass-back to the second guard (see Number 3, Chapter 4).

If the offense is high post like the University of Louisville, the pass-back can go to the center as shown in diagram 3.28. The options are basically the same.

Double-Screen Pass-Back "5"

With the high-post offense, a double screen can be used on the pass-back "5" option. It is really the "Double Head-Hunter Option" of Number 4. This is shown in diagram 3.29, when F passes back to g after G has made the 2 cut. On the

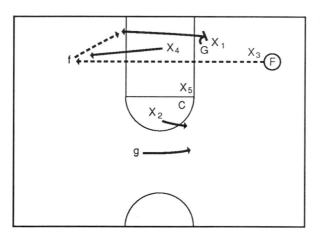

Diagram 3.30 Cross-Court Option

high post, a single screen is set when the forward passes to the high post. If the forward passes back to the second guard, then the center and forward screen for the first guard.

Cross-Court Option

This is a simple yet difficult option: simple, because it is an option that the defense dictates; difficult, because a cross-court pass is necessary. When the defense fronts the guard on his 2 cut along with help-side defense covering a lob pass, the cross-court option can be carried out. Diagram 3.30 shows F, seeing the defensive action of X_1 and X_4, throw the cross-court pass to f. When f receives the pass, X_4 must recover. Then G pins X_1 to his back and breaks to the opposite low post to receive the pass from f. The danger and difficulty of this option is the cross-court pass. It must be a swift, high, two-hand overhead pass. The options for f continue as if G would have originally cut to his side.

2 Outside Option

Instead of cutting inside, the guard cuts outside of the forward as shown in diagram 3.31. The forward F hands off to the guard G. The opposite forward f and center C both come to the low and high post, respectively. After the handoff, the forward F runs his man closely to C, hoping to rub him off the center. G can throw an alley-oop pass to F, hit f low, or hit C in the high post. If C is hit in the high post, both F and f look for a high-low pass.

The alley-oop pass to F should not really be a lob pass, but a two-hand overhead pass, thrown at the corner of the backboard. The height of the pass is determined by the size and leaping ability of the receiver. A lob is too slow

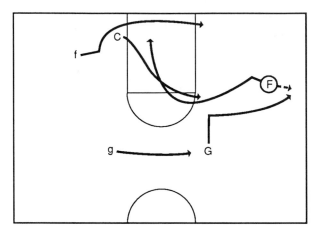

Diagram 3.31 2 Outside Option

and has a better opportunity to be intercepted. The rub-off by the forward is really a form of a back-screen 5 play (explained in Chapter 6 on Number 5).

When f comes across the baseline, he should look for the ball like any low-post option. G should dribble down if he needs to improve his passing lane to f. If f doesn't come across when the guard goes outside, then the alley oop is nullified because of congestion.

The center shouldn't try to screen F's man, but come to the ball. It is F's job to run his man into C — C should front pivot immediately upon receiving the ball. He then looks for either forward, F or f, in the low-post area.

Low-Post Number 2

Instead of breaking back out to receive the pass from the guard, the forward may just post. When he takes his two steps in and reverse pivots, he just stays in the low-post area. The guard simply drives to the corner to improve the passing lane. The low post is discussed also in Number 4 (Chapter 5).

RULE: If the forward posts, the wing or guard should drive to the corner to get a better angle to pass to the forward.

RULE: When the forward posts near the baseline, the forward should be *diagonal,* not square, with the baseline.

RULE: Post men should keep their arms spread to keep the defense ``off.'' One hand should be used as a target for the ball.

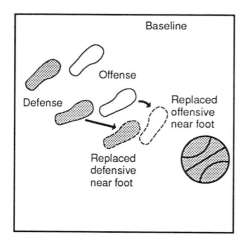

Diagram 3.32 Diagonal Offensive Post Established

Baseline Post

The low-post offensive player should keep his lead foot (foot nearest the ball) in front of the defensive player if he is behind him. Diagram 3.32 shows the forward posting his man diagonally to the baseline. Anytime the defense moves his foot toward the ball, the offensive forward moves his lead foot outside the defense. This should increase the area between the baseline and the defense; therefore, the area for driving and powering to the basket is increased. A slight move to the ball may be necessary in maintaining the post.

Outside Post

If the defense recovers to cut off the baseline or overplays the baseline, the outside post is used. This is not as good as the baseline post, because of help coming from sagging guards. However, sometimes you must take what the defense gives you. If the defense has overplayed the baseline, then the back foot of the diagonal low post is brought forward in front of the lead foot of the defense as shown in diagram 3.33.

Shots in Low Post

The step-over hook is an excellent move when the baseline is cut off. If the baseline is cut off early, the post man should post outside and the hook (right from the left side, left from the right side) is a natural move. If the baseline has been cut off after the post man receives the ball, the step-over is done like the outside

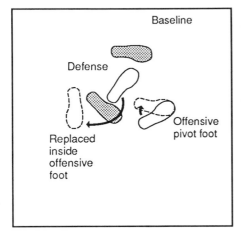

Baseline

Defense

Replaced
inside
offensive
foot

Offensive
pivot foot

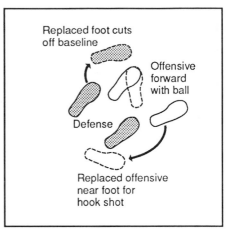

Replaced foot cuts
off baseline

Offensive
forward
with ball

Defense

Replaced offensive
near foot for
hook shot

Diagram 3.33 Outside Post – Step-Over Move   **Diagram 3.34** Fake Baseline – Step-Over
Hook Move

post move. The post man fakes to the baseline and steps over the lead foot of
the defense and hooks the ball into the basket as shown in diagram 3.34. The
defense finds himself blocked out as the offense sweeps to the basket.

The turn-around jump shot and the step-under are excellent moves when
the baseline is cut off. These are the same moves the cutting guards are taught.

"Fronted" Post Pin

If the defense completely fronts the post man, then the low-post man should
"pin" the defense with his hip and upper arm. Care should be given so that the
offense doesn't push off. This is why the lower arm should *not* be used in pinning
the defense. The pass should be a high pass to the low-post man. The "pin"
should be held until the pass is directly overhead. If the offense releases the pin
too soon, this allows the defense enough room to intercept the pass. This also
helps in keeping the offensive post man from pushing off the defensive man.

RULE: When pinning a fronted defensive post man, wait until the high pass is
directly overhead before releasing the pin.

DEFENDING NUMBER 2

As was said previously, if the offense doesn't use the first cutter, his man can help
on defense much more. He can trap the forward, sag to the middle to jam the
second options (either the forward drive or second guard).

However, good teams will try to make all options work if everyone is capable of scoring. This makes the defense more difficult, yet not impossible.

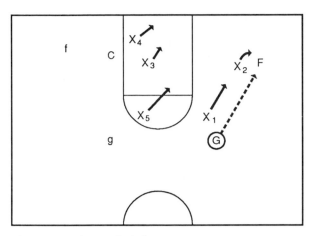

Diagram 3.35 Step to the Ball

Defending the First Pass

When defending the forward, or any player, we don't want him to receive the ball where he wants to. Yet, we don't want to open ourselves to too many back-door lay-ups.

We have our defensive forwards on ball-side keep their defensive hand (hand nearest ball) out to deflect a pass. Their inside hand should be free to "feel" for the backdoor cut. If the backdoor cut is made, the defense should face that ball and then change defensive hands protecting the high baseline pass to the backdoor cutter. However, the defense shouldn't open to the ball until the offense reaches the free-throw line area.

Defending the First Cut

As soon as the pass to a forward is made, the defensive guard should step toward the ball. All the defensive players should step toward the ball. We want to help on defense as much as possible. The sag towards the ball gives zone principles with the man-to-man. All defensive players should be in the center of the floor or nearer to the ball. They should be able to view their man and the ball. This will enable them to easily step in the passing lane on any pass as shown in diagram 3.35.

The defensive guard should have his defensive hand up. This is the hand nearest the ball. If a player reaches for the ball with his defensive hand, his body should be pulled toward the ball not his opponent. When the cutter G is to a point when the defense X_1 is even with the ball, as shown in diagram 3.36, X_1 momentarily fronts G and changes defensive hands. A simple change of head

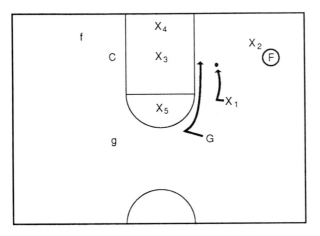

Diagram 3.36 Point Where X_1 Changes Defensive Hands

position will accomplish this. Team defense must help, if a high backdoor pass is made. This point on diagram 3.36 is where offense usually likes to get the ball to the cutting guard, G. Naturally, the degree of closeness the defense can stay to the offense depends upon each one's quickness.

Defending the Baseline Drive Option

We naturally force the ball to the middle by overplaying the baseline side of the forward. When we are overplaying, we like to split the baseline leg of the offensive man with the defensive body. The closeness again depends upon the quickness, shooting, and driving ability of the opponent. If the forward is weak, we can help more on the cutter, put more pressure on the pass-back, etc. We are normally driving a man where we can get help.

Baseline Drive Trap

If we are in a trapping defense, we would then encourage a drive to the baseline. Diagram 3.37 shows F driving the baseline on X_2. X_4, who is defending f, comes across and cuts off the baseline on F's drive. X_2 completes a double-up. X_1 doesn't follow G out and looks for interception on a pass to f. Some teams are constantly looking for this trap. I feel that your team must be looking for the trap in order to be effective. In most cases, it is easier to get help and recover in the middle. You are committed to the trap or double-up if you encourage baseline drives.

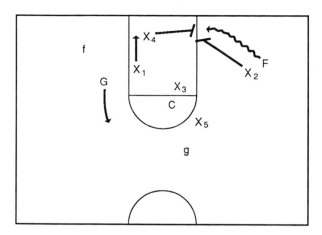

Diagram 3.37 Baseline Drive Trap

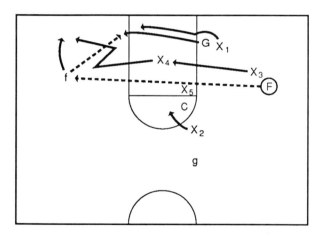

Diagram 3.38 Defending Cross-Court Option

Defending Cross-Court Option

The help-side guard X_2 and help-side forward X_4 must always look for cross-court or skip passes. They can be intercepted, if anticipated. Help and recovery of X_4 is very important. If G does receive the ball in the low post, then X_4 must help X_1 and recover again to f as shown in diagram 3.38. The second recovery is an "ins-and-outs" defense discussed in Number 4.

Defending Pass-Back "5" Option

The ball will return to the second guard more easily, if you are defending against the dribble-back, using the sagging guard. If the forward isn't a good dribbler or driver, then the pass-back should be denied.

   When the ball is returned to the second guard, there are two ways to defend the "5" option. We always switch on a forward-forward 4 play ("the defending Number 4 play"). If there is going to be a low-post height advantage, or the offense is using the option to get the ball into the low post, we use the head-hunter or down-screen option of Number 4 defense (see "Defending Number 4" in Chapter 5). The double screen passback "5" or double headhunter Number 4 is also discussed in detail in Chapter 5.

   Since this is basically a baseline screen, the defending of Number 3 principles are also involved (see "Defending Number 3" in Chapter 4).

Defending the Second Guard Option

When the forward is coming up, the guard should be sagging toward the ball. If the forward is using the reverse pivot, we try to go over the top. If the forward uses the close-out pivot, we instruct the guards to go third man, between the forward and our defensive forwards. Our defensive forward X_2 should help the guard X_5 slide through. If the offensive guard g reverses off the forward's screen and takes the jumper, the defensive forward X_2 might have to help and recover. We would rather have the forced jumper than the lay-up or the mismatch (diagram 3.39). This is true unless the guard is the star. Then we would jump switch on him at all times.

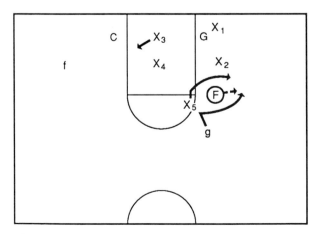

Diagram 3.39 Slide-Through Defense — Close-Out Pivot by F

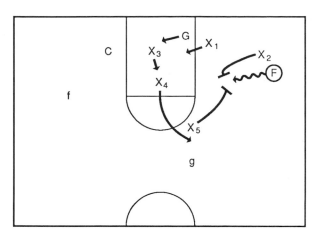

Diagram 3.40 "Fire" (Double-Up) on F – Second Guard Option

Double-Up on Second Guard—"Fire" Situation

A gambling option to the second guard play is for the defensive guard to aggressively double up on the forward dribbling up as shown in diagram 3.40. The offensive second guard is obviously open. Whenever a double-up occurs, the player doubling up yells "fire" and the rest of the team is playing "zone." If the "zone" can react and cover the passing lane to the guard as the forward panics, a turnover can occur. The element of surprise is the secret to the success of the gamble. A tie-up or bad pass is the desired outcome.

Defending 2 Outside-Handoff

When the guard goes outside, the defensive guard X_1 should slide through third man like defending the second option of 2 inside as shown in diagram 3.41.

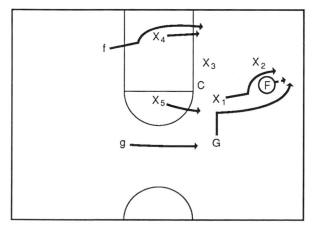

Diagram 3.41 Defending 2 Outside – Handoff

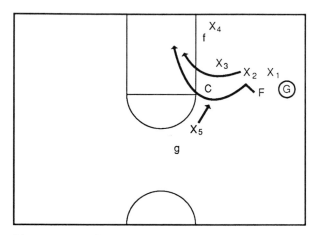

Diagram 3.42 Defending 2 Outside — Alley Oop

Alley-Oop Pass of 2 Outside

Putting pressure on the guard with a hand up in the passing lane will make this pass difficult to throw. The defensive forward X_2 should be in the passing lane to intercept this pass. X_3 should help X_2 through third man (diagram 3.42).

Baseline Option of 2 Outside

This should be defended like our low-post defense. This is discussed in detail in defending Number 4.

High-Post Option of 2 Outside

The degree of defensive pressure put on the high-post player depends on the driving ability of C. If C can't drive to the basket well, he should be played tight often receiving the ball with hands up in the passing lanes to f and F. Defensive players X_2 and X_4 should almost front f and F with their defensive hands (hand nearest the ball in the passing lane). The defensive guard X_1 and X_5 should help on C, ready to recover to G and g (diagram 3.43).

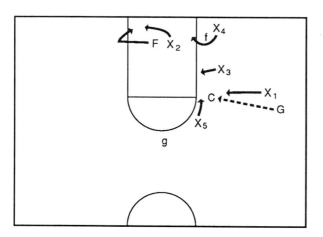

Diagram 3.43 Defending 2 Outside – Pass to C

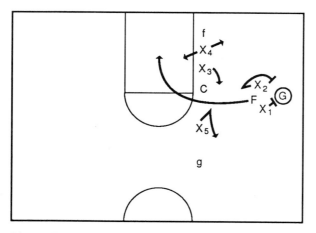

Diagram 3.44 "Fire" – Handoff of 2 Outside

"Fire" on Handoff of 2 Outside

When the forward F hands off to G, defensive players X_1 and X_3 can double up on G. This is done by X_2 jump switching on G and X_1 completing the double-up. Pressure must be extreme enough so that G cannot throw a good alley-oop pass to F (diagram 3.44).

Defending Low Post Number 2

This is discussed in detail in defending Number 4 in Chapter 5.

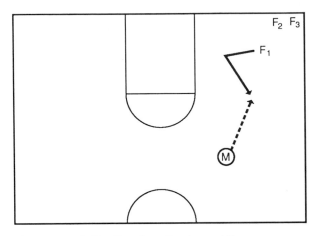

Diagram 3.45: Drill 1 Two-Step, Receive, and Pivot

DRILLS FOR NUMBER 2

Drill 1: Two-Step, Receive, and Pivot

1. Players line up, take two steps toward the basket, come back to the ball, receive pass from manager, pivot, and face basket (can shoot as option).
2. Add defense when proficiency is there.

Drill 2: Two-Step, Receive, Pivot, and Drive

1. Same as Drill 1 except drive is added. Care is taken to watch for *traveling* before drive.
2. Use as defensive drill, only concentrate on defensive fundamentals.

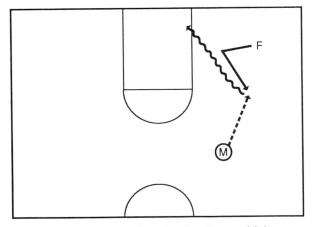

Diagram 3.46: Drill 2 Two-Step, Receive, Pivot, and Drive

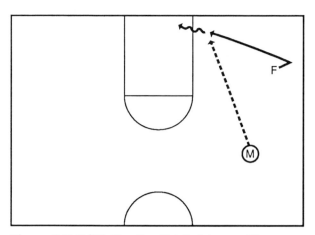

Diagram 3.47: Drill 3 Two-Step Out, Backdoor, and Score

Drill 3: Two-Step Out, Backdoor, and Score

1. Take two steps away from basket, backdoor, and receive ball.
2. Add defense; instruct defense to *overplay.*
3. After Drills 2 and 3 have developed proficiency, let player do either as defense "suggests."

Drill 4: Two-Step, Reverse Pivot, and Drive

1. Forward takes two steps in and comes to meet ball, reverse pivots on back foot, and drives to basket — PIVOT BEFORE DRIBBLE.
2. Add defense; instruct defense to *overplay.*

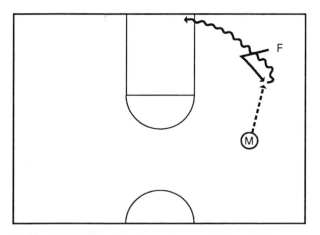

Diagram 3.48: Drill 4 Two-Step, Reverse, Pivot, and Drive

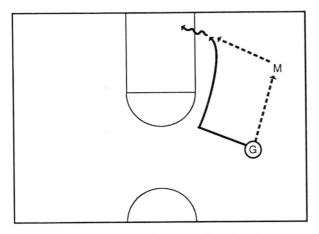

Diagram 3.49: Drills 5 and 6   Guard Pass, Two-Step, Return

Drill 5: Pass, Two-Step, Return

1. Guard passes to manager, or forward, takes two steps away, cuts back for ball, and drives for score.
2. Add defense.
3. This can be a defensive drill. If so, then only the defensive fundamentals should be concentrated on.

Drill 6: Guard, Number 2 Shooting

1. Same as Drill 5 except Number 2 shots are practiced.
2. No defense is used at first. Then "dummy" defense is used. Finally, straight-up defense is used.
3. Power lay-up — defense behind guard.
4. Turn-around jump shot — defense cuts off baseline.
5. Step-under — defense cuts off baseline, and tries to block shot.
6. Jump hook — defense cuts off baseline.

Drill 7: Guard Number 2, Partner Shooting

1. G passes to g, cuts to basket, shoots Number 2 shot.
2. g rebounds shot and throws outlet pass to G.
3. g breaks up middle of the floor and receives pass from G.
4. g passes to G and drill repeats with g cutting to the basket.
5. Start with power lay-up and continue with all Number 2 shots.

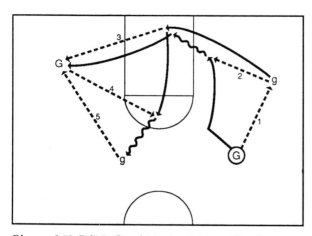

Diagram 3.50: Drill 7   Guard, Number 2 Partner Shooting

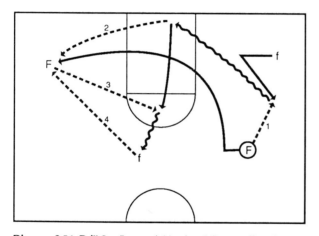

Diagram 3.51: Drill 8a   Forward, Number 2 Partner Shooting

Drill 8: Forward Number 2 Shooting

1. Same as Drill 2 except certain Number 2 forward shots are practiced – f rebounds own shot (diagram 3.51: Drill 8a).
2. No defense is used at first, then the dummy defense is added.
   a.   Baseline power drive – defense open to baseline.
   b.   Step-over hook – defense cuts off baseline.
   c.   Turn-around jumper – defense cuts off baseline.
   d.   Jump hook – defense cuts off baseline.
   e.   Step-under – defense cuts off baseline and tries to block shot.

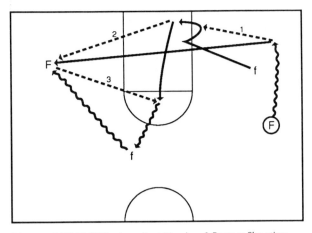

Diagram 3.52: Drill 8b Low-Post Number 2 Partner Shooting

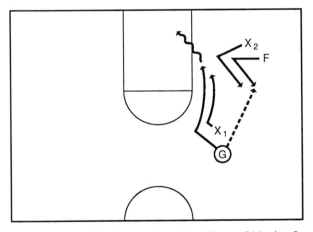

Diagram 3.53: Drill 9 Two-on-Two (Guard-Forward) Number 2

      f.   ''Earl the Pearl'' drive for lay-up — defense overplays drive.
      g.   Fake hand-off jumper — defense goes for the fake.
      h.   Do a. through e. from low post (diagram 3.52: Drill 8*b*).
  3.   Add solid defense.

Drill 9: Two-on-Two — Guard-Forward — Number 2

1.   Use the pass-and-cut option.
2.   Defense can be instructed to overplay, sag, etc.
3.   If this is used as defensive drill, concentrate on defensive fundamentals only.

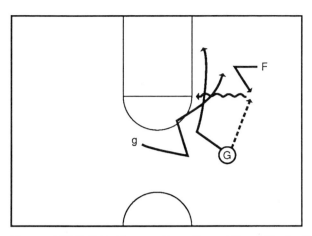

Diagram 3.54: Drill 10   Three-on-Three (Second Guard) Number 2

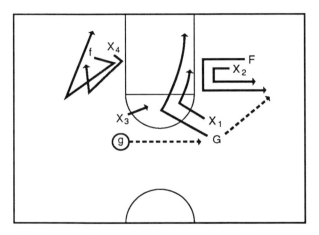

Diagram 3.55: Drill 11   Four-on-Four Number 2

Drill 10: Three-on-Three (Guard-Guard-Forward) Number 2

1.   Same as Drill 9 except add the second guard option.
2.   Drill on all phases of both options, including guard-guard backdoor.

Drill 11: Four-on-Four (Two Guards — Two Forwards) Number 2

1.   This is the same as Drill 10, except the ball can be reversed if one forward has been defended.
2.   Offense against help-side defense can be practiced.
3.   The defense can be instructed or they can play straight up.
4.   Concentrate on offense or defense, unless this is used as a competitive drill.

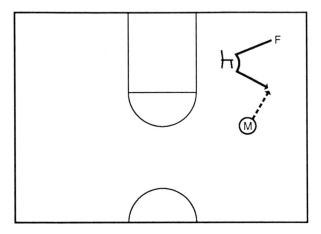

Diagram 3.56: Drill 12   Two-Step, Close-Out Pivot Chair Drill

Close-Out Pivot Drills

Drill 12

Use a chair to practice close-out pivot to open for pass. This is similar to the chair drill for Number 1 in Chapter 2. As the players break to chair, reverse or close-out pivot, and break back for pass. Two steps should be taken.

Drill 13

Give all forwards a ball to practice the dribble-up and close-out pivot. They all dribble and come to a jump stop. On command, they all step toward the coach and prepare to hand off.

Drill 14

Forward starts with ball and dribbles to free-throw area and jump stops.

1. Guard goes outside.
2. Guard goes inside.
3. Guard goes either way.
4. Add defense on guard.
5. Add defense on forward.

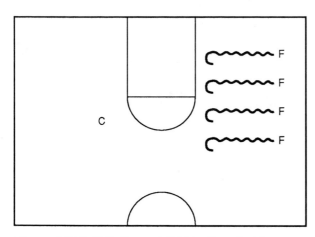

Diagram 3.57: Drill 13   Forwards Dribble, Close-Out Pivot

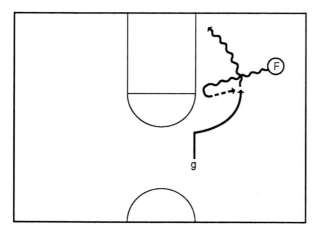

Diagram 3.58: Drill 14   Two-Man Close-Out Pivot

4

Number 3: The Cut Through

The third basic fundamental play of the Fundamental Five has been used by many coaches as their main offense, but is basically a zone play — cutting a player through to the opposite side of the court. It is a play I thought I had a monopoly on the development of early in my coaching career, but found out otherwise.

Virgil Sweet, former Executive Secretary of the Indiana Basketball Coaches' Association and famous expert on the free throw, used this play in his offensive system at Valparaiso High School. When I went to see Virgil at a clinic 25 years ago, my "bubble" burst; he was using "my" play. This did, however, give me confirmation that I was doing something right, as Virgil Sweet was, and still is, a respected authority on the game. And it did start to make me realize that there are only so many things that you can do offensively with the ball. I do not remember where Virgil got the play, even though we have been colleagues for quite some time, it has been used by many and probably was prior to 25 years ago.

The Basic Set-Up

A wing passes back to the point and cuts through to the opposite side. The point moves the ball to the wing on the opposite side, who passes to the cutting wing. This player is generally the team's best shooter. A screen is set by the opposite forward to open the cutter for the ball as shown in diagram 4.1. The play, as all the Fundamental Five, can be run from various set-ups. Diagrams 4.2 through 4.4 show Number 3 from other sets. Since I started using Number 3 as a zone offense from a 1-2-2 set against 2-1-2 zones, the diagrams in this chapter will be mostly from that set. Chapter 9 on zone fundamentals relates more to handling of zones.

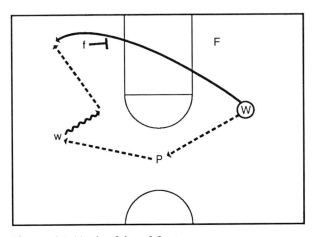

Diagram 4.1 Number 3 from 3-2 set

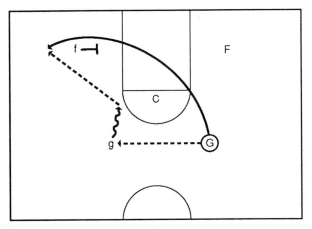

Diagram 4.2 Number 3 from High Post

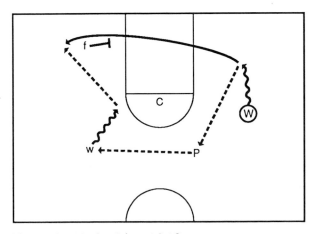

Diagram 4.3 Number 3 from 1-3-1 Set

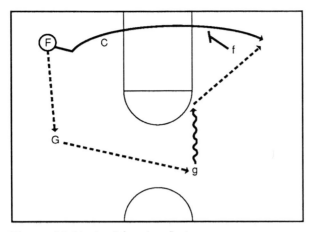

Diagram 4.4 Number 3 from Low Post

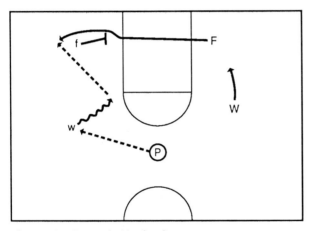

Diagram 4.5 Forward — Number 3

I found that Number 3 is an excellent way of getting into a stack offense after reversal of the ball. Therefore, there are as many man-to-man opportunities as zone. Also, the use of Number 3 against a match-up zone is included in chapter 9.

Actually, I started using this play, as in diagram 4.5, with the forward coming across, but it lessened the rebounding. I have used the point to go through to the corner as in diagram 4.6, but the fundamental principle is still the same.

Options to Number 3

As in any play, there are many options. The following options must be practiced in order to attain complete success of Number 3. These are situations that have

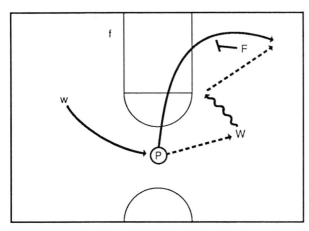

Diagram 4.6 Point Through — Number 3

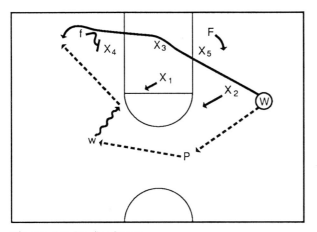

Diagram 4.7 Baseline Screen

developed during the running of the play that have caused the offense trouble during the years of use. The options are used when the defense either denies a pass or overshifts to "play the play."

The Baseline Screen

If the team is employing a zone defense, the screen to keep the defense from shifting quickly is used. This is shown in diagram 4.7. This usually opens W for a good corner shot. Naturally, the team must have good corner shooters for this to work. Our teams practice corner shooting every night because we run into many zones on the high school level of competition. The good corner shot for our teams has been as effective as any 15-foot shot.

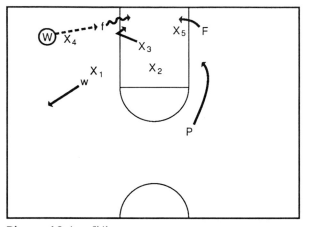

Diagram 4.8 Late Shift

The Late Shift

Sometimes the defensive forward shifts late because of the screen, but still can defense the cutter's shot. However, this generally opens the screener for a return pass. The forward should pivot to the ball, posting hard, because the opposite defensive forward or center will try to cover him. A power lay-up or similar low-post move can usually provide a score in this situation. Diagram 4.8 shows X_4 shift to cover W, then W passes to baseline side of f in low-post play. Note that if X_5 goes to cover f, F is open.

The Defensive Wing Shift

This type of shifting from a 1-2-2 zone or match-up can cause problems. Diagram 4.9 shows that with X_2 covering W, X_1 covering w, and X_3 shifting to P, the defense has matched up with no one apparently open. The development of the wing penetration rule helps eliminate this.

RULE: Upon receiving the ball from the point, the wing should penetrate with the dribble toward the basket, thus forcing the wing to cover him.

The defensive wing does not have time to shift to the corner if P quickly gets the ball to W. By W starting to penetrate, X_2 must cover him because X_1 has been covering P. This enables W to be open in the corner because X_4 has covered f. This penetration forces the defensive forward to cover the corner. It also

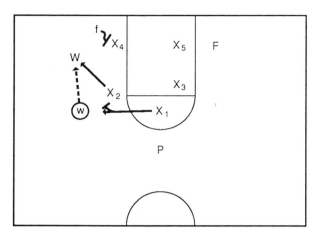

Diagram 4.9 Defensive Wing Shift — No Penetration

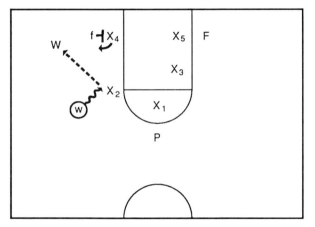

Diagram 4.10 Defensive Wing Shift — Wing Penetration

pulls a rebounder away from the zone as shown in diagram 4.10. If in a man-to-man situation, a slower forward may be forced to guard a quicker wing away from the basket. Also, the offensive forward will have a smaller guard switched onto him in the low-post position.

The Quick Forward Shift Option

As soon as the cutter starts, many teams will shift early. This is one of the better defensive moves against Number 3. Any zone team that is shifting well will cause any offensive team problems. A quick shift is shown in diagram 4.11. To counter this shift, diagram 4.12 shows that the low-post forward, f, must *step toward* X_4, since he is unable to screen X_5 and then break *toward* the ball with X_4 at his back. The ball is being received in the middle low-post area.

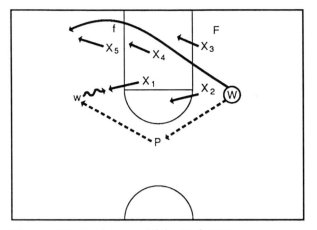

Diagram 4.11   Quick Forward Shift — No Screen

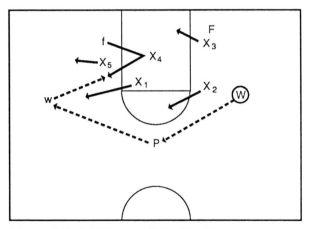

Diagram 4.12   Quick Forward Shift — f Pins X_4

The Flash-Pivot Option

Actually, anytime the forwards may break into the pivot area, the guard may pass them the ball. The forward can reverse pivot and drive if the defense is heavily contesting the pass, as shown in diagram 4.13. If the defense is playing behind him, as shown in diagram 4.14, he should front pivot then pass, shoot, or drive.

However, on an early shift as shown in diagram 4.15, the ball can be fed by either W or P into F, who breaks into the lane counteracting X_4's shift. Most teams want X_3 to cover the lane area, but since F generally is taller and coming in from the blind side, he can be hit with a *high pass*.

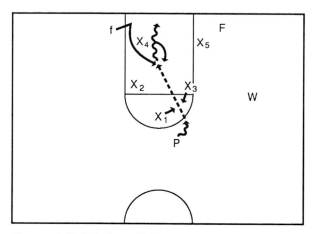

Diagram 4.13 Flash Pivot – Drive

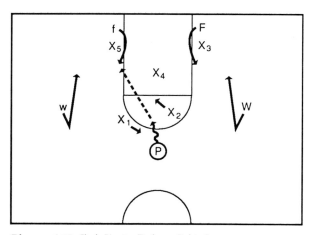

Diagram 4.14 Flash Pivot – Defense Behind

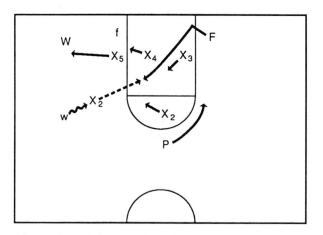

Diagram 4.15 Flash Pivot (After 3 Cut)

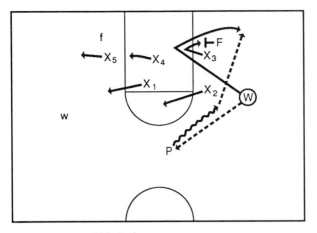

Diagram 4.16 Dribble-Back

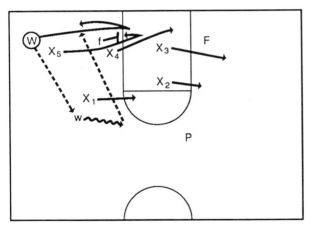

Diagram 4.17 Late Dribble-Back

The Dribble-Back Option

Another method to counteract the quick shift is a reverse action keyed by a dribble back toward the cutting wing's side. This option run occasionally will generally set up a regular 3 better as the defense will not be anxious to shift as early. Diagram 4.16 shows an early dribble-back: P fakes pass to w and dribbles back to F's side; F screens X_4; W reverses to corner for similar play.

This option can be run after the cut through. Many times the defense is expecting continuity and will quickly shift back after the cutter has been denied or at least defended well. Diagram 4.17 shows a late dribble-back after W has cut through and been defended well.

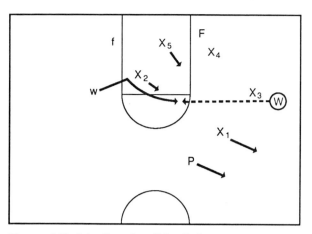

Diagram 4.18 Point Overplay — Wing Flash

The Point Overplay Option

A lazy or unawake offensive point man can find himself in trouble if he is not anticipating pressure on the pass-back from the wing. The main reason we pass the ball to the wing first is a free look at the forward who may be able to post and to get the zone shifting so it will be more susceptible to the screen. In doing so, teams have tried and been successful in stealing the return pass to the point. The point man cannot stand. He must move to receive the pass-back, sometimes out from the key, if the defense is applying pressure. In doing so, he opens the middle for the point overplay option, as shown in diagram 4.18. When w sees X_1 starting to pressure P, he should break into the key area yelling "free throw," one of our verbal location calls.

The point man must be careful that he is not too close to the point defense so that the top of the key is clogged up. He should force the defense to spread by getting into a good passing lane rather than one that can be intercepted without opening a better lane. Of course, if the defense is sagging deep in the middle to protect the flash-post option or the wing flash, the top of the key would be an excellent shot opportunity for the point man. Diagram 4.19 shows where P can step in and get an excellent shot when X_1 has sagged to jam the middle.

Number 3 Continuity Option

A continuity can be developed if the initial play and options are defended. Diagram 4.20 shows that if W does not have a shot or cannot get the ball to f, he passes it back to w. The ball is then passed to P who looks for W coming back

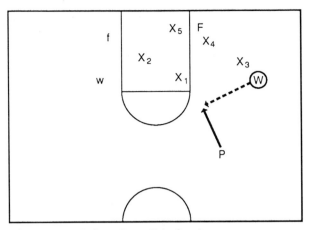

Diagram 4.19 Defense Sags — Point Step-In

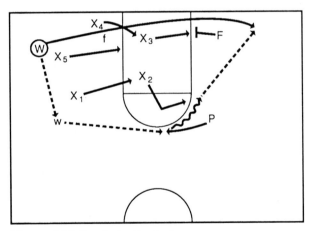

Diagram 4.20 Pass-Back — Continuity

off a screen from F. P may have a shot near the top of the key, if there is an extreme overshift. This would be like a point overplay. This continuity really follows our pass-back rule.

RULE: If the ball is passed back to the point guard, the passer cuts through to the other side.

Point Trap

If the point is trapped, the wings should break toward the ball. Good fundamental press knowledge of not panicking and facing the basket upon receiving the ball must be stressed to beat the double-up and trap. Keeping players spread

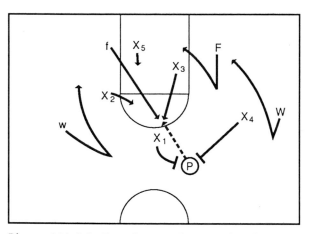

Diagram 4.21 Point Trap — Everyone Comes to the Ball

also helps so the offense has more room to move to the ball. Therefore, the defense has to spread and is not so awesome looking. A wide-awake point man can "see" the open man *before* the trap develops. Players must come to meet the pass. The play pattern must be disregarded and players must yell to him to alert the trapped player of his presence and the area he is cutting to (diagram 4.21).

Again, good fundamentals tell you to hit the middle and go weak-side. Note that f is coming from behind X_3. If he is hit, he should front pivot and look for w on the weak-side backdoor. Whoever gets the ball should get rid of it quickly.

RULE: If a double-up trap occurs, two quick passes should follow.

If a team gambles and doubles-up, someone has to be open. A good defensive team will help on the first pass, but it takes an exceptional team to recover to the second pass. Too many times the offensive team is satisfied with just relieving the pressure, not making the defense pay for the gamble. Diagram 4.22 shows that X_4's first reaction will be to the pass to f. If f quickly passes to W (or F, if he is open), X_4 won't be able to react to recover.

The Corner Trap

Some teams will trap the wing in the corner. The two quick pass rule will generally get a good shot. Diagram 4.23 shows if X_2 is overplaying the pass back to w, P will generally be open at the free-throw circle. The point P must come to meet the pass and w must keep a good passing lane.

F must keep X_3 occupied by starting to cut in the lane as shown in diagram 4.23. If X_3 leaves the lower key area to cover P, F should continue to cut in the lane for a pass.

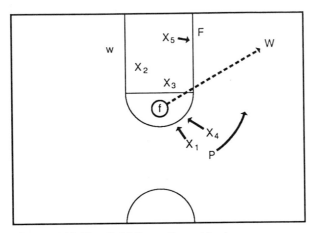

Diagram 4.22 Two Quick Passes (Second Pass)

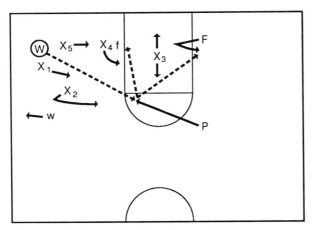

Diagram 4.23 Corner Trap (Second Pass-To for F)

DEFENDING NUMBER 3

Number 3 can be defended by the late shift, defensive wing shift, etc. As was mentioned previously, these have been effectively used, but options have been developed to counteract them. The effectiveness of the option depends on the execution of it. Likewise, the defensive execution may counteract the offense.

The scouting report may include weaknesses, such as corner shooting, poor screens, etc., that may decide which of the defensive options previously mentioned may be most effective. For example, if the team is not as effective outside as inside, the coach may decide to sag on a team who used Number 3. The outside shot is not "given," but the inside shot is protected. The options (previously given) that protect the inside must be used.

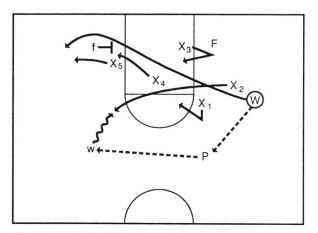

Diagram 4.24   Early Shift — X_2 Slides through to w

If certain shots are to be "given," they never should be wide open but should be hurried by an adjusted defense. If a team could not hit the corner shot on Number 3, no adjustments would ever be needed. Therefore, the zone must shift to hurry some shots and definitely not "give" others. If the scouting report states W is a good corner shooter and w is not, an early shift with X_2 sagging to prevent a pass to f, as shown in diagram 4.24, should work. If w is not a good shooter, then percentage is with the defense. You sag more from the poorer shooters.

The Slide Through

Since it is sometimes unadvisable to switch a wing or guard on a forward, the slide through must be used to counteract the screen. To slide through a screen in Number 3 is like the slide through in Number 2, and requires cooperation from your teammates and knowledge of the screen. The defensive foward X_4 steps up and verbally helps X_2 by calling out "screen" as shown in diagram 4.25; X_4 must step to the ball and let X_2 go through the third man; X_2 is ready to deny W the ball and X_4 can drop back to protect against f's flash pivot. The rest of the players help and recover.

The defending of the initial cut can be executed better if the defensive forward X_4 will not only step up to let X_2 through, but step out in the passing lane to force W farther into the corner. The defensive point guard X_7 should also sag to help clog up a possible flash-pivot option. However, X_1 must be ready for the ball reversal. X_1's depth depends on P's offensive ability and the inside play of the forwards.

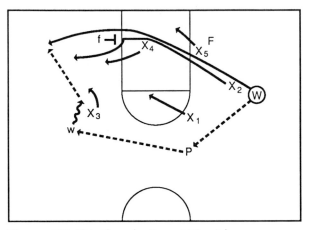

Diagram 4.25 Slide Through – Prevent Mismatch

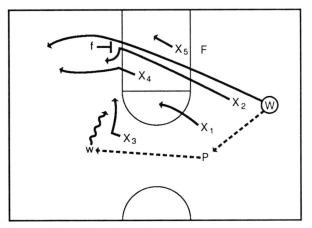

Diagram 4.26 Switch – Deny Pass

Jump Switch

The best method, providing that the height mismatch is not severe, is to jump switch. The denial of the pass to the cutter, W, is easier because X_2 is not worrying about sliding through. Diagram 4.26 shows the jump switch of X_4 onto W and X_2 fronting f to prevent a quick shift-flash post of f.

Defending Double Screen Number 3

Sometimes the offense in double stack will reverse the ball with a double screen Number 3. This must be switched to avoid confusion. Diagram 4.27 shows W

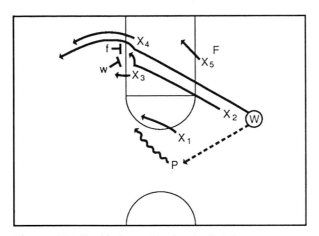

Diagram 4.27 Double Screen Number 3 — Switch

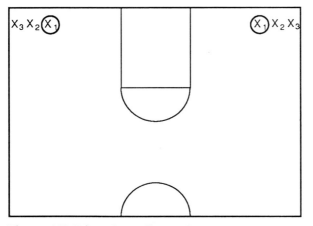

Diagram 4.28: Drill 1 Corner Shooting by Teams

coming to the double screen of f and w. W can go over the top or baseline. If he goes over the top, X_3 switches on W; if W goes baseline, X_4 takes him. X_2 covers the remaining player.

DRILLS FOR NUMBER 3

Drill 1: Corner Shooting by Teams

This can be a daily fun drill to develop good corner shooting.

1. Players are put in each corner by teams.
2. Players alternate shooting until one team makes ten shots.

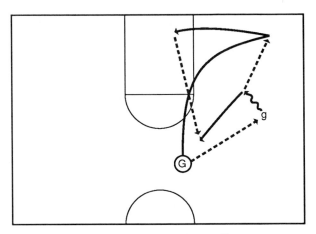

Diagram 4.29: Drill 2   Two-Man Number 3 Drill

3. Teams should "call out" when they make a basket: "seven," "eight," etc.
4. Players should follow and rebound their own shot.
5. Alternate corners after each win.
6. Losing teams can run a lap before going to the next basket.

Drill 2: Two-Man Number 3 Drill

This drill helps to teach dribble penetration as well as pivoting to receive the ball before shooting. The drill basically is for the guards, however all players can benefit from it.

1. G passes to g.
2. g penetrates with the dribble as G cuts to the ballside corner.
3. G pivots, receives pass from g, then shoots.
4. G follows shot, rebounds.
5. G passes out to g, who is now in G's original position.
6. Positions are now reversed and drill is repeated.

Drill 3: Four-Man (Plus) Number 3 Drill

This is one of our pre-game warm-up drills. It is exactly like the two-man drill except four lines are used instead of two. The same principles are drilled here as in the two-man drill.

1. Players rotate from A - B - C - D - A.
2. Ball starts in lines B and C.
3. A and D receive pass from B and C.
4. A and D penetrate as B and C cut to ball-side corner.

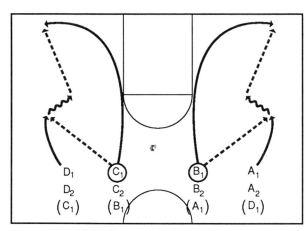

Diagram 4.30: Drill 3 Four Man Number 3

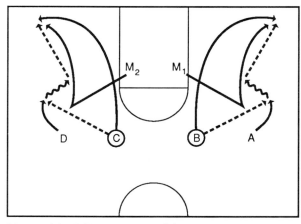

Diagram 4.31: Drill 4 Manager Drill for Number 3

5. B and C pivot and shoot.
6. B and C rebound their own shot.
7. B passes back to next B and C passes back to next C.

Drill 4: Manager Drill for Number 3

This drill is the same as two-man and four-man Number 3 drills as far as the offensive players are concerned. Managers are used as defensive players to get players to shoot, with defensive players trying to reach them. This simulates a late shift in defending the cutter.

1. Run drill like Drill 2 or 3.
2. Managers should guard A and D as they penetrate.
3. When B and C pass to A and D respectively, the managers switch to cover the shooters.

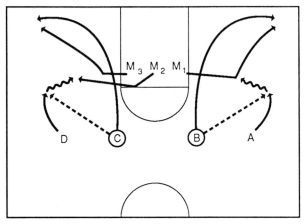

Diagram 4.32: Drill 5 Optional Three-Manager for Number 3

Drill 5: Optional Three-Manager Drill for Number 3

This drill simply adds one manager to Drill 4. The optional manager can play defense on either side of the court. A pass-back to the penetrating guard may be necessary if the optional defensive manager covers the first pass. The managers get quite a workout during these drills. Players can be used for the defensive managers.

1. Same offensive set-up as four-man drill (with one manager).
2. Optional manager is used for both sections of two-man drills.
3. Optional manager doubles-up on either corner shot, forcing pass-back, etc.

Drill 6: Spot Shots per Minute

This is a lot like the old ''around the world'' drill, only two balls and two rebounders are used. This is a good station drill.

1. Shooter moves from spot to spot, shooting without dribble, for one minute from spots the ball is shot from in Number 3.
2. One rebounder retrieves the shot while the other passes to the shooter.

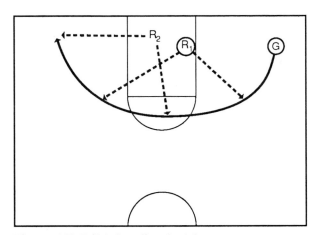

Diagram 4.33: Drill 6 Spot Shots Per Minute

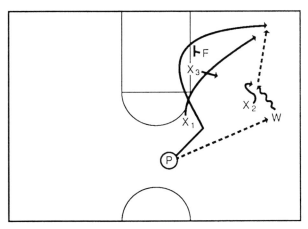

Diagram 4.34: Drill 7 Three-on-Three (Slide Through) Number 3

Drill 7: Three-on-Three Number 3 Drill

This drill can be either an offensive or defensive drill. A specific move such as baseline screen, late shift, quick shift, dribbler back, corner trap, or forward trap can be worked.

1. P passes to W.
2. W dribble-penetrates as P cuts off a baseline screen by F.
3. Specific moves can be worked on or simply straight defense.
4. Option: If offense scores or gets offensive rebound, they maintain possession of the ball ("make it, take it").

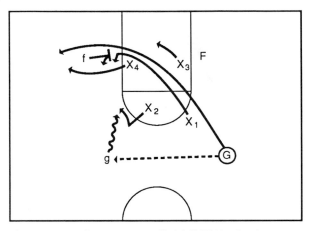

Diagram 4.35: Drill 8   Four-Man (Quick Shift) Number 3

Drill 8: Four-on-Four Number 3 Drill

This fits in with our eight-man group theory. Offense or defense can be concentrated upon as in the three-on-three drill.

1. Pass-back rule is in effect.
2. G passes to g.
3. g penetrates as G cuts off screen by f.
4. If G passes back to g, after receiving the ball in the corner, G should 3 cut along baseline to receive screen by F. This simply repeats the drill.

5

Number 4: The Pick Opposite

The easiest way to score is to free a man under the basket and give him the ball. All of the phases of the Fundamental Five have this in mind. However, one of the most popular moves today is the pick opposite, or screening away from the ball. In fact, the pick opposite's use in the passing game has made it more popular than the pick and roll. However, all of the Fundamental Five, except the initial option of Number 2, involve screens.

When Fred Taylor was at Ohio State, he called this the "head-hunter." It has been called many things, but it is still basically preventing one defensive player from guarding his man because the offense has screened him out. Bob Knight of Indiana University uses this as the crux of his passing game. Obviously, some of Fred Taylor's "head-hunting" had some influence on him. Where the idea originated is irrelevant, but it must be learned in today's game.

The pick opposite gives definite movement without the ball. It gets players moving away from the ball, yet promotes a pass to be received while moving to the ball. It also creates mismatches when the defense switches to counteract the screens. However, to be effective, like any of the offensive moves of the Fundamental Five, it must be executed properly. Diagrams 5.1 through 5.5 show Number 4 run from five of the many set-ups.

FUNDAMENTALS OF NUMBER 4

Setting a Good Screen

Many of the same fundamentals for Number 1 are adapted to Number 4. The screen must be wide and must be set on the defensive man, no matter where

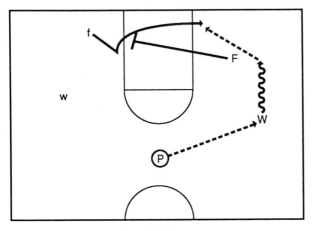

Diagram 5.1 Number 4 from 3-2 Set

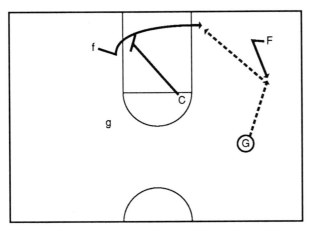

Diagram 5.2 Number 4 from High Post (f Could Come High)

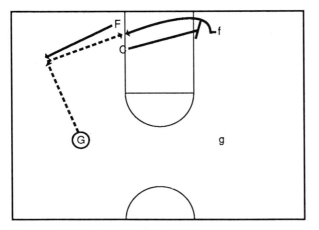

Diagram 5.3 Number 4 from Single Stack

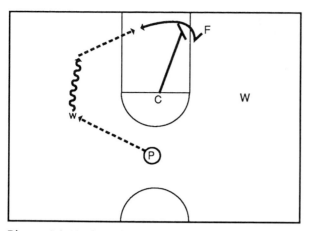

Diagram 5.4 Number 4 from 1-3-1

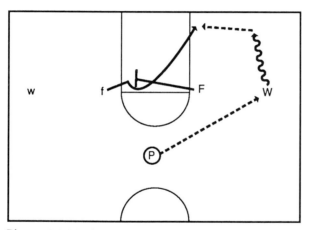

Diagram 5.5 Number 4 from 1-4 Set

the offensive player is. Since the screener will be facing the defensive man, he can set the screen as close as he desires without touching him. The knees should be flexed and the screener should be prepared for contact.

A roll, like in Number 1, can be used to "widen" the screen. The roll or reverse pivot in the direction the defensive player goes gives the screener good offensive rebounding position, as well as leaving him open for a return pass. The defensive player is behind if a switch is made. This is a definite advantage to the screener. If a switch is made, the screen has been a good one.

Difficulties of the Screen

There are certain difficulties of a good screen that must be overcome before the screen can be effective. The screen cannot be held if the defense is sagging in the lane because of the three-second rule. The screener must not move, other than a direct pivot, after setting the screen. If the screen is not wide, it is easily stepped around or over. An offensive player (the screener) has his eyes off the ball for a brief period of time and must be encouraged to roll quickly.

The Offensive Receiver

The primary responsibility of freeing the receiver has been placed on the screener. However, the receiver must do some fundamental things to receive the ball in scoring position. A head and shoulder fake just before breaking toward the ball will aid the screener in his pick. A hand out for a target toward where the passer should throw the ball is helpful for the passer. Always step toward the ball when receiving it. The same movements and options of Number 2 receiver will work in Number 4 regarding low-post and forward position. (Refer to forward receiving ball, low-post moves, chapter 3.)

Shots from Number 4

In Number 4, players receive the ball in the low post, medium post, or high post. They also find themselves in a one-on-one position from the wing or corner.

Low Post

The same low-post shots as for Number 2 are used here: the baseline power lay-up, the step-over hook, the turn-around jumper, the step-under, and the jump hook. Since the ball is received in the same place as the guard in Number 2, it would be redundant to repeat information here.

Flash Post

Since players break into the high-post area in Number 4, certain shots and moves need to be practiced. The front pivot turn-around jump shot, the front pivot and drive, the reverse power pivot drive, and the drop-step pivot and drive are the ones recommended for both high and medium post. The moving hook and jump hook are also used in the medium-post area.

When breaking off a Number 4 or simply flashing into the post, the forward comes to the ball hard with a jump stop. This way either foot can be the pivot foot. A reverse power pivot or front pivot is used if the defense is behind the forward. These were discussed in Number 2. Care must be taken that the shoulders are squared with the basket on the shot. The forward now is in attack position. He can shoot, pass to an open man under the basket, or drive to the basket.

If the defense tightens up so the jump shot cannot be shot, the forward should be ready to drive. Since the forward comes to a jump stop, he can pivot either way. Some players drive better off one foot than the other. We encourage use of either foot, but are more concerned about the player not traveling on the pivot and drive and about the direction of the drive, which should be off the lead foot of the defense. If the defender comes to the offense with his right foot forward, the offense should drive right and should be as close to the defender's lead foot as possible.

The reverse pivot and drive is also known as a drop-step. It is used when the defense is overplaying the forward. When the defense is reaching for the pass to the forward, the offense should reverse pivot after receiving the pass and drive to the basket. The forward actually closes out the defense with a wide pivot. Care must be taken to pivot *before* dribbling. This pivot is the same as in Number 2, when the pass to the forward is denied.

If the forward breaks in the medium-post area, the over-the-rim moving hook can be shot quickly while moving away from the defense. The hook is a good shot at this distance. Because the player is in the lane, he may not have a good angle to use the backboard as in Number 5 shooting. He is also moving away from the basket. The back of the rim should be looked at rather than the front, because of the player movement. The brain has a mental picture of the distance when you first sight the basket. As you move away, the distance of the shot is slightly increased; therefore, if you sight the front of the rim, your shot will usually come up short.

Because of the short distance, the jump hook can be used. In fact, if perfected, this may be the best shot around the basket. The only problem may be that in moving to get the ball, the forward may travel. The jump hook keeps the player closer to the basket for a rebound.

NUMBER 4 OPTIONS

Low Post

The 4 play is designed to get the ball into the low-post area. This is the first and primary option. The screen on the forward's man should be set so the forward can move to the low post if at all possible. Diagrams 5.1 through 5.5 show this primary option. (Low post is also discussed in chapter 3 on Number 2.)

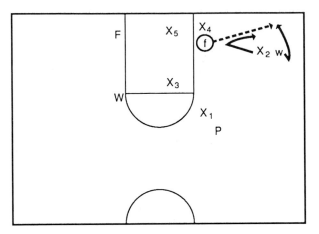

Diagram 5.6 "Ins and Outs"

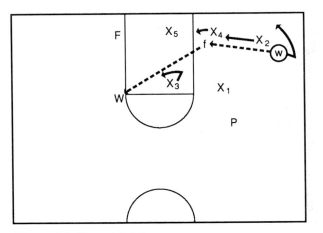

Diagram 5.7 "Ins and Outs"

Ins and Outs

"Ins and Outs" are exactly what the term describes — the ball going inside and back out. When the ball goes inside, the defense is going to collapse. If not, the offense should be one-on-one low, obviously. When the defense helps, the offensive low-post player can return the ball to the player whose defense is helping. This player should be ready to shoot the ball on the return pass. If the defense recovers, another pass to the low post may open up. This needs to be practiced.

The passer may have to move some to be open for the return pass. The passer's man, X_2, usually follows the ball to help X_4. However, as shown in diagram 5.6, W should never leave the vision area of the post man F.

Actually, f could pass to any player on the perimeter. Diagram 5.7 shows f with the ball received from W; f passes out to W (or P) because he has seen X_3 sag deep.

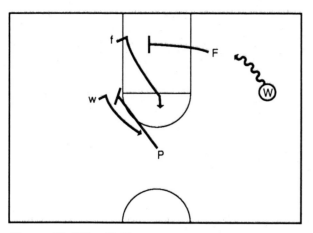

Diagram 5.8 "Clear Out"

Clear Out

If the forward or center has screened away from the ball, a side has been cleared out for a possible one-on-one drive, as shown in diagram 5.8. As the forward comes off the screen, he should see the wing starting his drive. Instead of going to the low-post area, the forward clears to the high-post area. If the defender of the forward switched, or helps too much, the forward yells "free throw." This is to let the wing know he is open at the free-throw line.

RULE: If a player goes one-on-one, do not bring your man into his area.

When you just clear the forward for the wing to go one-on-one, the defense will adjust quicker than if they are concerned about a Number 4. If the forward just clears, the defense may sag or even zone. If the defense is concerned about the 4 play, the wing has an excellent opportunity to beat his man without defensive help. This is obvious because the defense is concerned about opening up a pass to the low-post area.

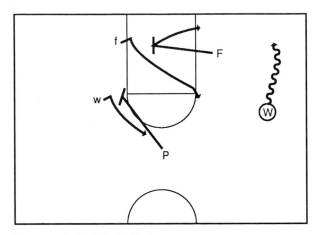

Diagram 5.9 ``Roll-Back'' Option

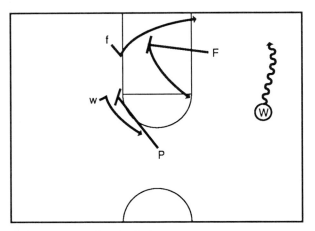

Diagram 5.10 ``Roll-Back'' Option

Roll-Back Option

After the forward has screened for the opposite forward, he can roll back to the ball. However, he must roll opposite the cutting forward, as shown in diagrams 5.9 and 5.10. The pivot is a reverse close-out like Number 1, with the pivot in the direction of the cutter's defensive man — this helps to get the defense screened even better. Even if he doesn't roll back, he should pivot. By rolling opposite, the passer has two post men to pass to, one in the high post and one in the low post. Care must be taken so that the two offensive players are far enough apart so that one defensive player can't play both passing lanes.

RULE: The screener on Number 4 should roll back opposite the cutter far enough to form two passing lanes.

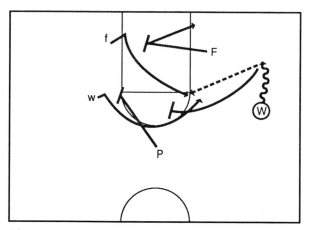

Diagram 5.11 ``Forward Split''

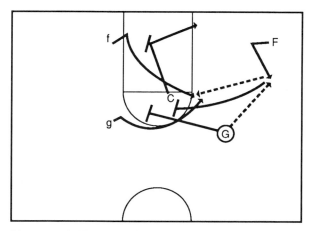

Diagram 5.12 ``Forward Split''

The Forward Split Option

If the defense is denying the ball well in the low-post position, we look for the medium or high post. This can be on the cutter or the roll-back. If the forward received the ball in a position he cannot score, we can try the forward split (diagrams 5.11 and 5.12). W passes to f, who is cutting into the high-post area. W cuts above the post following his pass. This clears the low-post area for a pass to F. W sets a screen, a Number 4, for w, who has interchanged with P.

Since a player is in the low post, the cutter off the split is basically limited to a jump shot. The forward gives the cutter the ball with a close-out pivot, like in Number 2. Diagram 5.12 shows a forward split from the high-post set. Note that in both cases a high-low can occur with f and C.

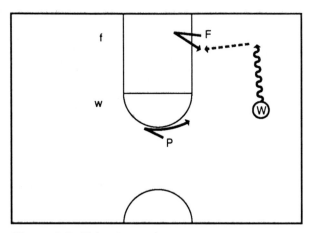

Diagram 5.13 "Fake 4"

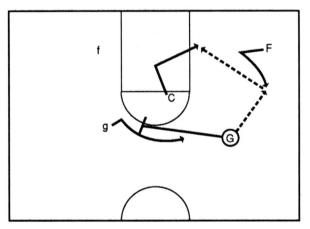

Diagram 5.14 "Fake 4"

The Fake 4 Option

Instead of the forward going opposite to pick, he comes back immediately for the ball himself. Diagrams 5.13 and 5.14 show examples of this and they work well when the defense is constantly switching or being lazy in the switch.

Again, we feel that at least two steps should be taken before cutting back. A good fundamental fake will set up an easy basket against a lazy defense. Execution is still the key.

The fake 4 option also can set up the clear for the man with the ball. It helps to disguise a definite clear out for a one-on-one. Once a fake 4 is used successfully, the defense tightens up. The clear out to the high post will bring the defense up (diagram 5.15).

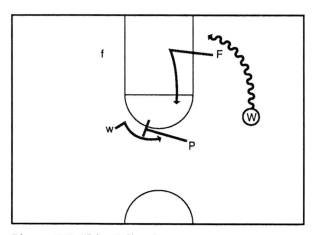

Diagram 5.15 "Fake 4" Clear Out

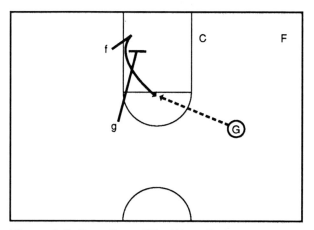

Diagram 5.16 Down-Screen "Head-Hunter"

The Head-Hunter or Down-Screen Option

If the defensive team is automatically switching and they have an extreme weakness at guard, this option will give a big man, little man switch. Diagram 5.16 shows g screening for f. If f has a good shot, he takes it. He may drive on the smaller or weaker guard.

After the guard down-screens, he breaks out to the corner. If f receives the ball too high for a good shot or move to the basket, he can pass to g for a Number 2 play as shown in diagram 5.17. This works even better if f has a "little man" switched on him.

RULE: On a down screen by a guard, the offensive guard should "roll" first the direction the forward cuts. Then he cuts to the near corner.

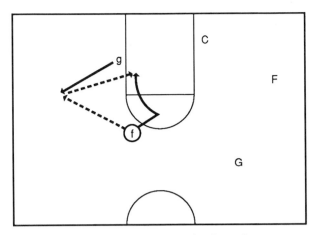

Diagram 5.17 Number 2 Cut Option After Down Screen

As g ``rolls back'' to the corner, he pivots like the forward would in Number 4. In this way, he helps to close out the defender even more to promote a switch or at least a delay to deny the ball. Also, g is in a better position to receive the pass as he has checked his defensive man before breaking out.

Double Head-Hunter Option

This is simply a double screen to free a shooter for the ball. It does provide somewhat of a clear out for the passer and obviously is the advantage of the double screen. The screens should be set on the shooter's defensive man. The option can be used as a specific part of the offense, or when the defense is doing an excellent job of ``beating the pick'' on an individual basis.

This can be used as an option of Number 2's pass-back Number 5 option (see chapter 3). The University of Louisville uses this ``double down'' as part of their high-post offense to free the guard who has cut off the high post. Diagram 5.18 shows forward F passing back to off guard g. Then both F and the high-post man C screen for the original cutter G. G can cut either way.

If G cuts to the baseline side, then F follows the down-screen roll rule and ``rolls'' to the baseline side. However, he simply posts there, looking for a return pass from G. C should also ``roll'' to the baseline side to force a switch on G's man. However, as shown in diagram 5.19, C then can step back to the high-post area looking for a pass from G.

If G would fake the use of the baseline and come back over the top, as shown in diagram 5.20, then the ``rolls'' would be to the middle. G usually gets open near the top of the key. C rolls into the medium-post area, hopefully with G's man switched on him. F stays low. F would break out to forward position if g can't hit G or C to start a new 2 play; f backdoors as soon as C gets the ball.

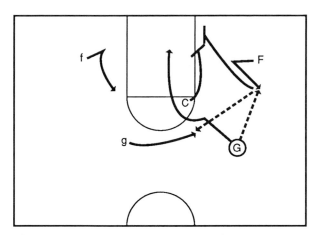

Diagram 5.18 Number 2 Cut Pass-Back Double Head-Hunter

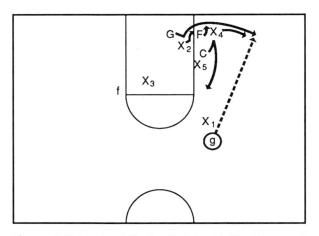

Diagram 5.19 Number 2 Cut Pass-Back Double Head-Hunter — G to Baseline

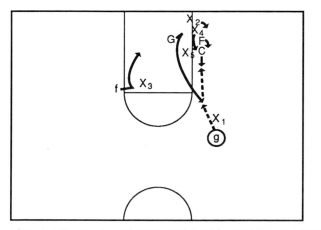

Diagram 5.20 Number 2 Cut Pass-Back Double Head-Hunter — G (Overplayed)

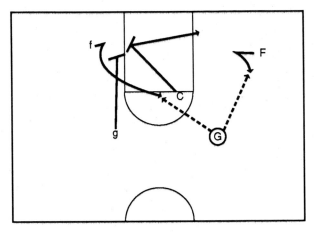

Diagram 5.21 Double Head-Hunter — f to High Post

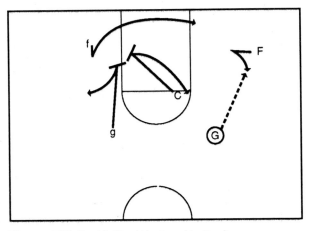

Diagram 5.22 Double Head-Hunter — f to Baseline

If the double head-hunter is used as an initial down screen to free the forward in the high-post area, the options are basically the same. These are shown in diagrams 5.21 and 5.22. If f comes over the top, off g's screen, both g and C "roll" to the middle. Then g rolls out, similar to F's move in diagram 5.20. However, C will roll back to get open at the low post for a high-low pass from f or low-post pass from F. C would not necessarily have to start from the high post; C could come across from the low post to set the initial screen.

If f goes low, to the baseline off C's screen, then the "rolls" are to the baseline. Diagram 5.22 shows f going to the low-post area and C rolling back to the high-post area; g waits, then rolls back to guard position.

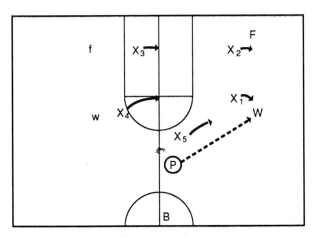

Diagram 5.23 Line B – Step to the Ball

DEFENDING NUMBER 4

Again, it must be a team effort defensively to stop any team offense. The calling out of a pick opposite is just as important as in the pick and roll. This is not only for the player screened to see the screen coming, but for the rest of the team to be able to help.

Scouting an opponent is always a must. Through a good scouting report, you can tell whether a forward-forward switch will hurt you. As a general rule, we will use a forward-forward switch.

The Forward-Forward Switch

This must be a hard switch. The defensive hand (hand nearest the ball) must be up and there is hard denial of the ball in the pivot area. The receiver is almost fronted when the switch is made. The switch forces the offense to go high or away from the ball.

The forward who defensively has sagged toward the ball makes the play more difficult to execute offensively. Anytime the ball is passed or dribbled to one side of the floor, our players are instructed to step to the ball. They should be at line B which is what we called it when I coached at New Albany High School because of the mascot "Bulldog" picture in the middle of our floor. If your center circle has any decoration in it, you should name it. The line down the center of the court is imaginary. See diagram 5.23. Players should be able to see their man and the ball. Players should also be within one or two steps of the passing lane, depending upon the quickness of the opponent, his ability, and the distance he is from the ball.

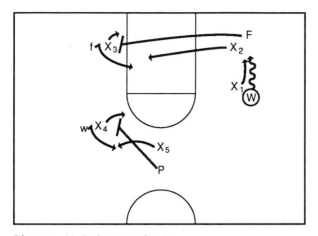

Diagram 5.24 Defense Not Sagging

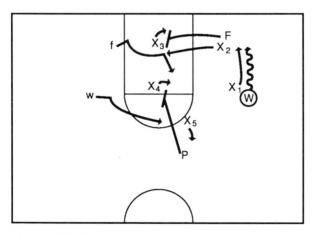

Diagram 5.25 Defense on Line B

In diagrams 5.24 and 5.25, the difference is shown between the sagging and tight defense. In diagram 5.24 X_3 is so close to f that when X_2 switches, f still has enough room to get the ball in the scoring area. It is not that X_3 isn't to guard f closely, but not so far away from the ball that the screen is more effective for the offense. In diagram 5.25, when X_2 switches, he can force f away from the ball. He can even get help from X_4 because he drove f into X_4's passing lane. This also cuts down on the area W has to go one-on-one, by jamming the key area as a zone would.

Since the defense doesn't want the low-post option, the defensive forward being screened, X_3, steps to the baseline and "forces" the screen to be topside. This helps X_2 to deny better topside, knowing in which direction f is most likely

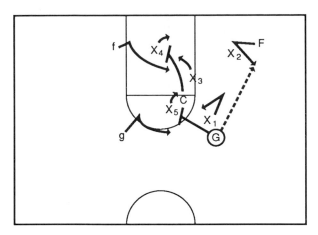

Diagram 5.26 Two-Guard Front — Defensive Guard Sag

to come. Obviously, if X_2 calls out the screen, X_3 is better prepared to do this. The call "step right," similar to defending Number 1, is the best call (see "Defending Number 1" in chapter 2).

Defensive Guard Help

The defense on line B helps to make the offense go away from the middle to receive the ball. The guards, on a two-guard front, are to step to the ball so that they are in position to see their man and the ball as shown in diagram 5.26. This enables X_1 to help on the drive by F, then recover to switch on g. It also clogs the middle passing lane to f — you don't want the ball to go inside.

The other defensive guard X_5 should be stepped toward the ball. He will sag even deeper as G passes to F. This enables X_5 to protect the middle even more, then switch to G. I do not expect X_5 to screen out G for rebounding as long as G stays outside. X_5 "looks" for G and then looks for the long rebound.

The defensive hand (hand nearest to the ball) of each guard is up. This also discourages passes to the middle. The pass outside is permitted, even encouraged, except when we are in a trapping defense.

The Low Post

The best defense of the low post is to prohibit the ball from getting there. The forward-forward switch should force the cutter out of the low-post area.

If the ball is received in the low-post area, the defense must protect the baseline power shot. Force the post man away from the baseline toward help defense. The amount of help needed must be determined by the ability of the post man.

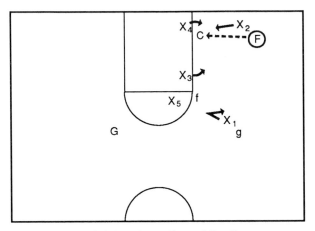

Diagram 5.27   Help in Low Post — "Ins and Outs"

Ins and Outs

If the ball is passed into the low-post area, the defensive corner man should help in containing the post man as shown in diagram 5.27. Note that f has posted high and that X_3 must deny f a pass from either F or C. Therefore, X_2 must help on C. The only times we don't help on C is when C is totally inept at the position or when F is an outstanding defensive player. In those cases X_4 contains C individually.

RULE: If the ball goes to the low post, the near defensive forward (or wing) helps until the ball is passed back out.

Since X_2 knows the pass will probably go back to F, he should *not* completely turn his back on F when helping on C. Instead of turning completely, X_2 should reverse pivot and slide diagonally to help on C. When C returns the ball to F, X_2 will only have to front pivot and slide to be back in defensive position on F. F will be open, but will not be in as good a scoring position as C was.

When the ball is returned to F, X_4 should be on the baseline side of C, semifronting C. The defensive hand (hand nearest the baseline) should be in the passing lane. This should force the ball outside or a more dangerous pass to the inside.

Note in diagram 5.27, that X_1 and X_5 have sagged considerably when the ball is in the baseline area. X_1 is still near the passing lane back out to g. However, a pass-back to g is taking the ball out of the scoring area. The only time X_1 won't sag as deeply is if g is a star player.

RULE: When you are guarding a star player, do not help. You are trying to prevent the star from receiving the ball.

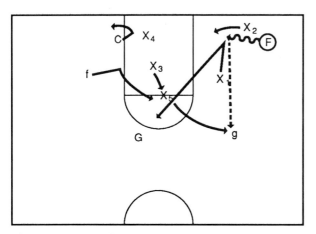

Diagram 5.28 ''Double-Switch'' Recovery – Clear Out

In the same respect, we always want to be ready to help on the star. If the star gets the ball in the low post, stronger help is needed and F may get open for a shot.

Clear Out

Guarding a good one-on-one player is one of the hardest things for a defensive player to do. One-on-one practice helps, but team help, as in the defensive guard play, will help. Diagram 5.26 shows that when G picks X_5, and X_1 helps on F, g will be open at the top of the key. The amount of sag depends on F's ability to drive and g's ability to shoot. Our principle is basically to stop the close-in shot. We, therefore, prefer to stop the drive by having X_1 helping on F's drive.

If g is getting the ball and hitting the shot, we may have to ''double switch'' the guards as shown in diagram 5.28. The guards must talk on this. Actually, X_5 just rolls off screen and returns to guard his original man, g. Player X_1 had switched, but moved to help X_2 on F's drive. When X_5 recovers to guard g, X_1 returns to guard G.

"Fire" Situation

Since the clear out is designed for the best one-on-one player, it is susceptible to a trap or ''fire'' situation. ''Fire'' is the call for a double-up by two players and the rest zone. The forward F starts his one-on-one move to the baseline. If we are really trying to trap F, X_2 will deny the outside move and open up the baseline as shown in diagram 5.29. It aapears that X_2 has given F the line. However, X_2 angles his slide to cut off F. By denying him the outside, he forced him inside. He now has the baseline to help cut off F.

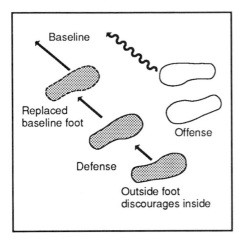

Diagram 5.29 Defensive Footwork for "Fire"

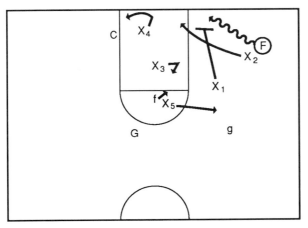

Diagram 5.30 "Fire" on Clear Out

After X_2 has cut off F, X_1 comes and doubles F on the baseline as shown in diagram 5.30. Player X_5 covers the first pass back to g and the rest of the team zones.

Some teams have had success with the forward X_4 coming over for the trap and X_5 covering C. The ability of your players and the opponents may determine which trap is best for you. Yelling "fire" helps the defensive team to know the trap is coming and when to play "zone."

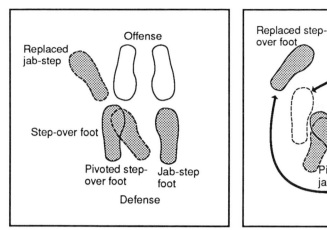

Diagram 5.31 Jab-Step – To Defend "Roll"   **Diagram 5.32** Completion of Jab-Step and Roll

Defending the Roll-Back

This is one of the best offensive options available and therefore one of the most difficult to defend. Since we are switching and forcing the cutter away from the ball, the roll-back is to the low-post area. A good screen is going to "head-hunt" and screen out the defender, as he would for a defensive rebound. The defense must talk so that the switch is confirmed early. The defender guarding the roll-back must react quickly.

The best maneuver is the same as our offensive rebound move, the jab-step and roll. These are shown in diagrams 5.31 and 5.32. The move is a cross-over step to the baseline foot of the screener, with a pivot and roll in front of the screener. After the jab-step, the defense pivots and rolls his defensive hand in front of the screener. He is then on the baseline side of the offense and forces the roll-back player up out of the low-post area.

The Guard Split Option

On a normal guard split we always switch our guards (diagram 5.33). Because of line B defense, player X_1 should be sagged near the center C. As G passes to C, X_5 steps to the ball. Both X_1 and X_5 are in position for a tie-up of C as well as for the switch of the crossing guards.

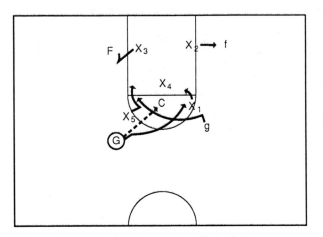

Diagram 5.33   Defending Normal Guard-Guard Split

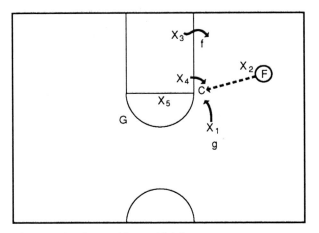

Diagram 5.34   Forward Pass to High Post

The Forward Split Option

When the forward passes to the high post after the roll back as shown in diagram 5.34, a forward split could occur. As soon as the ball is passed to C, X_1 and X_2 step to the ball as guards would on a guard split. X_3 must shift to protect a high low pass from C to f. X_2 must also be aware of a back door cut by F if f clears the low post area.

If the forward receives the ball from C on the split as shown in diagram 5.35, then X_4 will switch on C if C uses a close out pivot. X_2 will switch onto C. Note that X_1, by stepping to the ball, has forced F very high. The switch only puts a forward X_2 on a center C, therefore eliminating some of the offensive effectiveness of the play.

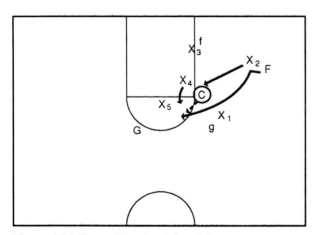

Diagram 5.35 Forward Receives Ball on Split

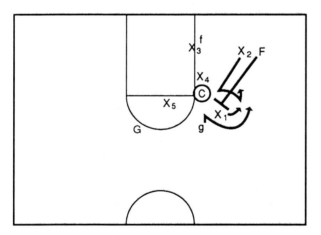

Diagram 5.36 Forward Screen on Split Defense

If the forward F screens X_1 as shown in diagram 5.36, then an over the top defensive move as in Number 1 is used. The defensive forward X_2 helps X_1 to outside like a Number 1 play. This forces the cutter, g, away from the high post, C. If g goes inside, X_5 should help and recover or call a switch with X_1. If F is using a good roll back after his screen, we may be forced to jumpswitch X_2 and X_1.

The Fake 4 Option

Since the screen really is not set, no switch is necessary. The defense must be careful not to switch too early. The defensive forward is waiting to jab-step on the screen. Talking on defense, ''I'll take him after the screen,'' is a good reminder

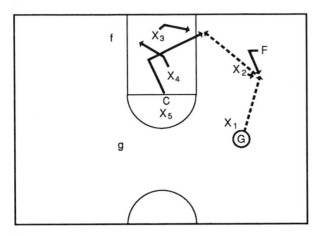

Diagram 5.37 ``Early Switch'' Gets C Easy Basket

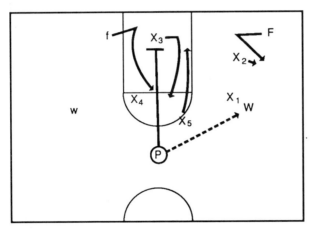

Diagram 5.38 Down-Screen Defense — Slide Through

not to switch too early. If the defense switches soon, the offense will be open for an easy basket as shown in diagram 5.37. This is because C has too much room to maneuver on X_3, who has stepped to the baseline.

Head-Hunter or Down Screen

Since we run into a guard-forward switch, we usually do not want to switch. This is one play where the forward must slide through the screen. We also want the offense to go high-middle rather than low-middle. In diagram 5.38: X_3 steps to line B as the ball is passed to W; X_3 steps to the inside of the screen set by P; X_5 will help X_3 through by going farther inside; X_3 slides through third man.

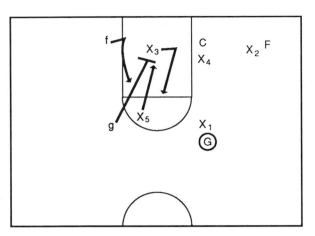

Diagram 5.39 Down-Screen Defense — Step to Inside

When the down screen occurs on the weak side of a low-post offense as shown in diagram 5.39, the forward f wants to receive the ball in the medium post. The defense on the ball side is denying the ball so help must come after the pass. Therefore, X_3 must force f up higher after stepping to the middle. By stepping to the ball, f can fake up and go backdoor; X_3 must be ready for this. X_5 helps to force f higher, but is ready to recover to g.

Switching

There are times when the screen and "roll" of the offense is effective enough to open the shooter off the down screen. Sometimes you may have to switch to eliminate this. I've seen coaches lose ball games because they kept harping "just execute." The switch is easier. It is more effective in cutting off the pass to the forward (or baseline player) coming off the screen. Referring back to diagram 5.39, if X_5 switches hard on f, he can stop the pass to him. However, X_3 will need to jab-step and roll as was shown in "defending the roll-back." Also, the fake 4 option can occur. It is probably easier to switch on all screens, but care must be taken to prevent lazy defense.

Actually, switching is the best method of defending the down screen because of help-side defense. Since the down screen 4 generally occurs away from the ball, this helps the offense, if the defense is following his man rather than playing the basketball. By switching, the defensive help-side forward is staying near the basket to help on a Number 1, 2, etc. Also, the defensive guard will switch to guard a player playing perimeter. The off ball-side switch is almost zone defense away from the ball. Therefore, away from the ball, we always want to switch on down-screen 4 plays.

RULE: On defending down screen 4 away from the ball, switch men.

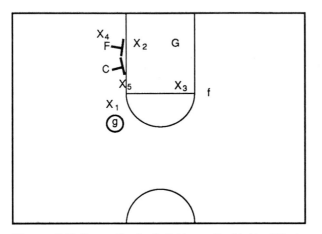

Diagram 5.40 Preparation for Switching on Double Head-Hunter

The Double Head-Hunter

Since the offense has added another screen to open the baseline shooter, they obviously want to get him the ball. The defense is similar to a baseline 4 play. In diagram 5.40 F and C are screening for G. G can go either way but whichever way G goes, either X_4 or X_5 switch and X_2 uses a roll-back jab-step defensive move to front the screener. Normally G will go baseline and X_2 sometimes can beat the double screen by anticipating it. This is because of the congestion in the middle. However, if F is using the roll-back type screen, X_4 still may have to switch. Communication, as on all switches, is important.

The amount of sag or defensive help X_3 can give depends on the position of f. If f is out in the guard position, he can give a lot of help on G cutting to the middle. However, if f comes to the scoring area as shown in diagram 5.40, X_3 must play f honest.

This switching occurs on any double screen. The defensive player being screened must be ready to recover by the jab-step and roll to defend the offensive player he is switching onto.

DRILLS FOR NUMBER 4

Drill 1: Chair Drill for Screen

This drill is used when beginning to teach the screen. It can be used as a station drill because it can be done anywhere. This can be a down screen as well as a cross screen.

1. Place a chair anywhere on the floor.
2. Players are in line X_1 X_2 X_3 etc.

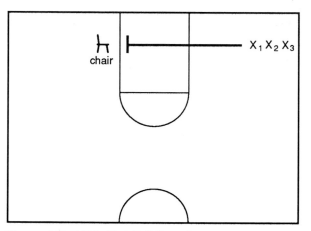

Diagram 5.41: Drill 1 Chair Drill (Screen)

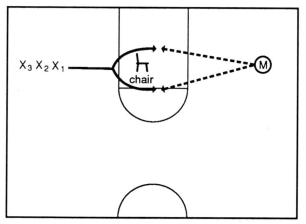

Diagram 5.42: Drill 2 Chair Drill (Receiver)

3. X_1 goes to chair and sets screen as close to chair as possible.
4. Coach calls for roll-back "left" or "right," checking for proper pivot, etc.
5. *Option:* Second player in line, X_2, can have ball and pass to X_1 on roll-back.

Drill 2: Chair Drill for Receiver

This drill is used to help the receiver (of the screen) to get the proper movement, head and shoulder fake, hand out for target, step to the ball, and balance to shoot the basketball on receiving it. This can be for a down screen as well as a cross screen.

1. Place a chair in the area where screen is most likely to occur.
2. Players are in line opposite the ball (X_1 X_2 X_3 etc.)

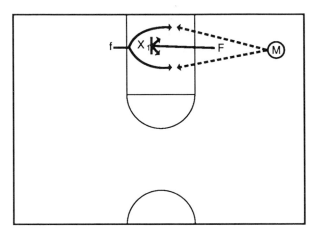

Diagram 5.43: Drill 3   Three-Man Drill (f Either Way)

3.   The ball is in a manager's hand opposite the line. This could be the
     player after being receiver, or a coach.
4.   Player X_1 fakes one way and goes opposite off the chair screen. Coach
     can determine which way.
5.   Player receives ball for shot in medium- or low-post area.

Drill 3: Three-Man Drill for Number 4

This drill uses only one defensive player with two offensive ones. The purpose
is to set the screen so that the receiver is open. The emphasis of Drills 1 and 2
are given. This can be done for down screens as well as cross screens.

1.   Player f has defensive player X_1 on him in good defensive position,
     sagging or tight, depending on the situation the coach wants to work on.
2.   F comes across (or down) and screens X_1.
3.   F rolls the direction f goes to screen X_1 out in order for f to be open.
4.   f should be open for shot and X_1 should fight through to get f.
5.   *Option:* The roll-back pass to F can be worked on.

Drill 4: Six-Man Drill for Number 4

This can be an offensive drill or defensive drill. It is simply three-on-three using
Number 4. It can also be done with a down screen as well as shown in a cross
screen.

1.   W starts with the ball.
2.   The dribble-down with W is optional to the drill. W could start in the
     corner or out in front.

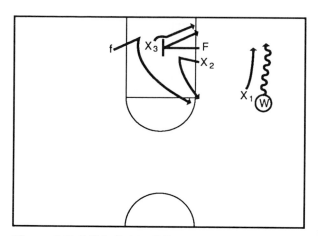

Diagram 5.44: Drill 4   Six-Man Drill

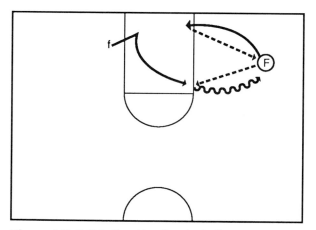

Diagram 5.45: Drill 5   Two-Man Shooting Drill

3.   f can be told to go baseline or over the top.
4.   Fake 4 can be added to this.

Drill 5: Two Man-Shooting Drill for Number 4

This drill is like all of the two-man shooting drills, continuous use of the players shooting.

1.   f fakes down and comes up or vice versa (as if coming off a 4 screen).
2.   F passes to f.
3.   f shoots, F rebounds and passes back out to f.
4.   The players have replaced each other and drill continues.

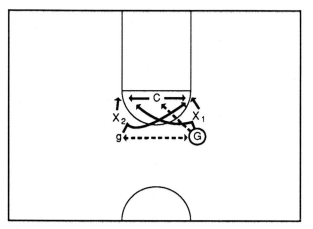

Diagram 5.46: Drill 7 High-Post Guard Split

5.   *Option:* Use of dribble-down by F.
6.   *Option:* F starting outside for a down-screen option.

Drill 6: Individual Shooting Drills

1.   Refer to shots from Number 4 on pages 114 and 115 and individually practice them.

Drill 7: High-Post Guard Split Drill

This is basically a pass-and-guard split with concentration on handoff and close-out pivot. The center should practice moving to the ball. It is best to start without defense first.

1.   G passes back and forth with g.
2.   G (or g) then passes to C.
3.   G and g split the post.
4.   *Option:* Use defense on guard only.
5.   *Option:* Use defense on C only.

Drill 8: Forward Split Drill

This drill(s) is run the same as the high-post split, only the forward passes to the post.

1.   f breaks from opposite post.
2.   F passes to f.
3.   F screens for G.
4.   G cuts off post for pass from f.

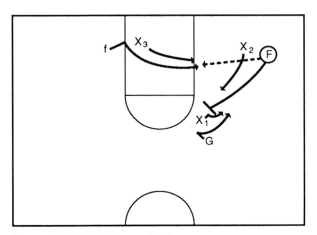

Diagram 5.47: Drill 8 Forward Split

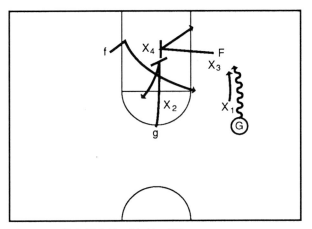

Diagram 5.48: Drill 9 Double Head-Hunter

Drill 9: Double Head-Hunter Drill

This drill should be practiced after single head-hunter or single down screens have been drilled. Drills 1 through 4 should be practiced on down screen first. There should be no defense at first, then dummy defense is added. X_4 should try to fight through screens at first (when teaching offense). This will force F and g to roll back and help close out X_4. The center can be added (to screen, pass, etc.) after four-man skills have been accomplished.

1. G has ball and starts dribble-down.
2. F and g head-hunt f's man.
3. f comes baseline or over the top.
4. F rolls opposite f.
5. g pops back to guard position.

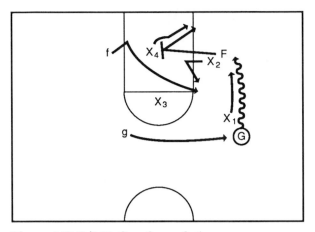

Diagram 5.49: Drill 10 Cross-Screen Option

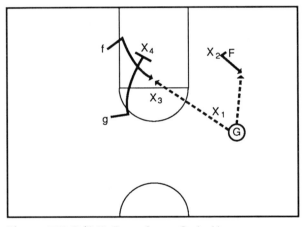

Diagram 5.50: Drill 10 Down-Screen Option(s)

Drill 10: Four-on-Four Number 4 Drill

This is another four-on-four series to practice the Fundamental Five. All factions of Number 4 can be practiced, both offense and defense. The clear out for a guard can be practiced here from a fake 4 option.

This can also be used for the "fire" situation on the cross-screen 4, fake 4, or clear out. The man guarding F, X_3, fakes going with F and doubles up on W. X_4 must jab-step over F's screen. X_2 looks to intercept pass to f or g.

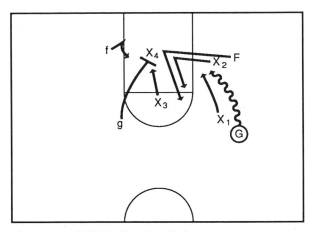

Diagram 5.51: Drill 10   Clear-Out Option

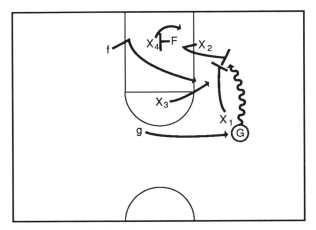

Diagram 5.52: Drill 10   ''Fire'' Option

6

Number 5: The Shuffle Cut

The Drake Shuffle or Auburn Shuffle was one of the most popular continuities of the 1950s. The shuffle cut starts many offenses and is the fifth of the Fundamental Five. Against a tight man-to-man defense, Number 5 can release a player for a close-in shot. It requires more team continuity than the other four plays. However, if executed properly, Number 5 will pay dividends.

When the Fundamental Five was in the process of being developed, the Lowell High School team I was coaching was playing a very aggressive, very quick team from Gary, Indiana. We had not yet used Number 5 at Lowell; however, I remembered from my own high school that the shuffle cut worked well in releasing the pressure of the "do or die" man-to-man defense. We beat the Gary Edison team for the first time ever, and the shuffle cut, Number 5, became part of the Fundamental Five.

The use of big guards is extremely conducive to the use of Number 5. Three of our recent All-State players: 6'8" Richie Johnson, 1980, (Evansville University); 6'7" Bubby Mukes, 1982, (Evansville University); and 6'4" Ric Ford, 1984, (Oglethorpe University) were big guards. The shuffle cut was used to open these players for the ball and they all scored well on this maneuver.

The shuffle cut, as well as the other members of the Fundamental Five, can be run from various set-ups (diagrams 6.1 to 6.7). It basically releases a guard or forward away from the ball. This is especially true if the defense isn't switching or helping.

Since teams tighten up their defense during delay tactics, Number 5 has always been a part of the control aspect of our game. The zone team that is not ready to come out and play you tight may have difficulty with a good 5 play. Number 5 produces lay-ups and close-in shots that you want during the delay situation.

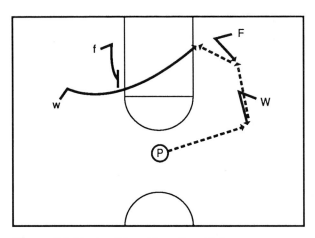

Diagram 6.1 Number 5 from Three-Guard Set

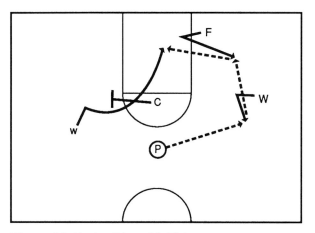

Diagram 6.2 Number 5 from 1-3-1 Set

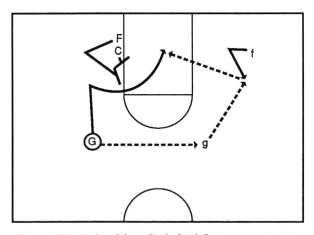

Diagram 6.3 Number 5 from Single-Stack Set

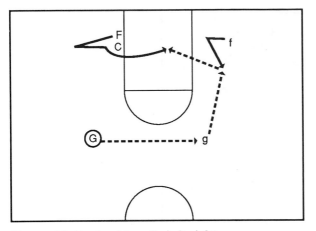

Diagram 6.4 Number 5 from Single-Stack Set

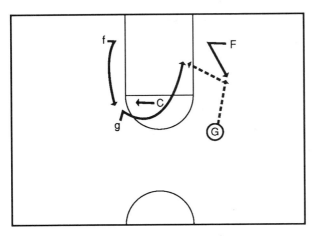

Diagram 6.5 Number 5 from Two-Guard High Post

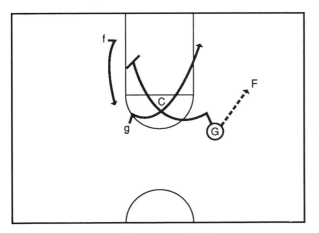

Diagram 6.6 Number 5 Option from High Post

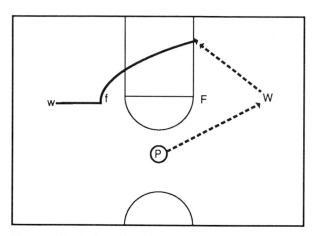

Diagram 6.7 Number 5 from One - Four

Shot Off Number 5

Since forwards are coming across the middle like Number 4, their shots are basically the same (see chapter 5). However, guards and wings are sometimes shooting from a different angle than the other four plays. Many times they may be able to angle and power like in Number 2 shooting (see chapter 3 on Number 2). However, since they are moving toward the ball, they may find themselves moving past the hoop.

The reverse lay-up and moving hook are two shots that the 5 cutter should have and both are shot past the basket.

Reverse Lay-Up

The ball is shot with the inside hand and inside foot. The players are taught to turn in the air to help protect the lay-up with their body. The shot is used when the defense is heavier on the outside hand.

The offense simply continues under the basket and "reverses" the lay-up.

The reverse lay-up can also be used when the defense is outside and expecting the hook. The offense protects his lay-up with the body against the shifting defense help.

Players must project themselves to the basket as their body momentum is carrying them away. This momentum forces the shooter to place his shot nearer the center of the backboard square. We discourage unnatural spin to make the ball reverse and encourage simply better ball placement on the backboard.

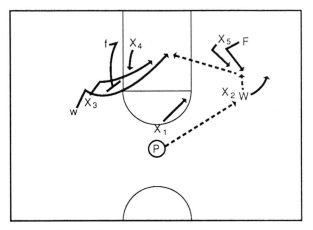

Diagram 6.8 Basic Number 5 – Pass from F

The Moving Hook

In most situations in a Number 5 cut, the defense will be behind the cutter. The moving hook is a natural shot for a number 5 cutter. The moving hook is a good shot for the guard who has the forward switched on him. The shooter is moving away from the defense and the ball is even farther away. The moving hook, as in the reverse lay-up, must also be placed nearer the center of the backboard to take care of the momentum. This is one of the things some athletes have never been taught and therefore miss shots they could have easily hit.

A good stationary hook should be taught before the moving hook. The same principles of protection, body turn, and follow-through are based on the moving hook. As in all phases of fundamentals, these need to be reviewed at times.

FUNDAMENTALS OF THE SHUFFLE CUT

It is the responsibility of the *cutter* to rub his man off the screen. At least one step should be taken away from the ball, even if the screen is nearer the ball than the cutter.

The timing of the cut is important. The most frequent mistake is that the cut occurs before the forward gets the ball. The defense that does any adjusting at all can defend the cut. In diagram 6.8, F should use the two-step moves that are described in Number 2. W cuts outside to help take out his man from sagging into the passing lane. The opposite wing, w, cuts after f gets the ball by taking a two-step move to the baseline and then tries to rub his man off f.

Problem of the Early Cut

Some coaches will let a wing or guard throw to the cutter. This, I think, makes a more difficult passing lane and increases the possibility of the defensive sags. Diagram 6.8 shows that W doesn't have the passing angle that F has. Also, P's man, X_1, can sag and prevent the pass. X_4 also is sagging to clog the middle. Of course, if the defense is tight on everyone, then the lane will be open. However, if F is being extremely denied, the backdoor forward option (see Number 2) is probably the best option, rather than forcing the early pass and cut.

Taking Out the Sag

Since the ball is passed to the forward, the play has a similarity to Number 2. Diagram 6.8 shows that W's man, X_2, is being kept honest after the pass to F. W starts a two-step move, then goes to the outside of F, like Number 2 outside. X_2 then is forced to play W honest.

If P's man, X_1, sags too far, P should step up to shooting range. F simply "freezes" X_1 with a fake pass to W and returns the ball to P for a good shot.

If f's man, X_4, sags too deep, f can move to the ball for a quick shot. This also helps set up the Number 2 outside option.

Diagram 6.9 shows the 2 outside options from the three-guard set. The same principle applies to all sets. The same options of Number 2 outside apply here. When F hands off to W, he does a 5 cut, off f, coming across the lane. If F is open, W throws a high pass to him. Another option would be to pass to f for a high-low option.

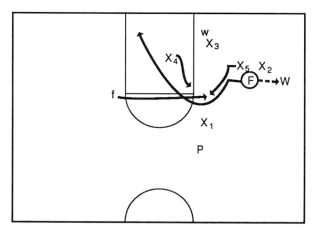

Diagram 6.9 Number 5 — Number 2 Outside Option

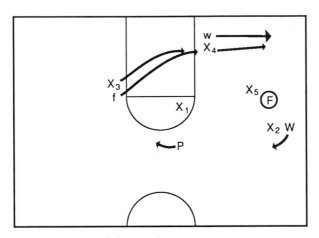

Diagram 6.10 Switch f to Low Post

The Switch

If the defensive forward (guarding the screener) switches, there should be a definite height advantage develop for the offense. The weak-side screener, f, must take his man, X_3, immediately to the ball and basket before the defense can switch back as shown in diagram 6.10.

The cutter w should clear the area, if there is a good switch. By doing this, he accomplishes two things. First, he takes the defensive center farther away from his man. Secondly, the area is less congested for the taller center to move on the smaller defensive guard.

If w has taken his man into the screen to force the switch, X_3 should also be behind f. This should enable F to hit f easier. However, f must keep X_3 behind him by the diagnonal low-post pivot. He should also call for the ball when a switch is made. This is especially true if there is a definite height advantage. The first cutter w must see that his man is cleared from the low-post area. F could pass to w to pass to f, if the passing lane needed to be improved.

If f is fronted, there shouldn't be much backdoor help. A high pass should get the ball to f, if he pins him. However, if the defense does sag, the ball should be reversed before the defense can switch a forward back on f. Diagram 6.11 shows W coming back out front when the switch is recognized. P reverses to the weak-side wing when W comes out. F passes to W who, in turn, reverses the ball to P; f comes across low with the smaller defensive player still on him.

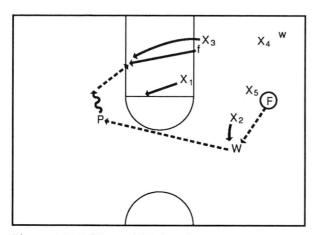

Diagram 6.11 Ball Reversal if Defense Sags

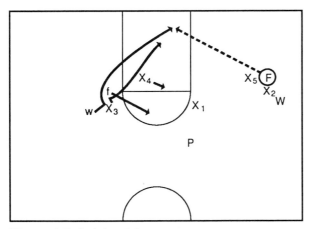

Diagram 6.12 Backdoor 5 Cut

The Backdoor Cut on Overplay

If the defense starts to overplay the play by beating the screen early, w should fake high and go backdoor (diagram 6.12). The screener f should then break high in case of a switch. It is the responsibility of the guard to set up the backdoor. A step with the inside foot (right on left side of floor and vice versa) will usually back up the defense more. Then a quick step with the outside foot as close to the screen as possible will usually run the defense into the screen or make the defense turn to find the cutter.

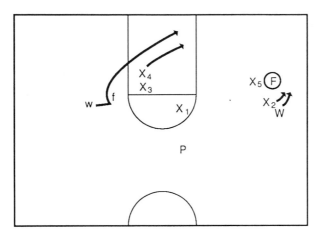

Diagram 6.13 Sag Prevents the Top Cut

DEFENDING NUMBER 5

Prevent the Top Cut

As was previously stated, Number 5 works better against a tight man-to-man defense than against a sagging one. Anytime the offense forces the defense to tighten up, Number 5 is going to be more successful. If the offense scores on this play, it will be a lay-up. The defense must be good. There are those who never switch and will try to go over the top. They will try to play "belly-up and over" (see "Defending Number One" in chapter 2). They better be aggressive. This gives the ball-side offense too much room for other options. Since the player making the cut doesn't have the ball, like in Number 1, he also can go either over the top or backdoor much easier.

   By stepping to the ball, the defense is waiting for the cutter to come over the top, as shown in diagrams 6.13 and 6.14. Anytime the defense can direct the offense or eliminate one of its options, it is doing a job. Since the top cut is eliminated, the defense must prevent the backdoor.

To Switch or Not to Switch

"To switch or not to switch" — that is the question. Personnel as well as philosophy enters here as in the other five plays. If w posts well and X_3 is weak defending the post, X_4 and X_3 should switch in the 5 cut as shown in diagram 6.13. This is true also if there is a height advantage and X_4 can guard the post better. The defensive forward, X_4, who is switching, should help the guard, w, by saying,

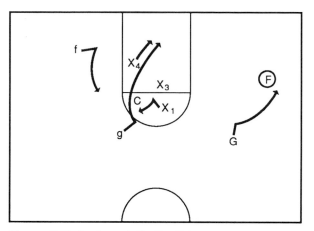

Diagram 6.14 Sag Prevents the Top Cut

``I'll take him, if he comes.'' Of course, X_3 will have to front f rolling down the lane. If w is a better scoring threat than f, it definitely is worth the switch.

In Diagram 6.14, X_4 could pick up the cutter, g, X_3 could stay with C and X_1 would pick up f. This is done if g has the option of screening f, or if f comes to the top. This is basically a match up zone situation. However, X_1 could end up defending a taller player and X_4 could be guarding a quicker one. Again, it depends on the threat of the guard, g, scoring on the 5 cut, especially if he gets the ball low. Normally it is easier to switch because X_4 is usually better in defending the low post. It depends again on the scouting report.

Slide Through on High Post

If we don't want to switch guards and forwards (Chapters 2 and 3 on Number 1 and 2), we feel the slide through on a cutting guard works best on a high post set. This takes cooperation between the defensive guard and center. The center must let the guard know the screen is being set and help the guard slide through the screen on the back door cut.

Since we have decided to prevent the top cut, we will force the offense to alter their screen. By sagging to the ball, the center, C, will have to set his screen closer to F to be effective at all. Diagram 6.15 shows this. This could force a 3-second call. The center setting the screen either must go higher or get out of the lane sooner than he might like to. This is especially true of teams that screen the man rather than putting the majority of the responsibility on the cutter.

The passing lane to the cutter is jammed more if the defensive forward or center also steps to the ball. This also helps to close down the driving area of F.

When the screener C comes up to start the 5 play, the defensive center X_3 should provide the room for the slide through by X_1. By stepping to the ball,

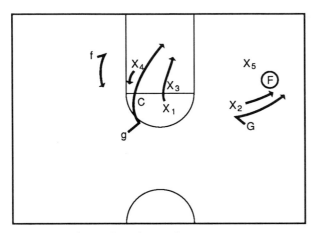

Diagram 6.15 Slide Through on High Post

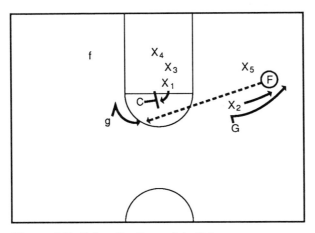

Diagram 6.16 X_1 Sags Too Deep – Fake Cut

X_3 should be in good position to help X_1 slide through. If g goes over the top, X_1 should be in the passing lane from F to g. If g back cuts, X_3 should almost push X_1 through so he will reach g before he can receive the ball. X_3 must then be ready to recover to defend a pass to C from F (diagram 6.15).

There is a possibility of g faking the cut if X_1 sags too much, as shown in diagram 6.16. g fakes the cut and C tries to screen X_1 from recovering to g. If X_1 has sagged too far, he can't recover. To prevent this, X_1 must stay near the passing lane from F to g. It is still better to give g the shot outside, rather than the lay-up.

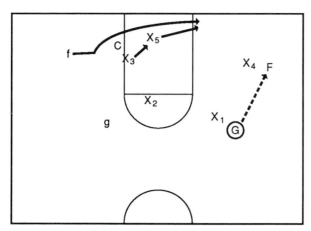

Diagram 6.17 Switch on Low Post Number 5

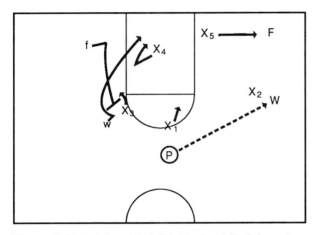

Diagram 6.18 Switch on Weak Side Number 5 (Back Screen)

Switch on Low Post

If the 5 play is run from a low post, as shown in diagram 6.17, we will switch as we would on a 4 play. This is true even if it is a guard forward 5 play. When G has the ball, X_3 should be topside of C, sagged to the middle in the passing lane. If F comes over the top, X_3 takes him. If F back-cuts, X_5 switches with X_3.

Switch on Weak Side

If the 5 play is an off-ball 5 play that is sometimes called a back screen, we also switch. This is true on a guard-forward back screen of a high-post offense. Diagram 6.18 shows a back screen 5. X_3 and X_4 switch as the back screen occurs. Communication is important because even if X_4 picks up w automatically, f will be open. Therefore, X_3 must switch on f.

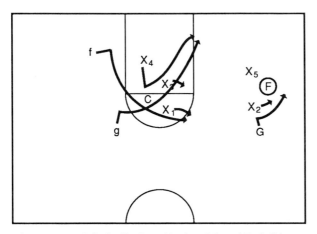

Diagram 6.19 Split Shuffle Cut – Number 5 From Weak Side

Defending the Split Shuffle Cut

Sometimes the offense will perform a double or split shuffle cut with a guard and a forward as shown in diagram 6.19. To defend this a switch must be done by the guard X_1 and forward X_4. Fighting or sliding through in this case causes the offensive players too much confusion. The defensive forward X_4 should be sagged to start with. He will take the first cutter low. This is because f could fake high and come low. X_3 steps to the ball, allowing a gap for a slide through for X_1, if f also goes low. This is not generally done by the offense, because of the congestion; however, X_1 should prepare himself for this possibility. If confusion arises, the shot that will be open will be an outside shot high rather than the 5 cut low. "Protect the basket first" is a pretty good rule on any defense.

A very effective split shuffle cut is the one shown in diagram 6.20. This has been called the "wheel" offense because, diagrammed, it looks like the spokes on a wheel. It is a 54 offense, a 5 play followed by a 4 play. The offensive guard G splits off the center and gives a moving screen for g as he cuts; g does a 5 cut off the center C. G then down-screens x_4 for f. There is a continuity that follows this. Defensive guard X_2 can easily be screened on this play. Therefore, defensive guards X_1 and X_2 switch. Then, X_2 will switch on f as he comes up high; X_4 will switch on G. In case of a fake-out by the guards, X_4 must be ready to guard coming across the baseline. X_4 should sag to ball side as in normal help defense. When G (or g) has the ball, the defensive guards X_1 and X_2 should be offset. X_1 should be defending G when he has the ball and X_2 should be back helping on C. As soon as G passes to F, X_1 steps to the ball as if defending a 2 cut. When G goes backdoor, X_1 yells "switch" and X_2 takes G. X_1 is ready for g coming over the top or a backdoor 5 cut. X_2, by sagging inside, jams G and slows down this cut. Defensive center X_3 should also be to ball side, sagging after G passes. X_1 and X_3 are now pushing g's 5 cut outside the lane.

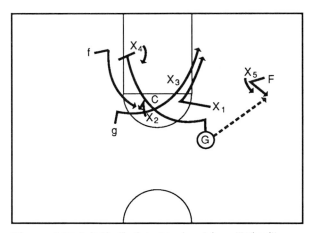

Diagram 6.20 Split Shuffle Cut — Number 5 from "Wheel"

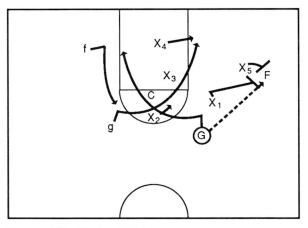

Diagram 6.21 "Fire" on Split 5

"Fire" on Split 5

This must be a planned defensive play. When G passes to F, X_1 jumps to the ball as shown in diagram 6.21. X_1 and X_5 double-team F. X_4 looks to intercept a pass to g. X_2 looks to intercept a pass to G (if G doesn't cut) or the pass to f, coming up. X_3 looks to intercept a pass to C on a lob to f. This is effective, if not done too often, as in the case of all half-court traps. If defensive center X_3 is quick, it is sometimes better to let X_3 cover g cutting and X_4 to come from behind to intercept a pass to C from F. Your personnel will dictate this to you.

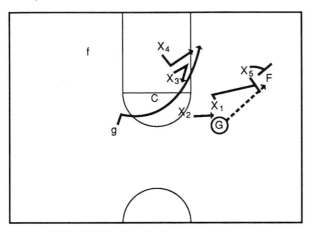

Diagram 6.22   "Fire" on Number 5

"Fire" on Regular 5

The double-up could be used on a single 5 cut as well, as shown in diagram 6.22. The defense is the same as the split 5 cut except X_2 picks up G, if he doesn't go guard outside. Either X_3 or X_4 picks up g. Obviously f is open, but a cross-court pass must be thrown. X_3 and X_4 look for this.

DRILLS FOR NUMBER 5

Drill 1: Chair Drill Over the Top

1. Manager M has ball.
2. Player G takes two steps and breaks after planting outside foot and cutting as close as possible to chair.
3. Both sides should be used, right and left.
4. Specific shots can be practiced: hook, reverse, lay-up, power lay-up, turn-around jumper, step-under, and jump hook.
5. Coach can call shot after player starts move.

Drill 2: Chair Drill Backdoor

1. Same as Drill 1 except backdoor cut
2. Player G takes two steps inside and cuts backdoor as close as possible to chair.
3. Both sides should be used.

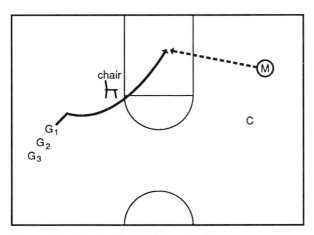

Diagram 6.23: Drill 1 Chair Drill Over the Top

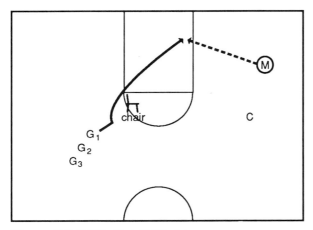

Diagram 6.24: Drill 2 Chair Drill Backdoor

4. Practice all Number 5 shots.
5. Coach can call shot after player starts move.

Drill 3: Double Chair Drill

1. Same as above, only use two chairs.
2. Should be done only after Drill 1 and 2 are mastered.
3. Can alternate over-the-top and backdoor cuts.

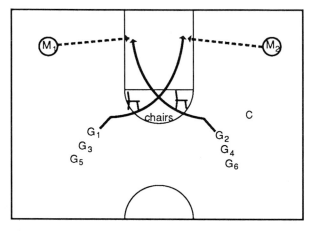

Diagram 6.25: Drill 3 Double Chair Drill

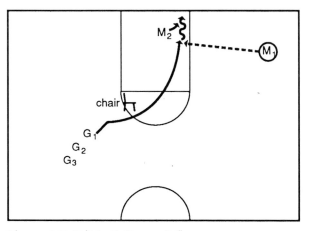

Diagram 6.26: Drill 4 Air Dummy Drill

Drill 4: Air Dummy Drill

1. Manager 2 has a football air dummy like in baseline Number 2 shooting.
2. If manager 2 is outside, reverse lay-up shot.
3. If manager 2 is inside or behind after cutter receives ball, cutter shoots hook.
4. Pass can be delayed so player posts and Number 2 shots are practiced.
5. Pressure of air dummy applied is varied so players won't alter their shots.
6. Use backdoor as well as over the top.

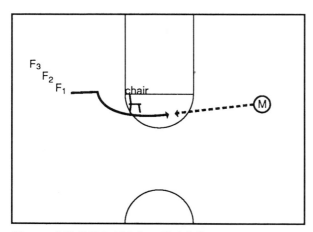

Diagram 6.27: Drill 5 High-Post Chair Drill

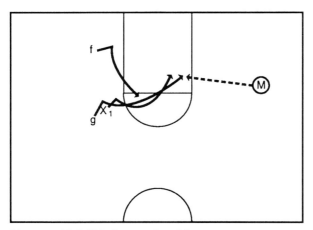

Diagram 6.28: Drill 6 Two-on-One Offense

Drill 5: High-Post Number 5 Shooting

1. Same as Number 3 high-post shooting except 5 cut off chair before shot
2. Same options: jump shot, fake and drive, reverse pivot and drive

Drill 6: Two-on-One Offense

1. Manager has ball.
2. Defense is instructed: play tight, force a certain direction, etc.
3. Offense may have only one move; over the top or backdoor.
4. Offense can go either way.
5. Use both sides.
6. Use two managers as in double chair.

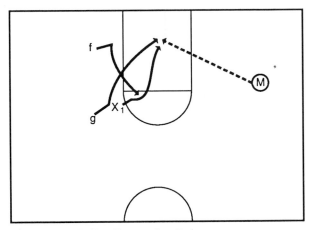

Diagram 6.29: Drill 7 Two-on-One Defense

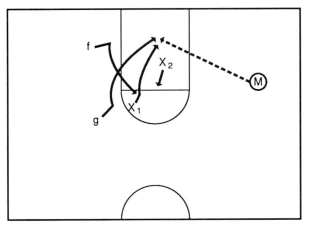

Diagram 6.30: Drill 8 Two-on-Two Offense and Defense

Drill 7: Two-on-One Defense

1. Same as previous, only defense is stressed.
2. Defense plays sag into passing lane and forces backdoor.
3. Offense could be limited to over the top, backdoor, or both.

Drill 8: Two-on-Two Offense and Defense

1. Concentrate on one or the other.
2. Use same options as two-on-one drill.
3. Practice slide through defensively.

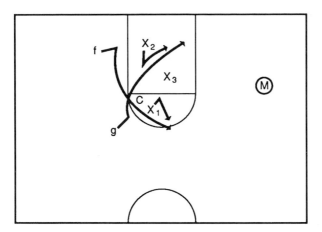

Diagram 6.31: Drill 9 Three-on-Three (Switch)

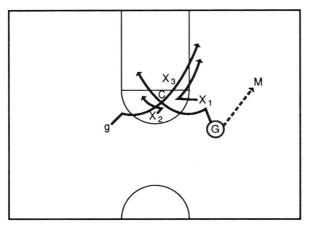

Diagram 6.32: Drill 10 Three-on-Three from Top

Drill 9: Three-on-Three Side

  1. Offense drill: defense must stay with man — g goes either way.
  2. Offense drill: defense may switch — g goes either way.
  3. Defense drill(s) like 1 and 2

Drill 10: Three-on-Three from Top

  1. Offense: defensive plays, no switch
  2. Offense: defense switches, offense may back-cut as well.
  3. Defense: offense must split — practice switch.

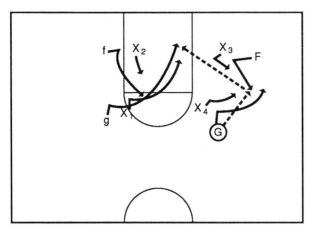

Diagram 6.33: Drill 11 Four-on-Four (Over the Top)

4.   Defense: offense may back-cut; switch on crosses only; slide through on back cuts.
5.   Add C as third option on offense (defense).

Drill 11: Four-on-Four Drill

1.   Effective way to involve eight players in a station drill or group work
2.   Adds defense on passer plus adds dimension of one-on-one move from forward
3.   As always work both sides; work both switch and slide through.
4.   Rotate players, if desired to have players play both guard and forward: G plays F, F plays G, f plays g, g plays f; rotate four times then defense becomes offense.
5.   Control offense or defense as in two-on-two drill.

Drill 12: Double-up Offensive or Defensive Drill (Use Both Split and Single 5 Cut)

1.   Same as Four-on-Four Drill
2.   Could be Five-on-Five Drill
3.   If offensive drill, concentrate on two quick passes from F. The first player to receive a pass from F should get rid of the ball quickly.
4.   If defensive drill, F should drive occasionally.
5.   If defensive, nearest passing lanes should be covered.
6.   If offensive, defense should be directed to cut off certain passing lanes.

Drill 13: Five-on-Five Drills

1. Use different offensive set-ups.
2. Control offense to work to certain side only.
3. Control defense to deny certain side only.

7

Fast Breaking with the Fundamental Five

The Fly Fast Break

I believe in the fast break. My philosophy has always been to run if the opportunity is there. The fast break is the first offensive action that I teach in the fall and has to be a part of any effective offense. This type of offense is the one most frequently used in the game today. Even if a coach does not like the running game, he must practice against it. In Indiana high school basketball, I cannot recall any championship team that did not have the running game as part of their offense. In fact, I cannot recall any NCAA championship team who did not run when the opportunity was there. The running game of the pros goes without mention.

Some coaches believe you run or you set up — there is no in-between. I feel you can run and use our offense to end the break. If you can run and continue the offense without setting up, the offense will have these additional advantages of the break:

1. Quick shots before the defense sets up
2. More offensive players (three-on-two, etc.)
3. Offensive rebounding may be easier because the defense has not set up.
4. Driving area seems to open more against sagging defensive teams and the zone because the defense hasn't set up yet.
5. Teams who are going from a zone press to a man-to-man defense do not have as much time to get into a man defense. More mismatches occur.
6. Screening is easier because defensive adjustments haven't been set up yet.

You can create opportunities for the break. If you play any kind of pressure defense, you are certainly hoping for an easy break. I believe in both the traditional and sideline break. There are certain basic rules which I feel apply to both:

1. Get the ball out quickly, either by a pass or the dribble.
2. Don't force the ball anywhere.
3. Get away from the dribbler.
4. If a man is open ahead of you, get him the ball, then fill a remaining lane on the break.
5. Keep spread as much as possible and come to the ball and/or basket at the end of the break.
6. Try to force the defense to commit themselves and then take advantage of it.
7. Beat the defense down the floor. The more "numbers" you have on the opponents, the easier it is to score.

FREE-THROW FAST BREAK

It goes without a great deal of explanation that when an opponent is shooting a free throw it is an excellent opportunity to set up a fast break. It gives the basketball team the closest thing to football in setting up a play. We "huddle" inside the lane before the referee hands the ball to the shooter. This huddle is done both offensively and defensively.

After the free throw has been attempted, the ball should change hands. Approximately 65 percent of our opponents make their free throws. Of the 35 percent remaining, 80 percent (28 percent of total) or better should be controlled by the inside team, *if they block well.* This leaves less than 7 percent controlled by the shooting team. Therefore, it is definite situation to prepare for having the basketball.

In our huddle, the regular free-throw fast break (diagram 7.1) is set up as follows:

G Big Guard (small forward classified today by some coaches as a 3 man). He is the best passer and ball handler of the front line personnel. He also takes the ball out, if we are being pressed. Ideally he and f and F could interchange. G on the free throw is always right, if he is right-handed.

P Point Guard. He is the best ball handler. He also boxes out the inside offensive man 5 before he breaks out for the outlet pass (1 man by some coaches).

g Fly guard — He is the second-best ball handler. Ideally he and P can switch depending on which side the ball is rebounded on. He should be a good corner shooter. He boxes out the shooter before releasing (2 guard by some coaches).

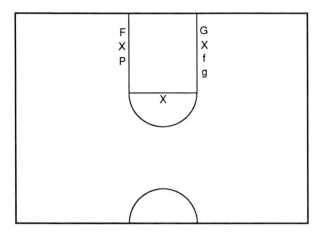

Diagram 7.1 Free-Throw Set-Up

f Low-Post Player. He should be the first big man down floor. He is the player
     we want to get the ball to on the low post. He also helps (like P) to
     block out the inside forward on his side 4 (5 man by some coaches).

F Forward (other low-post player). Ideally he and f can interchange. He must
     box out before going downcourt (4 man by some coaches).

Corner "Fly" Break from Made Free Throw

The movement of a made free throw is relatively simple. As shown in diagram
7.2, G will grab the ball out of the nets and throw it to P or g, whoever is open.
The front-line people will move opposite the outlet pass. f breaks downcourt
and moves the low post on ball side. F, the second front-line player downcourt,
moves to opposite block low-post position. G trails a guard position opposite
ball side. As g gets the ball and starts to dribble to the corner, he calls out "corner"
verbally. P follows as trailer on ball side.

It must be pointed out that G could throw the initial pass to g. The offense
would remain the same with P trailing g. This long pass may get g a lay-up or a
two-on-one would be more likely.

Aid to Forward Getting the Ball

As the forward f comes to the block, there may be a defensive player already
there waiting to defend him. The forward f should step across the defensive
player's foot that is nearest the baseline. This will enable F to establish a post

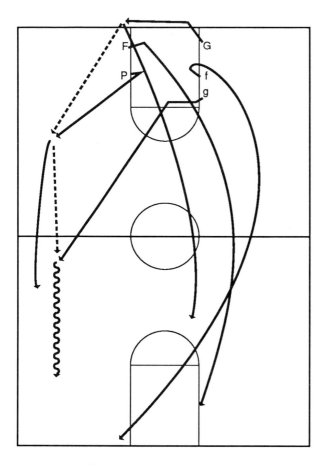

Diagram 7.2 ``Fly'' Fast Break from Free Throw

position on the defense. He can ``pin'' the defensive player if he does this. Diagram 7.3 shows f coming across to the baseline side of defensive player X_2. The dots show the legs established on a diagonal post.

If the defense overplays the baseline, f must step over the lead foot of the defensive baseline player. This establishes an inside post rather than a baseline post. Because of the break, the defensive help has not been established yet. The most important part of this is that f gets the ball on the blocks. Diagram 7.4 shows defensive player X_2 established near the baseline. When f sees this he cuts so his legs (dots) are positioned to post himself for the ball. This is simply an inside diagonal post position.

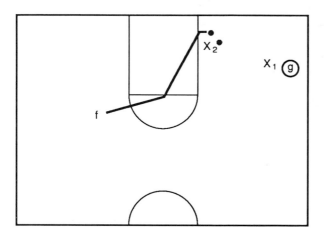

Diagram 7.3 Dots Show Feet of Forward Coming Across

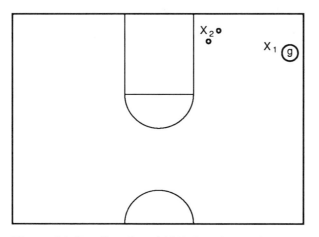

Diagram 7.4 Dots Show Feet of f if X₂ Overplays Baseline

Left-Side Break

I have always used the right side of the floor for the break because most of the time G was a right-handed player. It is easier for a right-handed player to move to his right to throw the ball long to the fly man. However, as shown in diagram 7.5, if G is left-handed or if we simply want a change to confuse the opponents, the left-side break can easily be run.

If our opponents overplay the guards to the point we are having extreme difficulty getting the break going on the right side, we can run a left-side option.

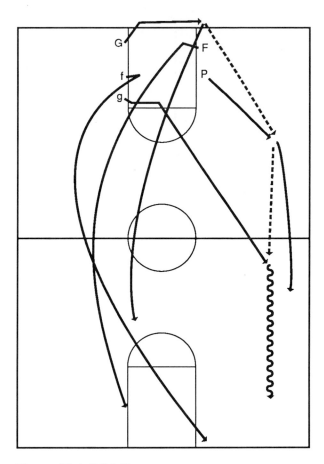

Diagram 7.5 Left-Side Fly

Diagram 7.6 shows f receiving an outlet pass from G and g reversing early to become the fly on the left side. Note F starts left, but changes direction to complete the break as the first big man downcourt.

CORNER "FLY" BREAK FROM THE MISSED FREE THROW

Rebounded by F

If the ball is rebounded by F as shown in diagram 7.7, the movement is basically the same as if the basket was made. F looks for P and g as outlet men. F becomes the defensive protector. G becomes the second big man down and goes to the opposite block.

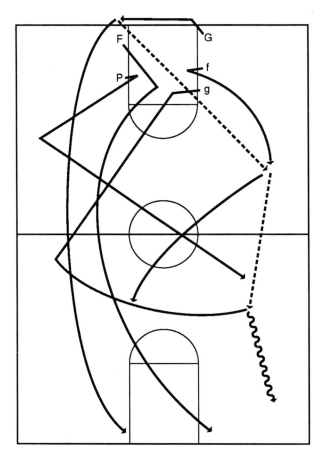

Diagram 7.6   Left-Side Fly — P and g "Denied"

The same situation could occur as on a made free throw that the guards are overplayed defensively. A corss-court outlet pass, usually from a release dribble first, to the opposite forward f produces a left-side break as shown in diagram 7.6. As soon as F reverses the ball, g "flies" to ball side.

Rebounded by G

If the ball is rebounded by G, a left-side break develops. The easiest and probably the best way is to have g be the outlet man as shown in diagram 7.9. P then becomes the fly man. The first big man down the floor should be f. He goes to the ball-side block. If F beats f downcourt, they reverse positions.

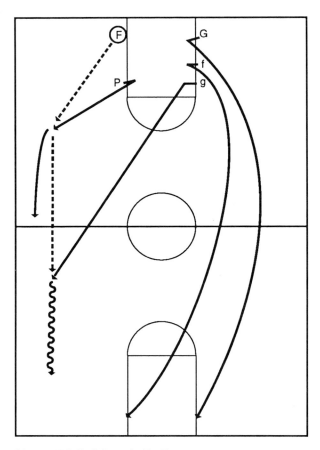

Diagram 7.7 Fly Rebounded by F

If P is the best ball handler (maybe the *only* ball handler), P breaks for the outlet and g continues to the fly position as shown in diagram 7.10. This is done when we *rule* certain players have certain positions on the break.

Use of Single Outlet Man

Actually, if the outlet man P sees the break is not available, he can simply slow down the game. The outlet man is the floor general. He determines the flow of offense and can direct the attack. The big advantage of one outlet man is this control factor. He is always looking for the ball on the rebound and the other guard is always flying. The use of a single outlet man and a one-guard offensive front are synonymous.

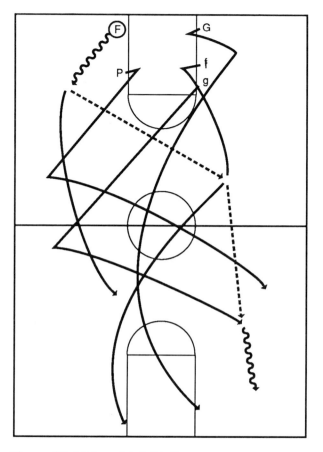

Diagram 7.8   F Rebounds Left-Side Fly

The disadvantage of the single outlet man is that the defense can guard the outlet man before the break is started. They know, as the offense does, which man the ball is to be passed to. Therefore, the defense can overplay the outlet pass. This can cause early reversal or even slow the break completely.

However, if the defense is that concerned with the slowing of the break, it can affect their offense. The opponent must be looking for the outlet man. Sometimes this concern can cause an offensive player to be out of position to receive a pass because he is concerned about where the outlet man is. Many times the fast break is slowed down early in the game when the defense is doing this early checking. However, as the game progresses and the player(s) responsible for stopping the break realizes he is not in the offense because he is concerned with the break, he will start to get more involved in offense and the outlet

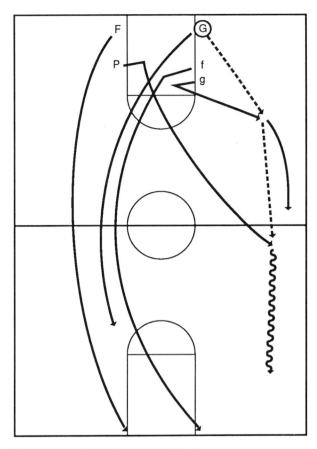

Diagram 7.9 Fly Break Rebounded by G

man will open up again. The fast-breaking team must be looking for the break even if the defense covers the outlet man a few times. As was previously said, the defense has a difficult time covering *both* the outlet and fly man.

Sometimes even another player other than the point guard can be placed as outlet man and the point man can become the fly guard. This change may open up the defense for some easy baskets and cause further defensive adjustment. If the defense is overplaying the break in the backcourt, the break opens up more in the frontcourt, if the ball gets by the initial pressure. Also, the long pass sometimes opens up more if the defense is covering one specific pass.

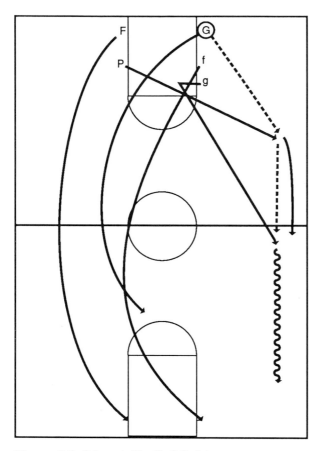

Diagram 7.10 Rebounded by G – P Outlet

Two-Man Outlet Pass

If two players are designated as outlet man, the player closest to the rebound is the outlet man and the other is the fly man. These players are generally the guards. Defensively, they should be outside men or defense the out men of the 2-1-2 zone, or the two man-to-man guards. One guard may fly to the corner and should be able to operate from there offensively. The other is the outlet man.

The advantage of using two men is the flexibility of using either player in fly or outlet. The defense must defend against the outlet pass, not a pass to a specific player. The outlet pass can be made quicker because the pass is made to the closest person, whereas with one specific outlet man, the outlet man may be away from the rebound side defensively. If either guard can handle the corner position or the outlet ball-handling position, the dual outlet is best.

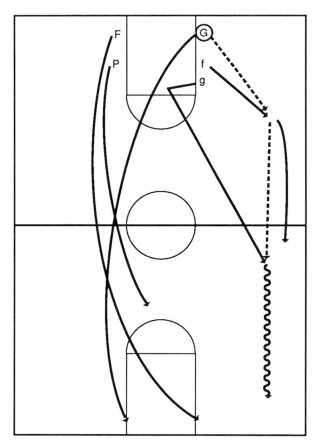

Diagram 7.11 Two Outlets, One Fly

Two Outlets, One Fly

Sometimes the coach may want to designate one player as fly guard and two players as outlets. This provides immediate release by the fly guard. The situation may determine when g releases — he may release on the shot or after checking his man from the boards, etc. Diagram 7.11 shows that f and P are designated outlet men (closest to rebounder is outlet, the other becomes defensive protector). In this situation, G and F always go to the blocks; whoever is downfloor first takes the ball-side block. This is a good situation if your team has only two big men whom you want on the blocks or in the post position.

One Fly

If it wouldn't matter which players come to the blocks, a very simple adjustment can be made. One player can be designated as fly guard g, or first player down-court is designated to go to the corner as g. The player the ball is "outletted" to becomes the point guard P. When the ball is "outletted," everyone except the fly guard goes away from the ball, the second player downcourt takes the ball-side block, the third player takes the weak-side block, and the rebounder is the protector. This is not a bad set of rules, especially if your team is talented and somewhat equally sized. All of the options remain the same. In reality, the guards usually are outlet and fly, and forwards are opposite most of the time in this set of rules. It's usually easier to start teaching with specified positions and then go to the one fly rules.

Rebounded by f

This is generally a middle or center rebound. Both g and P can outlet to determine by fly side as shown in diagrams 7.12 and 7.13. These diagrams show g and P interchange the fly and point depending on which side the ball is outletted to. The first big man downcourt is taking the ball-side block, the second takes the opposite block, and the third is defensive protector. Obviously, we can rule that specific players take certain places on the blocks. This may be easier in first teaching the break. However, it is quicker if the first big man takes ball-side block, etc.

Ruled Option Rebounded by f

If we have ruled that f will always go to the block, then he will break to the block on ball side. If we have ruled that g will always be in the corner, then a pass from P to g must occur, as shown in diagram 7.14. If P gets the ball from g soon enough, our traditional "middle" break will occur. However, sometimes P has to go down and back (even if we aren't ruled that g must be in the corner). P is coming back to the ball and it is quicker for g to drive to the corner than for P to reverse pivot and drive there. This option can be used anytime the defense denies the pass to P early.

Rebounded by P or g

Where P and g rebound the ball obviously determines the outlet pass. The re-bounder P could easily throw to g if the ball is rebounded in the middle as shown

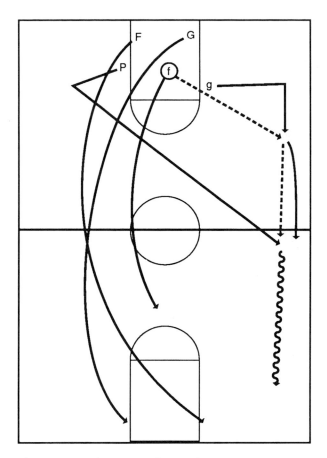

Diagram 7.12 Rebounded by f − g Outlet

in diagram 7.15. Then g drives to the corner to complete the corner break. Likewise, if P was the outlet, he would drive to the corner the ball was outletted on. Forwards go opposite. g could be looking for a traditional two- or three-man break, especially in this case, with the first forward down.

If you have ruled that g will always fly, then g will outlet to P and then fly as shown in diagram 7.16. This is similar to the down and back shown in diagram 7.14.

If P or g rebound and outlet to a forward, as shown in diagram 7.17, the forward quickly passes to the other guard who breaks to ball side. Then all forwards break opposite the ball.

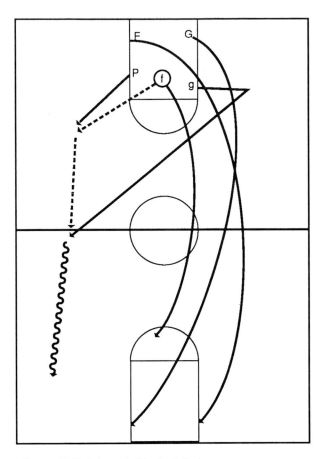

Diagram 7.13   Rebounded by f – P Outlet

TRADITIONAL TWO- AND THREE-MAN BREAKS

As you can readily see, there are many situations where the ball could easily be taken to the middle of the floor for a traditional three-lane break. Anytime it is possible to do this, we will. Instead of "corner," the verbal call is "middle" and three lanes are filled. If we are out quick enough to have a two-man break, "two" is called. The verbal call usually is made by the outlet man, who is slightly behind the play. However, all players should call out verbally so proper lanes will be filled. Even though the ball is outletted to one side of the floor, we still may go to the middle if a player is ahead of the ball. The ball can be thrown, on occasion, across the middle and the two-man break occurs. Steals, as well as rebounds, create fast-break situations that must be altered from the controlled break. However, the "middle" break can be practiced from our fly situation.

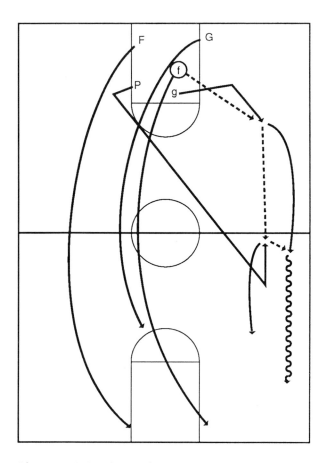

Diagram 7.14 P and g Interchange

Traditional "Middle" Break

If P can get the ball to g in the middle of the court before he reaches the sideline, as shown in diagram 7.18, a traditional three-lane middle break occurs. The frontline people still start opposite the outlet. G will provide defensive protection for a possible fast break by the defense. F comes to the post position as a trailer. The quickness of the break determines F's action. It must be noted that F may have beaten f on the break and f could be the trailer. It would be rare that G, on a made basket, could pass the ball in and beat f *and* F on the break. However, the rule is the last man downcourt should be defensive protector. Communication between players can change the defensive protector.

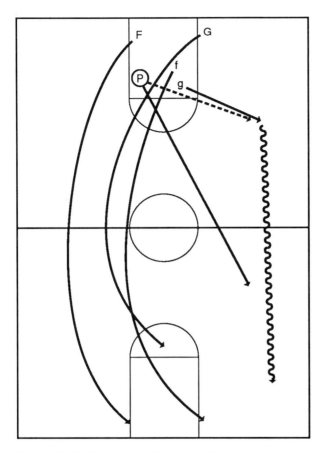

Diagram 7.15   P Rebounds g Outlets and Flies

Trailer Options on the Middle Break

Assuming F is the trailer on the break, there are some options that flow from the traditional break. The first one is shown in diagram 7.19. If we don't get the shot, we are set to go into offense as if we had executed the fly — a guard is in the corner, F is in the low post, etc.

F also has the option of screening for the off ball side as shown in diagram 7.20. Note that F can roll back after the down-screen 4 and we are again in the same set-up as the fly. It should also be noted that everything can be mirrored to either side of the floor.

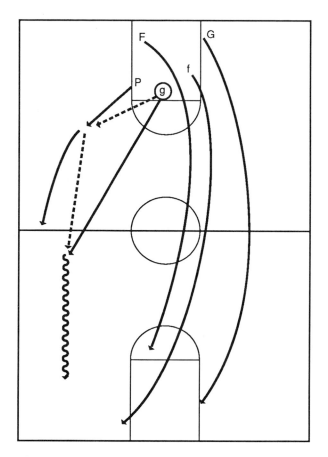

Diagram 7.16 g Rebounds and Flies

F may also trail on ball side. On a middle break, we're trying, as in all breaks, to get the ball down quickly. F, as in diagram 7.21, may simply 2 cut to the basket if P is defensed wide. Note that g has followed the pass to the edge of the free-throw area after the pass to P.

RULE: The middle man on a three-lane break stops near the free-throw area where the defense stops him. He follows his pass to the edge of the free-throw lane for a return pass.

If the defense has jammed the ball side on the break, F could go opposite or screen for P. Diagram 7.22 shows F using Number 1 for P. Normally, an outside Number 1 is not effective because of help defense. However, because the defense is not set up yet, Number 1 to the middle can be effectively used. This is especially true if P is an excellent shooter.

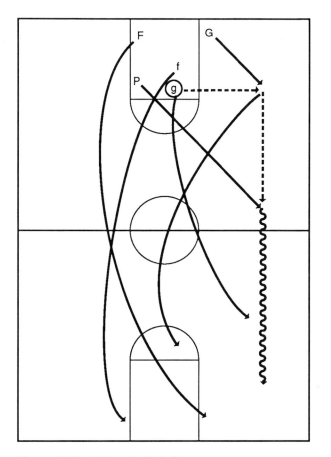

Diagram 7.17   g Rebounds, G Outlets

Sometimes F is trailing to the point that P is moving for his shot. Then F just goes to the boards. If P returns the pass to g, as shown in diagram 7.23 F can down-screen for P and roll to the basket. On the return pass, note that f is going to post low. This all depends upon how quickly F is downcourt.

Guard to Protector

If the guard (point or fly) has the ball in the middle lane of the break, the break is performed like the previous middle break diagrams show. G, the forward taking the ball out of bounds or the rebounder, has been the last man downcourt. G has defensive protection against the opponent's fast break.

It is obviously better if the bigger players are on the offensive boards. Therefore, *if* G and g can *communicate,* G will go to the boards and g will assume

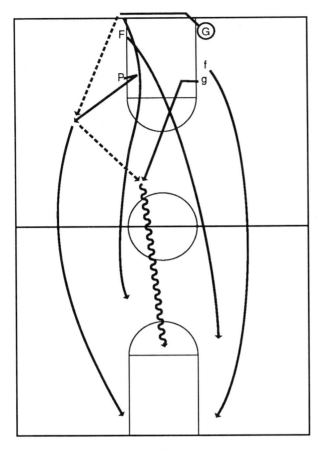

Diagram 7.18   Three-Lane Middle Break

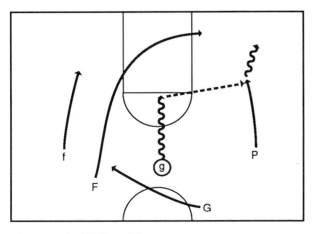

Diagram 7.19   F Trailer — G Protector

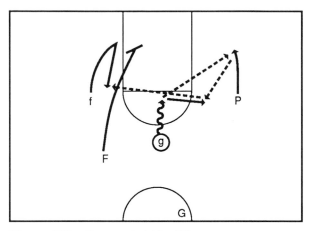

Diagram 7.20 g Reverses to f After F Screens

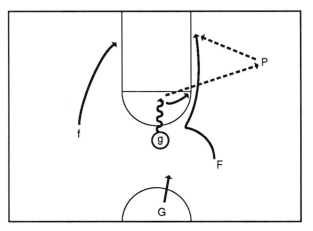

Diagram 7.21 P Is Contained — F Trails to Post

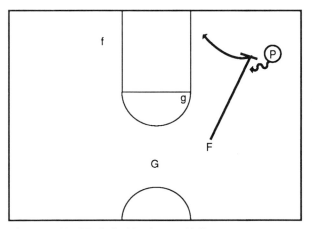

Diagram 7.22 F Trails for Number 1 with P

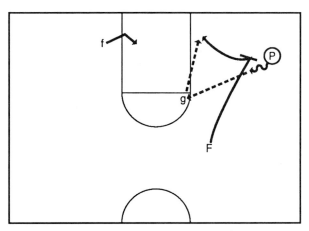

Diagram 7.23 F Screens and Rolls – P Returns Ball to g

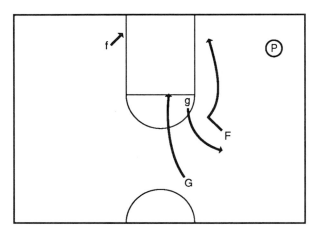

Diagram 7.24 g to Protector

the defensive protector; g then moves out the guard position and this gives G an opportunity to be another offside rebounder. This, as shown in diagram 7.24, generally occurs when the break has been somewhat slowed.

However, if there is a true three-man break, the middle man must board. This is after the shot has been taken by the wing player. He goes directly to the boards from the position he has passed. This is shown in diagram 7.25. The shooter comes back to the middle for the rebound to fill the third rebounding position.

RULE: When shooting a shot from the wings, follow the shot to the middle for the long rebound.

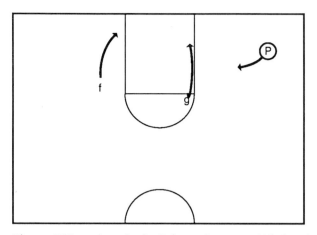

Diagram 7.25 g rebounds *after* P shoots; P goes to middle for rebound

Forward in the Middle

If the defense has completely overplayed the outlet side of the floor or, simply, if P sees f (any forward) breaking open downcourt, he can pass to him (see diagram 7.26). This could be a two-man break as well as a middle break. P should trail as protector and F should go to the boards, P should call out "protector" so F will go to the boards or to the block as if he was the first trailer, and f will go directly to the boards on a shot.

Forward Corner Break

If the ball is reversed early enough that the forward goes to the corner, the second big man downfloor (F) goes to the near block as shown in diagram 7.27 F started away from the outlet. When he sees f driving to the corner, he simply 2 cuts to the ball, almost as if he had passed the ball to f. Normally, this would be a middle break with f driving to the middle. However, f may have streaked down the side and continued to the corner; f should communicate "corner" to help F.

   Obviously, this puts one of the guards on offside rebounding. This is not all that bad, because G as a trailer can down-screen for P. This brings P back out to guard and may provide a good shot for P, as shown in diagram 7.28. This gets the guards out if the set offense is a two-guard front. If we are in a ruled offense, whatever ball reversal we have set up will follow with f being the fly guard.

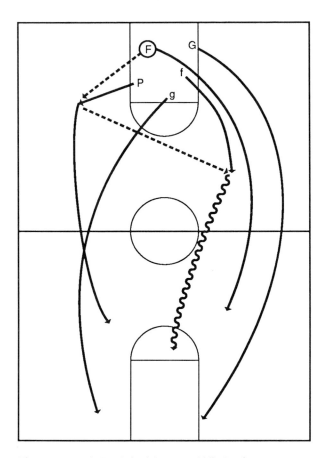

Diagram 7.26 Fly Denied — f Open — Middle Break

THE "FLY" FAST BREAK

The "fly" is a designated sideline fast break. It started from the success we had from the free-throw fast-break pattern. Each player has a definite spot to go to from the break. The fly is a very quick way to advance the ball down the floor in an organized fashion. The options are *identical* to the free-throw break. However, the fly man can release earlier than he normally does. In fact, a release of one of the players may even result in a "cherry," "snowbird," or similar type of basket.

The releasing of a player is not necessary to perform the fly. However, it can provide a gamble that will obtain good results. The offense cannot send everyone to the boards and it does seem to open up the game. In fact, it will weaken offensive rebounding because of the threat. We will release a player

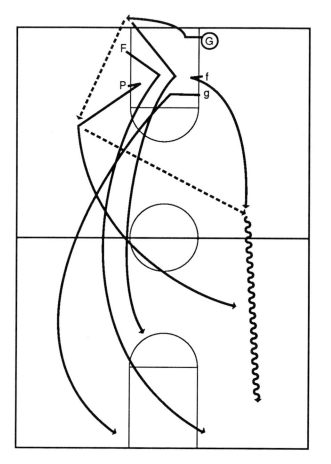

Diagram 7.27   P Reverses Ball — Forward Corner Break

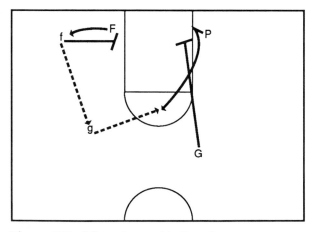

Diagram 7.28   G Down-Screens 4 to Open P

anytime he attempts to block a shot on the outside, since his recovery to his man or rebounding usually is fruitless. Our players are trained to release down the side of the floor and our long passes are always thrown to the side. The rebounder knows we are looking for a release, either planned or from an attempted shot block.

RULE: Never throw a long pass down the middle of the floor; likewise, never release down the middle.

There is a twofold reason for this rule. One is that the defense always tries to recover down the middle and does not want to come out of the basket area to try to intercept. The second is the offensive player on receiving the ball knows where he is in reference to the basket. Too many times the offensive player gets the pass and is too far under the basket and tries an impossible shot recovery or simply loses control of the ball trying to recover from where he is in reference to the basket. If you are going down the right side of the floor, you know your first move is to the left, so you can concentrate on catching the ball.

Basics of the Fly

It is certainly not difficult to see that the rules from the free-throw break can apply to made baskets and rebounds from regular offense. The rules, such as designated point or fly, apply here as well. Teaching the fly is probably best done from the free-throw break since it is a very controlled situation. The following rules may be somewhat redundant to the free-throw break; however, I usually teach the free-throw break first and then relate this to scrimmage play.

1. The release of the fly man (g) is to the corner the ball is rebounded on.
2. The outlet man P moves to the side the ball is rebounded on.
3. The "low-post" man will break down the opposite side of the floor and roll down the lane to the ball-side block.
4. The "forward" F will break down the opposite side of the floor and end up at the opposite block.
5. The "big guard" G, generally the rebounder, will trail up at the opposite outside guard position. He assumes the same position as the in-bounds thrower of the free-throw fast break.
6. The outlet man should verbally call "outlet."
7. The fly man should yell "touchdown" if open on the release. This also signals that a sideline break is open.
8. If the ball is dribbled to the middle of the floor, a traditional three-lane break occurs. The player dribbling, usually the outlet man, yells "middle." If, as in the free-throw break, the fly man gets open in the backcourt in the middle, he calls "middle" for a three-lane break. If the fly man does not receive the ball, he continues ball side toward the corner.

9. Only the fly man and outlet man are ball side. The other three go opposite. If the ball is shot by the fly guard, our rebounding will be coming from the best side.
10. Unless otherwise decided, on a made basket, the *nearest* forward (other than fly or outlet) takes the ball out. The fly or outlet guard *never* take the ball out of bounds. This helps for presses as well as the quick release of the ball handlers. I have, on certain teams, designated one player, usually the big guard, to always take the ball out.
11. It's best if the fly guard and outlet point guard are interchangeable. If the ball is rebounded on the right side, then the player that is nearest the rebounder is the outlet and the other guard flies.
12. It is also best if the rebounder becomes the big guard. It is only natural he will be trailing opposite the ball. In initial teaching, it is probably easier just to designate where everyone goes on the break. However, your break will be quicker if the rebounder becomes the big guard and the first forward down becomes the low-post man, etc.
13. When introducing this to younger players who can't make the long pass downcourt, the fly guard should not break as long. He then dribbles farther to get to the good low-post passing lane.
14. Either guard has defensive protector. If one has the ball, the other should be thinking protector. If the two guards are out on the break, the big guard should be protector unless a verbal exchange can be given.
15. If the pass to the corner is stopped, the defense is overplaying. A cross-court pass to the lead forward may produce an easy basket. This could be done from the point guard after the outlet pass or directly from the rebounding forward. If it is from the rebounding forward, he has usually cleared the rebound by dribble. The forward, middle, or corner break is then run.

PRESS OFFENSE FROM THE FLY

If the defense goes into a surprise full-court press, the fly can make certain adjustments that can alleviate the pressure. This has to be recognized and reacted to by the offense and also has to be practiced.

Diagram 7.29 shows the basic set-up. The fly guard g must come back to post on ball side. F comes back to the middle of the floor. G serves as a pressure valve. As soon as any player gets the ball in the middle of the floor, he pivots toward our basket and looks downcourt. This concept also fits my personal philosophy that your press offense should have a ball handler in both front and backcourts.

The fly break could continue if, as in diagram 7.30, P passes to g coming back to help. g returns the pass to P, who continues down the side. The others fill their lanes for the corner fly break.

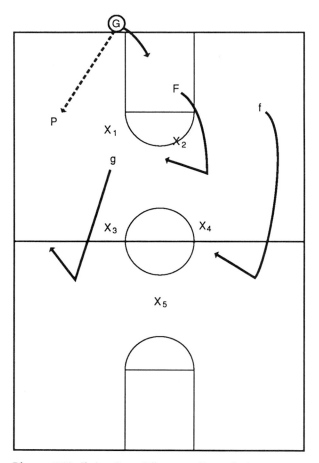

Diagram 7.29 Fly into Press Offense — g Comes Back

Fly Guard Back Options

The fly guard g may have to come back anytime the point guard P is in trouble with pressure. Diagram 7.30 shows the easiest and most natural way to relieve the pressure. Note that defensive player X_2 is inside g in normal defensive coverage. g should use a close-out pivot similar to the second option of Number 2 when handing off to P, if possible.

g can fake to P and drive to the middle as shown in diagram 7.31 to create a middle break. Trailer options by F can be created if the three-man break doesn't score. Note that g can anticipate the jump switch by defensive player X_2, who has moved to sideline side of g. This makes the fake even more successful.

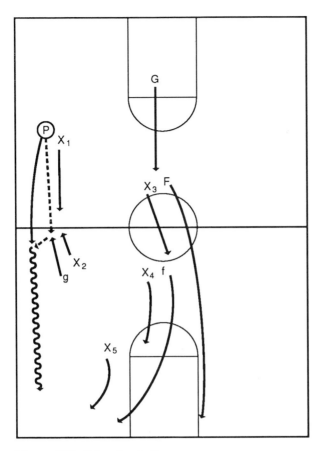

Diagram 7.30 Return Pass to P

g can also fake handoff, front pivot, and return pass to P going to the corner. Diagram 7.32 shows this continuation of the fly. F, f, and G go to their respective spots to finish the break.

g can also immediately pass to f (first forward down) and a forward corner break or forward middle break could occur.

These options all depend on how quickly players can get downcourt. The length of the outlet pass, the defense getting back, the speed of the teams, the quickness of the pass to the fly guard, etc. are all factors that determine the option. All of these options can be practiced with no defense and dummy defense.

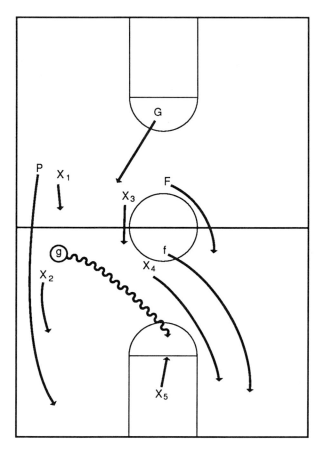

Diagram 7.31 g to Middle

GETTING INTO OFFENSE FROM THE BREAK

The ruled offense using the Fundamental Five is designed for the corner break. Chapter 8 on the ruled offense shows how the offense is run from the break. It also explains point dribble entry from the middle, reversing the basketball, etc.

A Single-Guard Set

If you have a single-guard set offense, the fly break can easily flow into the set offense. If the point guard has ended the break in the fly position, and the ball hasn't been entered to him, then the player who ended in the point position can interchange with him as shown in diagram 7.33. If your offense is a 1-3-1 set,

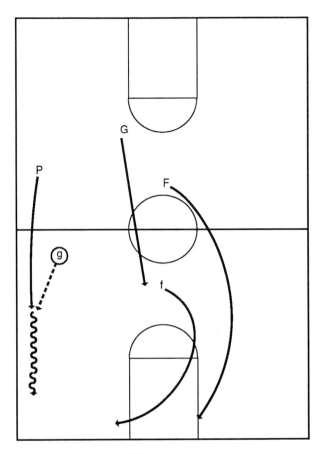

Diagram 7.32 g Returns Ball to P After Pivot

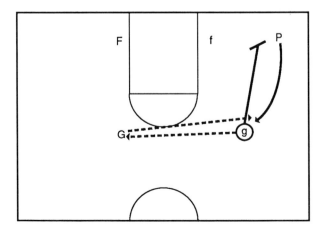

Diagram 7.33 Rotate P from Fly Back to Point

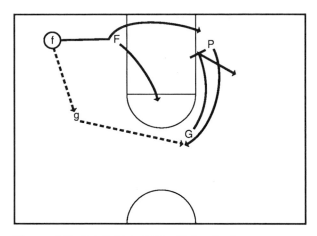

Diagram 7.34 Rotating into 1-3-1 with F as Center

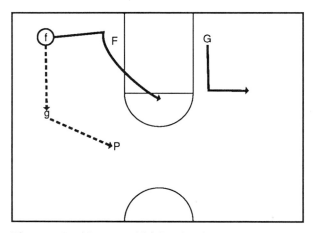

Diagram 7.35 f Rotates to High Post in 1-3-1

then P comes out to a wing and G goes to the opposite wing. F or f comes to the high post to complete the 1-3-1. In a 1-2-2 set, you are already there. In a 1-4 set, the forwards simply flash to their high-post positions.

If the first player down is fly, 2nd player to block, etc., or in a forward corner-break situation, the point guard could end up in the F position. This, as was pointed out in the forward corner-break section, is not all bad. G does a down-screen 4 for P to bring him back to the guard position. This gets P the ball out front and sometimes a good shot coming off the down screen. G sometimes is open on a roll-back. Also, f can come off a back-screen 5 to his forward position on the set offense of the 1-3-1. If F is the center, then F back-screens for f before coming to the high post (diagram 7.34).

If f is the center, the f comes high after tryng to rub his man off F as shown in diagram 7.35. The offense is now set for 1-3-1.

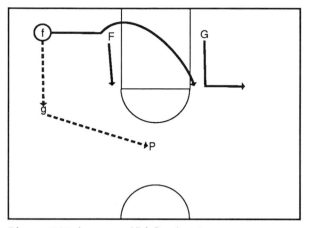

Diagram 7.36 f rotates to High Post in 1-4

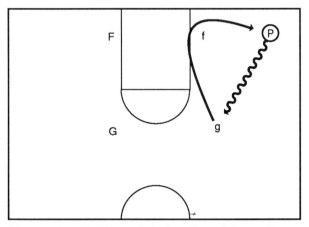

Diagram 7.37 P Dribbles to Point from Fly – g 5 Cuts to Corner

If you are in a 1-2-2 set then f continues across the lane as shown in diagram 7.34. However, if the offense is a 1-4 set, then f comes to opposite high post and F rolls back to the near high post as shown in diagram 7.36.

If the point has ended in the fly position with his dribble left, he may bring the ball out himself. To eliminate a double team by g's man, g must interchange with P. He could just go to the wing, but the danger of the double-up is created. Diagram 7.37 shows a good way for g to use a 5 cut to open himself at the end of the break with P dribbling back out to the point. This works like a stack offense.

G could also go to the stack position as P dribbles out as shown in diagram 7.38. If the offense is 1-4, the forwards could break to the high post after the guards have come off the low posts. This is what we do off the ruled offense when the point (fly) dribbles back out.

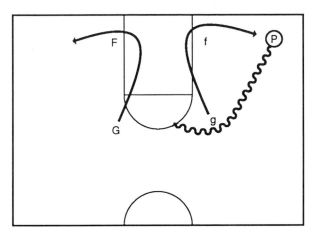

Diagram 7.38 P Dribbles Out from Fly — g and G 5 Cut to 1-4

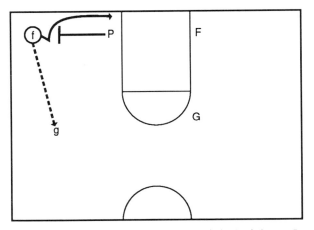

Diagram 7.39 P at Low Post — Rotate P to Fly by Back-Screen 5

Obviously, if your point guard and fly guard are interchangeable, a pass from the fly back to the point is all that is necessary. The other players then simply break to their respective positions on the set offense. This is true on all the above options.

Point at Low Post

If the point guard has ended in the low-post position by the first player down fly, second player down post, etc., then two exchanges are necessary to put the point guard back out front. The first is shown in diagram 7.39. If a forward, because he got out quickly on the break, ends up in the corner with the ball and the point P ends up in low post, a back-screen 5 can put f in the post position and P in the corner. We are now back to P in the fly position and ready for that option to get P back out front.

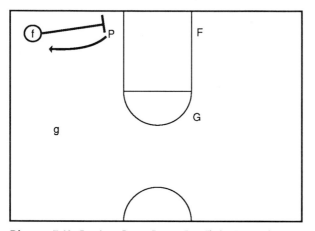

Diagram 7.40   P at Low Post – Rotate P to Fly by Down-Screen 4

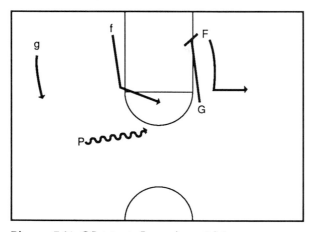

Diagram 7.41   G Rotates to Forward on a 1-3-1

f could down-screen 4 for P and the same interchange could occur as shown in diagram 7.40. Verbal communication must be had between f and P. This could be a pre-set call. In other words, P must back-screen 5 for f.

Rotating G into Forward Position

If G, the rebounder, is to be a forward on our set offense, he must be sure that one of the guards is in the defensive protector position. If either of the wings or point is the F position on the break, he simply down-screens 4 for that player as shown in diagram 7.41. If we are in a 1-3-1 set, F either stays low in the baseline position or rolls back to the high post; f does the opposite of F to complete the 1-3-1.

The same is true if we are in a 1-4 set. Note that g can stack with f in this situation before the forwards come up to the posts. Obviously in a 1-4 low post, they stay in the low-post positions. In diagram 7.41, F becomes a wing player and f is a post player to complete the 1-4.

DOUBLE-GUARD SET

Point Rotation to Double-Guard Center at Low Post

This is a very simple rotation as shown in diagram 7.42. If f is going to be the center, he flashes to the ball and continues to be ball side. G down-screens 4 for F and rolls back to the opposite forward position. As P dribbles across, g comes up to complete the two-guard front. This occurs when g passes back to P, as well as P not being able to pass to g. If the two-guard set is a low post set, then f remains at low post on this and all other options.

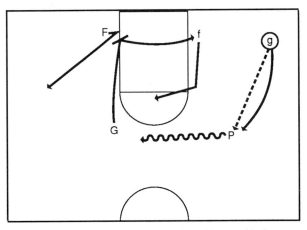

Diagram 7.42   Point Rotation to Two-Guard Front — f Is Center

If the center ends up at the F position, G down-screens 4 for F as shown in diagram 7.43. G rolls back to the forward position as F comes to the high post. As P dribbles across, g comes up to complete the two-guard front. f is already in the opposite forward spot. Note that all of this is mirrored to the left-side break as well.

Center at G

Many times the rebounder will be in the center and end up at the G position as in diagram 7.44. G down-screens 4 for F and rolls back to the center position. As P dribbles across, g comes up to complete the two-guard front; f is already in the opposite forward spot.

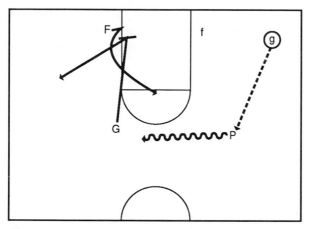

Diagram 7.43 Rotation with F As Center

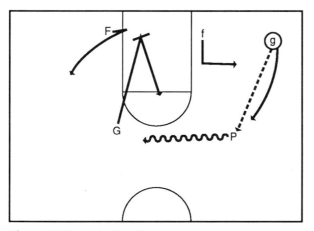

Diagram 7.44 Rotate G to Center

Guards Interchanged

If the guards are interchanged (P at g and g at P), it doesn't make any difference since we are in a two-guard set.

Guard at Forward

Using the normal rules of guards to outlet side, this won't happen. However, using first player fly, second player block, etc., this could happen. A forward could end up in the g position and a guard in the f. A cross-screen 4 by g (a forward on the set offense) puts f (a guard on the set offense) in the corner, as

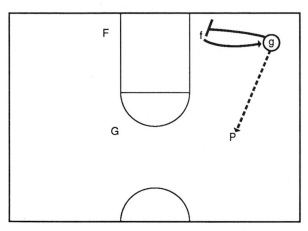

Diagram 7.45 Forward at Fly – Rotate Fly and Low Post

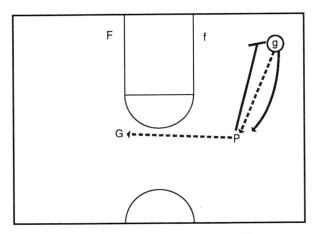

Diagram 7.46 Guards Are at g and f – Rotate P to Fly

shown in diagram 7.45. When P gets the ball, either from a return pass from g or by failure to hit g, we are now in the original situation from the break and are now ready for point rotation as shown in diagrams 7.42, 7.43, and 7.44.

If both guards end up low at f and g positions, this means that P, G, and F are all forwards. When P gets the ball, he reverses the ball to G, as shown in diagram 7.46. P then down-screens for g and g comes out to guard position. We are now in the same situation as diagram 7.45. P then screens for f (the other guard); f comes out to the corner. We are now in the original set-up for a point rotation.

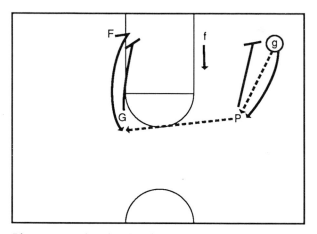

Diagram 7.47 Guards at F and g

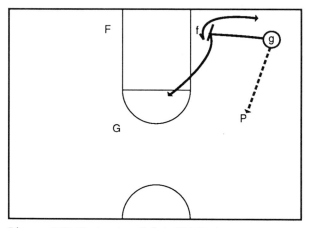

Diagram 7.48 Center at g – Rolls to High Post

Guard at F

If a guard ends up at F, then G down-screens 4 for F (the guard) as shown in diagram 7.47. If the other guard is at g, then P down-screens 4 for g. Now both guards are out front.

Center at g

The rotations we have done may leave the center at g. The center (g) cross-screens 4 for f and is now in the low-post position. If we are in a high-post set, g rolls off the screen, as shown in diagram 7.48, to the high post. This screening helps to open the forward and center for entries into the set offense.

Starting the Offense

The screens that are set not only get the players in position to start the offense, they provide offense. Good shots can come off these screens. They also provide entry into the set offense. Since teams realize that you can get shots from this, they will protect the basket, etc., and provide entry into the offense.

Guard at Forward

Forwards and centers may not be denied as much as they would otherwise. The guards must be ready to start the set offense when the ball is returned to them.

Obviously, if we run the rules of guards to outlet and forwards opposite, the adjustments are less. However, if your team is intelligent, are good ball handlers, and play multiple positions, the first player down fly, second player block, etc., may be good for your team. I usually start by teaching designated spots — fly, point, etc., — before I attempt to give more flexibility to the rules. A passing game or ruled offense fits into this much better because you do not have to rotate back to the set offense. A ruled offense designed to go with the fly break is explained in chapter 8 on "ruled offense." However, the rotation to the set offense has ruled-offense plays that provide good shots even before your set offense. They are similar to our ruled offense. Therefore, whether we are going to set offense or ruled offense after the break, the change is not great.

DEFENDING THE FAST BREAK

Philosophy enters the picture as to whether a pattern set-up play by the offense will slow up the defense and therefore slow up the break. Usually a fast-breaking team seems to defend the break better than a pattern club, perhaps because of its use in practice. Nevertheless, the fast break must be practiced whether it is run or not.

Rebounding

Strong rebounding is necessary for the break to get started. If the offensive team is battling the boards, the defense has to be concerned with just controlling the ball and not how quickly they can get the ball out. The team that "fires and falls back" is actually helping the fast-breaking team becasue the first phase of the break is easier for them. The team that rebounds strong offensively causes the defensive team to block out hard rather than just "check and go for the boards."

Covering the Outlet

One philosophy of stopping the break is to always cover the outlet pass. Make the forward or rebounder bring the ball down the court or at least dribble some. If this is done every time, the offense can adjust and still get the break going well for them. Since the defensive guards are constantly committing themselves, the offensive forward knows he cannot immediately look for the guard. Consequently, he always starts the break himself and looks for the guard (outlet man) after he has dribbled. The defense has more room to cover and a long pass to the outlet guard may make the break even more effective.

It is better to occasionally "check" the outlet pass hard and catch the rebounder in a careless "turn and throw" than to always be there. Since it is best to get the ball out quickly, the rebounder should always try to make an outlet pass. If the pass is picked off occasionally, the rebounder has to think, "Is that guard going to be there this time, or should I protect?" The time involved in this process can slow down a breaking team. At least it may affect the timing of the break.

Covering the Rebounder

This is similar to covering the outlet. If pressure on the rebounder is used off and on, he may become careless with his dribble and a turnover can result. Overplaying every time prohibits good defensive coverage on the scoring end of the court because the offensive team adjusts to the pressure.

Having Defense Back

Some offensive player(s) must be responsible for defense. Some teams have one individual responsible for defense. He is always back; however, this restricts his offense. He cannot drive or follow his shot if he is a primary defender against the break or release of a guard. We have some basic rules in the half court.

RULE: Against a zone, the wing, point, or guard who passes the ball is responsible for defense.

When Number 3 is being run or if we are breaking, generally, a guard is making the pass before a score. He is responsible for defense. As shown in diagram 7.49, P has defense if g shoots. This is true for all offensive situations. When a forward receives a ball in close, he should be scoring or too close to the basket for defense of the release man. Naturally, if the ball changes hands, the farthest man back should be ready to protect against the break.

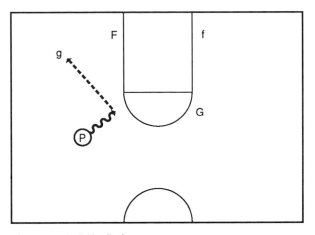

Diagram 7.49 P Has Defense

RULE: Against a man-to-man defense, the wing, point, guard, or sometimes forward who is rotated to the backcourt has defense against the guard release. In a two-man front, *one* guard should always be back. The guard without the basketball is the guard back.

This man-to-man defensive break coverage is designated by the offense and by who is "naturally" moving away from the basket. More talk rather than rule is sometimes necessary on the maneuver. This is because of the inside scoring opportunities that develop among the guards through man-to-man coverage. If both guards are out on the offensive break, the last forward down must be defensive protector until he can communicate with a guard.

Downcourt Coverage

The traditional two-man, I-formation coverage is used with defensive trailers primarily protecting the middle. Naturally, the defensive team that hustles can protect against the break better than the team that loafs. It is fundamental to try to stop the ball and force as many passes as possible. If a team is using Number 3 as a finish to the break, the defense is going to have to shift quickly and keep aware of the screens so that they can make the defensive adjustments to slow down the offense. The more passes the breaking team has to make before the shot, the more likely they are to make a mistake and, also, the more time that is available for more team members to get back. The breaking team wants to shoot — they do not want to pass and set up.

The defense should clog the middle first then cover the sides. Even though this may mean giving up a twenty-foot shot, it is better than a lay-up. Communication is the key. "You take 20, I've got 25" is the type of talk that will force

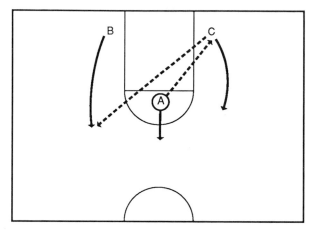

Diagram 7.50: Drill 1   2-on-1 Drill

the breaking team into taking bad shots or their set offense. If you can beat the breaking team down the middle with numbers, you can generally stop their break.

FAST-BREAK DRILLS

The drills that are included here are some of the fast-break drills that I have used. They are mainly the ones that prepare for the fly. Drills for the outlet pass, long pass, etc., have not been included. I did include one 2-on-1 drill and some three-man drills that relate especially to the fly and my fast break. Breakdown of the fly drills into specific phases may also have to be done to perfect the offense.

2-on-1 Drill: Drill 1

This is a simple drill to teach 2-on-1 fast-break offense and defense.

1.   Defensive player A stands at free-throw line with ball.
2.   B and C are on the blocks.
3.   A may pass to either B or C.
4.   As soon as A passes, the other player takes off and a 2-on-1 break is attempted.

The points of emphasis are:

1.   Ball should be passed if either offensive player is ahead of the other.
2.   Offensive players should call out "two."
3.   After passing top of opposite key, only one pass should be thrown and that should be a bounce or high pass.
4.   Defensive player A should challenge, drop back, defensive fake, take charge, etc.

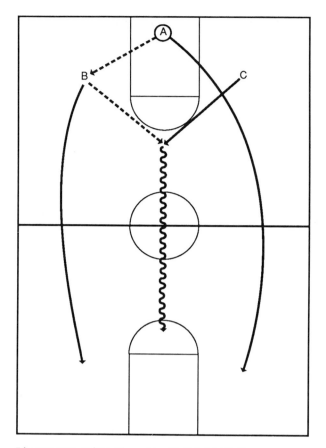

Diagram 7.51: Drill 2   Three-Man Outlet, Middle Pass

5. The head fake and drive should be worked on by the offense after reading the opposite key. The head fake is best when the dribbler looks at his teammate.

Three-man drills

These drills should first be done with no defense, then one defender, then two defenders. A trailer defensive drill 3-on-2 continuous adds a third defender. Forwards should basically be in the rebound line (initial middle line), but players obviously can be in any line.

Outlet, Pass to Middle: Drill 2

a. A puts ball on backboard and rebounds it.

b. B yells "outlet" and A passes ball to him.

c.   C yells "middle" and B passes to him as he cuts to middle.

d.   C dribbles to free-throw line while A and B fill outside lanes.

e.   This can be run to left and right sides.

The points of empahsis are:

a.   B and C come wide.

b.   C dribbles to key area, no farther than free-throw line.

c.   C follows pass to edge of key to either A or B.

d.   C goes straight to board after B's (C's) shot.
      C goes to board.

e.   B will come to middle following shot.

f.   The above points will be for all three-man middle drills.

Outlet, Dribble Middle: Drill 3

a.   A puts ball on backboard, rebounds, outlets to B.

b.   B yells "outlet," receives pass from A.

c.   C cuts across middle.

d.   B yells "middle" and dribbles to middle, others fill lanes.

e.   C can be instructed to start after outlet pass.

f.   This can be run from right and left.

The points of emphasis are:

a.   C is "covered" or late, therefore B must take ball to middle.

b.   Longer outlet pass also simulates B necessity to take ball to middle himself.

Outlet, Fly to Corner: Drill 4

a.   A rebounds, outlets to B, etc.

b.   B yells "outlet," receives pass from A.

c.   C cuts across middle early, yells "touchdown," receives pass from B.

d.   C yells "corner," dribbles to corner.

e.   A breaks to ball-side block.

f.   B follows to ball-side guard position, yells "protector."

g.   C passes to A in low post, (or)

h.   C passes back to B for shot, (or)

i.   C passes back to B, A flashes to ball for a pass

j.   A can pass directly to C on this drill. This can be option or another drill by itself.

The points of emphasis are:

a.   A must come to baseline at an angle. A will have a tendency just to come down the middle of the floor.

b.   On all three drills, emphasis is on "talk."

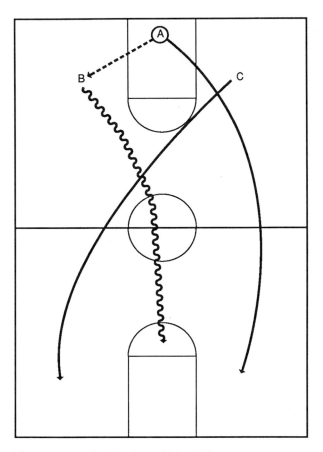

Diagram 7.52: Drill 3   Outlet, Dribble Middle

Outlet — Fly Come Back — "corner": Drill 5
a. C releases as A puts ball on board or slightly before.
b. B yells "outlet," receives pass from A.
c. C comes back to ball and receives pass from B.
d. C returns ball to B who drives to "corner."
e. A goes outside, then back to ball-side block.
f. OPTION: Manager M comes back with C staying on inside.

The points of emphasis are:

a. C comes back as if pressured (by M) and press offense is in effect.
b. C should close-out pivot if he hands off as if in Number 2.
c. The pass from C does not have to be handoff — can be after C
     pivots and faces basket.

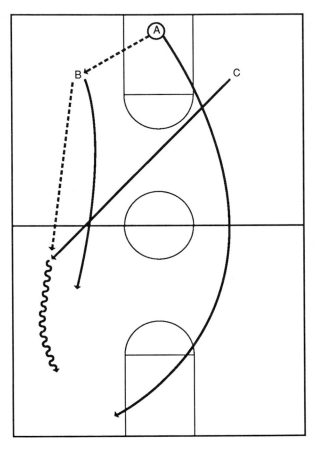

Diagram 7.53: Drill 4   Outlet, Fly to Corner

Outlet — Fly Come Back — "Middle": Drill 6
a.   Same as previous drill except that C does not give ball to B.
b.   C reverse pivots and drives to "middle."
c.   If using manager, manager (M) plays on outside of C as C comes back.
d.   C could hit B immediately after pivot and drive and "corner" would occur.

   The point of emphasis is that talk is essential to know whether to "corner" or "middle."

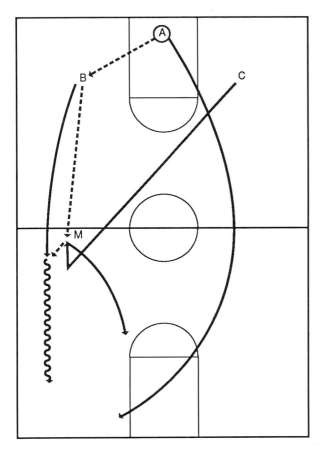

Diagram 7.54: Drill 5   Outlet, Fly Come Back — "Corner"

Five-Man Fly Drills

The following drills are first done with no defense, with players at the free-throw line positions, then with designated rebounder, usually G, throwing the ball on the backboard and no defense. Then we go to the made free throw (by coach or player) and no defense. After players have picked up the basic movement, two coaches and/or managers are given specific defensive assignments, e.g., defend low post, force the offense to reverse the ball, etc. Two other coaches or managers are back to defend the next break.

When first going 5-on-5, dummy defense is suggested. For example, the defense permits the first two passes, outlet and fly. Another example could be to definitely deny the pass to the fly and force the middle break. Another is the denial of the outlet pass. After the defense permits or denies the "dummy" request, regular defense is employed.

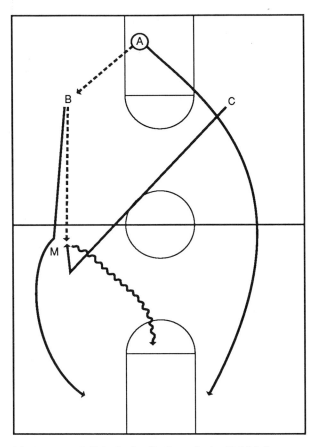

Diagram 7.55: Drill 6   Outlet, Fly Come Back — "Middle"

Basic Fly Drill: Drill 7
a. Players line up at designated positions.
b. G takes ball off backboard from directly out of boards, from made free throw, from coach's shot, etc.
c. P yells "outlet" and receives pass from G.
d. g comes across middle and receives pass from P after yelling "touchdown."
e. g yells "corner" on receiving ball and drives to corner.
f. f (first forward down) goes to block for pass from g.

Left-Side Free-Throw Fly Drill: Drill 8
a. F is designated to get ball out of nets and play is specifically run to left side of floor.
b. F "outlets" to g.
c. P cuts across the middle to side and yells "touchdown."

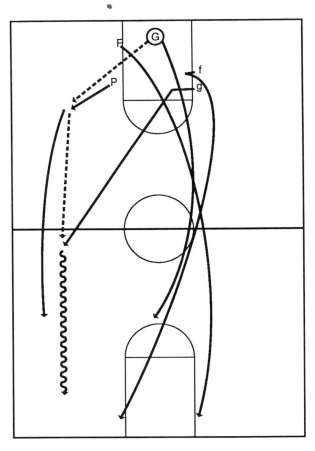

Diagram 7.56: Drill 7 Basic Fly Drill

d.   g passes to P, who dribbles to "corner."
e.   g passes to f, the first forward downcourt.
f.   G and F fill in second and third forward down positions.

The points of emphasis are:

a.   If the man taking the ball out is always to be the same player, then F and G must change positions on the left-side drill. Likewise with P and g.
b.   With defense, players can huddle before free throw and determine right or left break.

Option Drills for Right or Left Side

The following drills are started the same as the above drills. The specific options are practiced and the specifics are given in the chapter.

a.   Rebounded by F
b.   Rebounded by G

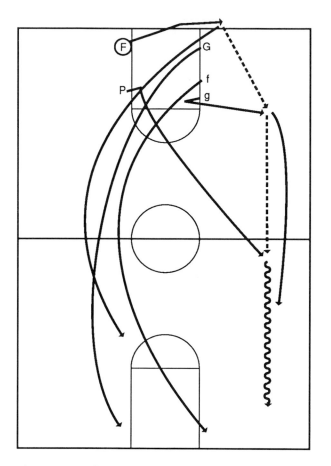

Diagram 7.57: Drill 8 Left-Side Free-Throw Fly

    c.   Rebounded by f
    d.   Ruled option rebounded by f
    e.   Rebounded by P or g
    f.   Specific ruled break by g
"Middle" Drills

These drills are started like all fly drills with five men. Instead of a corner break, a middle break is used. Just like basic fly drills, it is probably best to start from the free throw, even though the majority of time in a game the corner break would work better from a made free throw. Then go to the rebound on the backboard, etc., just as with the basic fly drills. The option diagrammed is fly guard to the middle. (Diagram 7.58, Drill 9) Other options that can be worked on as written in the chapter are:

    a.   P to middle
    b.   F trail to ball side (2 cut)

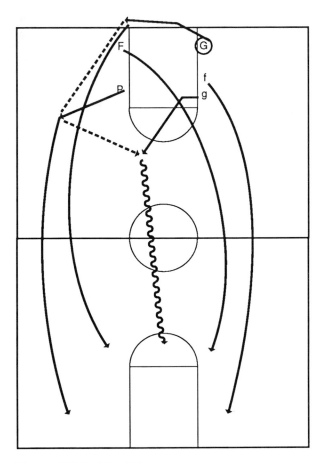

Diagram 7.58: Drill 9 Middle – g

    c.   F trail to weak side (off ball)
    d.   F trail to ball side (#1)
    e.   F trail to ball side (#1, roll back)
``Forward'' Drills

    As was pointed out in the text, sometimes the ball is cross-courted to a forward who can take the ball to the middle or to the corner (see ``Forward Corner Break'' in this chapter). Both of these need to be drilled as all the fly drills previously discussed.

    Press Drills from the Fly

The outlet-fly come back drills can be practiced against various pressses to work on adjustments to quick surprise pressure. The chapter on special situations shows some specific plays to get the ball in against the full-court denial presses. However, fast-break principles follow these plays.

8

The Ruled Fundamental Five Offense

Ruled offenses such as the so-called passing game, have become the most popular recent offense. The ruled offense doesn't depend on specific play patterns or continuities. For example, if a player passes to a forward, he always picks away from the ball (a Number 4), etc.

After we have trained our players in the Fundamental Five, their ability, along with their knowledge of the basic Fundamental Five, determine whether they can handle the freedom of a ruled offense. We still like to have two or three offensive sets (high post, low post, stack, etc.) while encouraging the "bread and butter" options that best suit our personnel. The use of 1, 4, and 5 are used to interchange personnel while 1, 2, 3, and 5 are used in ball reversal.

Hopefully, we are still able to run our fast break with Fundamental Five options off it. Nonetheless, we still must have rules governing the Fundamental Five options.

Entry
Fly Man or Corner

Our ruled offense is best entered from the fly fast break. Therefore, we are in a double low-post set and flow into offense from it. If we can hit the fly man, this is the best entry into the offense. As was discussed in the "Fly Break", the first forward down makes a 2 cut to the ball-side block. If the fly man is not open, the ball can be reversed to the big guard. This puts the offense in the dribble penetration phase.

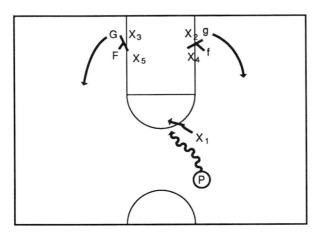

Diagram 8.1　Point Penetration in Double Stack

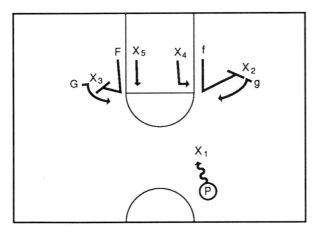

Diagram 8.2　Pressure — Forwards Flash — Down-Screen 4

If the fast break isn't available, we generally go to a double-stack entry from the low post as shown in diagram 8.1. This enables us to get into offense from both sides of the floor. The fowards simply screen for the guards. The fly guard stacks on the fly side (the side the ball was rebounded on) and the big guard stacks opposite.

If the point guard is pressured significantly, so that he can't penetrate far enough to make the entry into the guards, the forwards flash to the high-post area as shown in diagram 8.2. Then if they don't receive the ball, they down-screen 4 for the guards.

If one of the forwards receives the pass in the high post, he front pivots and looks inside for a quick score as shown in diagram 8.3.

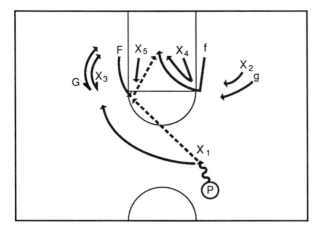

Diagram 8.3 Forward Flash – High-Low for Score

Obviously, if the point guard isn't contained defensively, we are going to be in a five-on-four situation offensively. His penetration should be as deep as possible. Some players can handle penetration deep into the free-throw area and still maintain good peripheral vision and ability to hit the open man. The degree of penetration will have to depend on the ability of your point guard.

Guard Dribble Penetraion

The fly guard is designated to be back on defense when the point guard penetrates deep into the free-throw area. Otherwise, the point guard is responsible for being the initial person back on defense. Since we will rotate any of the guards into the point position, the player at the point at the time of the shot, is responsible for defense. For an immature team, it's probably best to designate the point and fly guard. But obviously, you will have better flow if the latter point guard designation is used.

When the point guard penetrates deep, the forwards should spread by a two-step move to the outside, as shown in diagram 8.4. This is like a basic two-step backdoor move for Number 2. This move is also used in the four-corner delay offense. If a forward helps too much on the deep dribble penetration, the offense has a backdoor situation.

After the entry has been made, dribble penetration is also important. Not just dribbling to be dribbling, but going somewhere to help the offense. If the receiving guard dribble-penetrates to the corner, as shown in diagram 8.5, the forward on ball side posts. The fly guard usually uses this type of penetration depending where he receives the ball on the break. This phase is eliminated by some coaches because of the player's initial reaction to put the ball on the floor. The dribble penetration is used to improve the passing lane to the forward coming to the block.

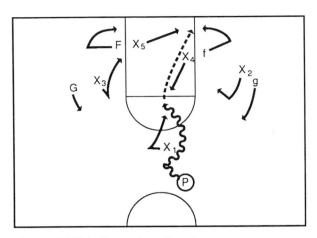

Diagram 8.4 Point Penetration – 5 on 4

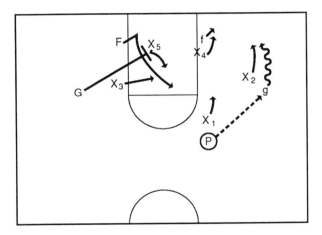

Diagram 8.5 Dribble-Down Penetration

If the receiving or entry guard g or G receives the ball above an imaginary line extending from the free-throw line, two types of dribble penetration can be used: the aforementioned dribble-down to the corner for the forward to post low or the inside penetration dribble (see diagram 8.6). If the guard penetrates inside as shown in diagram 8.7, the forward breaks out of the low-post position to receive a pass in a normal forward position. We are now ready for a 2 cut from the guard. Note that G and F are screening for each other opposite the ball.

We like to use the dribble penetration rule because we don't want the guards to give up their dribble. If the guard receives the ball in a good position to pass to the low post, we don't want the guard to put the ball on the floor. The dribble-down helps the passing lane. The same is true of the inside penetration dribble. If the guard has the basketball and is beyond the free-throw line

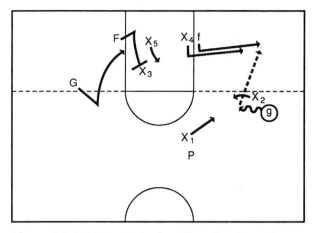

Diagram 8.6 Inside Penetration by g Above Free-Throw Line

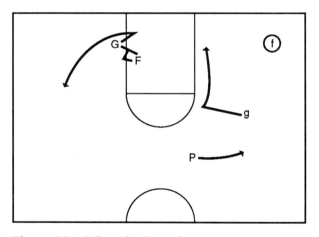

Diagram 8.7 g 2 Cuts After Pass to f

extended, the forward can break to the outside for a 2 play. The forward should definitely either flash post or go to the outside if the guard loses his dribble. We don't want the forward flashing on the dribble penetration inside to avoid the congestion.

If the guard hasn't initiated his dribble, then the forward f can initiate the play by his movement. If he flashes, interchanges with F, or posts low, the guard should dribble down. If the forward f, 2 cuts outside, a 2 play is initiated; g can dribble inside.

If the point guard dribbles toward the fly guard, a 3 cut occurs by the guard who is being dribbled at, as shown in diagram 8.8. This clears out the area for the dribbling point guard while providing motion in the offense.

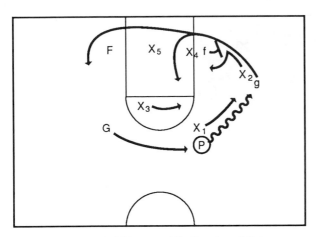

Diagram 8.8 Point Dribble toward Fly Guard — g 3 Cuts

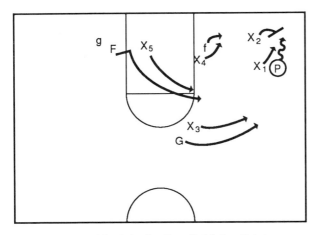

Diagram 8.9 Double-Up by X_2 — Two Quick Pass Rule to g

Diagram 8.9 shows the possibility of a double-up on the dribble-down defensive players x1 and x2. Two quick passes should provide g an open shot. When F observes the double-up he must come to the ball. P should pass to the open player — f, F, or G — who should in turn quickly look for g. If g has used the option to come to the high post, as shown in diagram 8.8, P should be able to pass to g directly.

Clear Out

A clear out for P can occur if f interchanges with F via a 4 play as shown in diagram 8.10. F should read that P is going one-on-one and come high. This forces

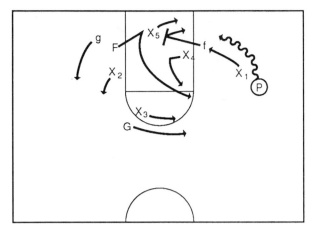

Diagram 8.10   Clear Out for P – f Cross-Screens 4

the defensive help on F to go high and further clear out for P. If P can't go one-on-one, he goes to corner for regular 4 play and f rolls back to low post. Otherwise, f simply posts and blocks out for rebound of P's shot.

Flash Post or High-Post Entry

Either forward has the option of breaking to the high-post area. This can be previously designated. The forwards can communicate as to which one flashes. Both can flash. As shown in diagram 8.11 (repeat of diagram 8.3), when P passes to f, F goes to the ball-side low-post area. Upon receiving the ball, f front pivots and faces the basket. f should look for F. If either G's defensive man, x3, or g's defense man, x2, has sagged to help on F, they (G or g) will be open.

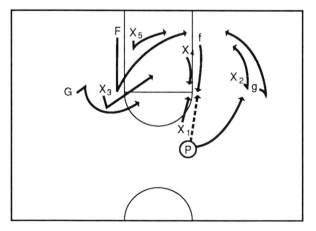

Diagram 8.11   Flash-Post Entry

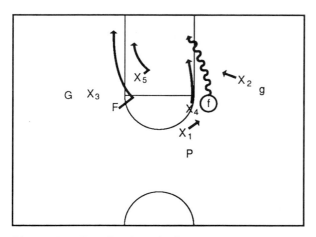

Diagram 8.12 Drop-Step Drive by f − F "Cuts" After Pivot

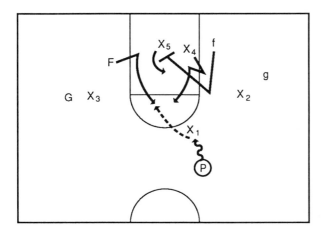

Diagram 8.13 Down-Screen 4 After f flashes

All players should be in f's vision and within range to score. Note in diagram 8.11, P has moved to the right. Too many times the defense sags to help on the low post and the other players are out of vision of f and out of shooting range to receive the ball from the high post. If the defense forces the high-post man to reverse pivot after front pivoting, they have won this battle.

If the defense has overdenied the pass to f, the f can drop-step (reverse pivot) upon receiving the ball and drive directly to the basket. F should not break to the opposite post in this situation, as shown in diagram 8.12. F should not cut until f front pivots.

If f doesn't receive the ball in the high post, he can down-screen 4 for either the opposite forward F, as shown in diagram 8.13, or for the guard g, as shown in diagram 8.14.

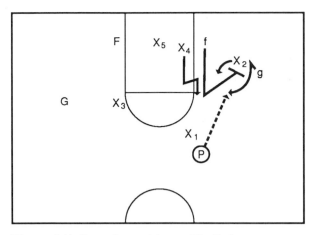

Diagram 8.14 Down-Screen 4 for g — After Flash

Low-Post Entry

If the ball is entered to the low post by dribble penetration or by pass from the fly or flash post, the low post should obviously try to score. However, the defense is going to try to help. The "ins and outs" described in Chapter 5, on Number 4 will help here as will all the options of Number 4.

INTERCHANGES

It is important to have player movement in a ruled offense while maintaining floor balance. Just interchanging doesn't do the job well. A screen must be set and used. Down screens and cross screens, as called by some coaches, are a form of Number 4. Back screens, a form of Number 5, can also be used. More detail of these fundamentals are discussed in the respective chapters. However, as a part of a ruled offense, certain rules are added to make them interchanges.

Interchanges can be done anytime. They are good when the ball is passed or dribbled. However, if you don't receive the ball in a two-second count, you should interchange. This is to avoid three-second lane violations as well as to provide player movement.

Our rules concerning interchanges will be affected by our personnel. We may never back-screen or down-screen a specific player. For example, our big guard (rebounder) on the fly fast break may be our best low-post player. Therefore, the back-screen 5 or down-screen 4, as shown in diagrams 8.15 and 8.16, not only gets the big guard low, but it increases the possibility of getting him open low. In the same sense, we may never back-screen 5 or down-screen 4 our best (sometimes only) ball handler point guard.

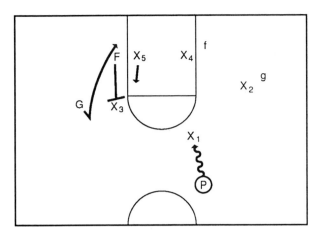

Diagram 8.15 Back-Screen 5 for G

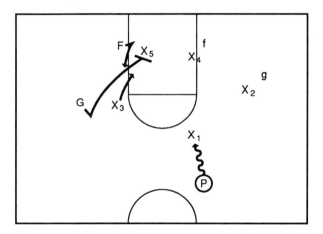

Diagram 8.16 Down-Screen 4 Interchange

Down-Screen 4 Before Reversal

When the ball is returned to the point guard, the reversal has *not* started yet. Down-screen 4 may occur again as shown in diagram 8.17 to free the opposite big guard, G or F, who is interchanging with G. This down-screen action may help occupy the defense so that g and f could have a low-post play before g passes to P.

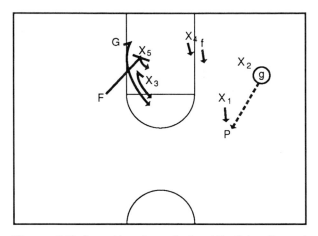

Diagram 8.17   Second Interchange by F and G – Before Reversal

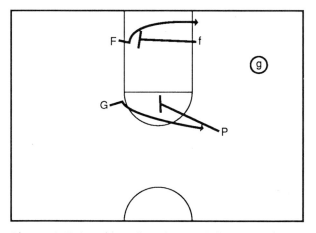

Diagram 8.18   Interchange Cross-Screen – Before Reversal

Cross-Screen 4 Before Reversal

This is a regular Number 4 as shown in diagram 8.18. The guards may or may not perform a Number 4. The roll-back by f will be determined by the type of reversal we have planned.

Diagram 8.19 shows g cross-screening 4 for f. f may receive the ball and not shoot if he is out of range. f can return the ball to P and repeat the screen for g, who is in the low post. Obviously, if g can score in the low post, he should get the ball there. This is the same option as in the 2 play pass-back from the forward (see Number 2).

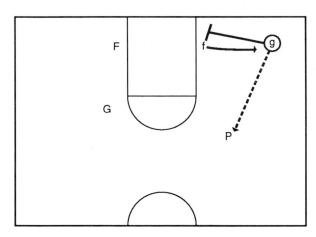

Diagram 8.19 Interchange of g and f – Before Reversal

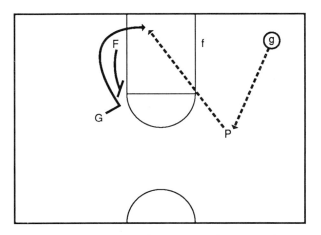

Diagram 8.20 Weak-side Back-Screen 5 ''Before Reversal''

Back-Screen 5 Before Reversal

There are two basic back-screen 5 options. The first is on the weak side of the floor as shown in diagram 8.20. When the ball is returned to P, F and G can perform a back-screen 5. This could be performed when G has the ball. This is done with an alley-oop type of pass. This is really a reversal, but not to a guard out front.

The other back-screen 5 can occur when g passes back to P as shown in diagram 8.21. In both of these options, the rule of breaking to the lane and out by the cutter must be followed. This is like the backdoor 2 cut rule. The cutter should pop out or interchange again.

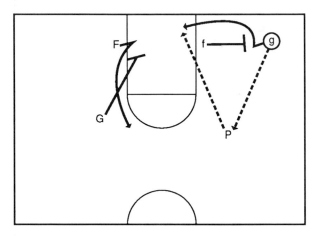

Diagram 8.21 Ball-Side Back-Screen 5 Before Reversal

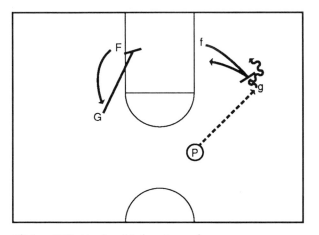

Diagram 8.22 Number 1 Before Reversal

Use of Number 1

Number 1 can be used anytime a good shooter has the ball. In the ruled offense, it simply is done when two players are somewhat isolated. The verbal call, "Number 1," is used either by the screener or the player with the ball. A guard-guard Number 1 is a form of interchange, whereas the guard forward simply has the players in the same place in the offense. The forward rolls back to his spot. If the guard doesn't get his shot or hit the roll man, the offense simply continues with the same rules. Examples of this are shown in diagrams 8.22 and 8.23. Diagram 8.23 shows a Number 1 ball reversal.

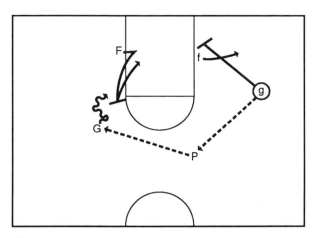

Diagram 8.23 Number 1 After Reversal

REVERSALS

Before the ball reversals are attempted, good interchanges must be practiced and somewhat perfected. Even though interchanges are designed to get good shots, the defense may be good enough to force a ball reversal. Sometimes patience through ball reversals will produce even better shots.

Ball Reversal from Corner

When the ball has been entered to the corner and interchanges have occurred, the ball is ready to be reversed. The ball could be returned to the point guard and entry could be done again. However, the 1, 2, 3, and 5 plays could occur with the ball being reversed to the big guard. This is designated from the bench, huddle, pre-game, etc. It still doesn't hurt for the offense to call out the number of the ball reversal.

2 Play Reversal

One of the easiest ways to reverse the ball is the 2 play. Diagram 8.24 shows the ball reversed to G who performs a 2 play with F. The chapter on Number 2 should be referred to.

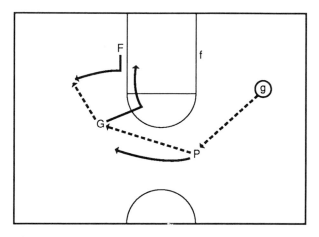

Diagram 8.24 Ball Reversed to G for 2 Play

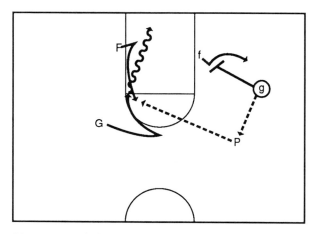

Diagram 8.25 Flash-Post Reversal

Flash-Post Option

Sometimes F can flash or has flashed to the post when the ball has been returned to P. If P passes directly to F, then G cuts off F for a handoff similar to the second option of the 2 play as shown in diagram 8.25.

If G doesn't get the ball, he goes to the low-post position as shown in diagram 8.26. This is almost an interchange with F. When F doesn't pass to G, it is now like the second option of Number 2, with one exception. F can front pivot and drive because he has his dribble left. As soon as F front pivots, f and g perform an interchange (either 4 or 5). We now have three good pass opportunities. If F passes to either P or g, he then interchanges with G. Obviously, if he passes

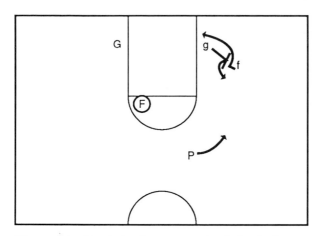

Diagram 8.26 F Looks for Open Man — After Facing Goal

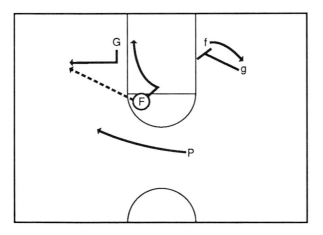

Diagram 8.27 G Breaks to Corner — 2 Play

back to P, we are back to the point guard penetration phase. F can pass to G breaking to corner, as shown in diagram 8.27. G has posted and broken to corner. A 2 play now occurs as if F and G had interchanged.

Forward Dribble-Back

This is the normal second option of Number 2. When the forward starts his dribble the cutting guard should clear to the weak side. Diagram 8.28 shows F dribbling to the key area. This creates several options: the normal second guard option to P; the high-low option of F to f; G should balance the floor, but look for a possible rub-off of his man on f; g provides defensive protection (as per the rule of P penetrating).

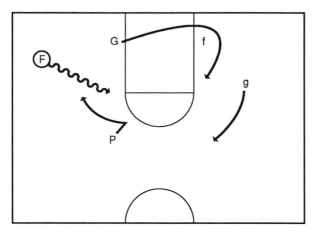

Diagram 8.28 Forward Dribble-Back

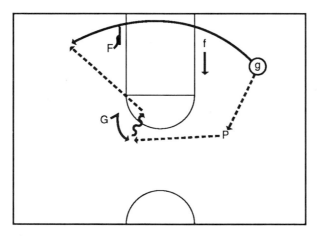

Diagram 8.29 Number 3 Ball Reversal

3 Play Reversal

The pass-back rule as discussed in the chapter on Number 3 is applied if 3 is designated as the ball reversal. When the ball is reversed, as shown in diagram 8.29, dribble penetration from the big guard, G, would be inside penetration. All the previous interchanges can be used before and after the ball reversal; g shouldn't begin the 3 cut until G has the ball.

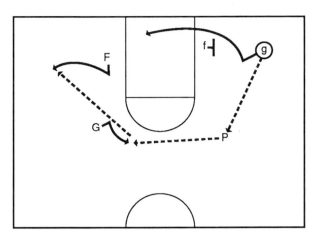

Diagram 8.30 Number 5 Ball Reversal

5 Play Reversal

When the ball is passed back to the point guard, the fly guard either stays in the corner or interchanges with the post. The 5 cut doesn't occur until the ball is passed to the opposite forward, as shown in diagram 8.30. If the forward has broken to the sideline, the fly guard (or post man, if they have interchanged) 5 cuts off the post man. The options now are the same as if we had performed a 2 cut (dribble-back, forward pass-back, etc.) with g as the cutting guard. g doesn't cut until F has the ball.

Flash Post 5

If the forward f breaks to the high post instead of the sideline, a high-low post situation develops. A roll-back situation for f as shown in diagram 8.31 develops.

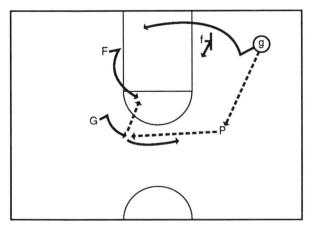

Diagram 8.31 F Can Pass to Either g or f

The fly guard continues to the corner. If the high post f passes to g, then F 2 cuts to the low post and now the offense is mirrored as shown in diagram 8.32. After G has passed to F, he interchanges with P to complete the mirror effect.

The movement of the forward can be pre-determined. He can always come up (or out). He can alternate. This, as many ruled offenses, can be left to the players' discretion as to where the defense is.

Skip Pass 3 Option

If the defense is a zone or sags quickly when the ball is beginning to be reversed, the skip pass option can be used as shown in diagram 8.33. Since g doesn't cut

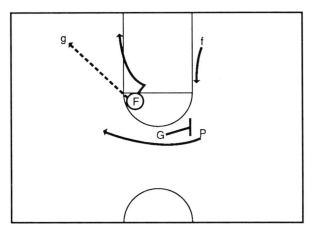

Diagram 8.32 F 2 Cuts to Complete Reversal

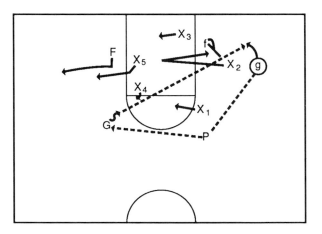

Diagram 8.33 Skip Pass 3 — Defense Sags

until the opposite forward F has the ball, this can be quite effective. Upon receiving the ball, G sees the quick defensive adjustment by X_2 (g's man or the zone shift). G then penetrates to put further concentration by the defense to the middle. f, recognizing this option by G's dribble and by X_2's and X_3's sagging, screens X_2 from recovering to g. G then throws skip pass (skipping P) to g for a corner show. The 3 play corner options can follow here. However, if g returns pass to F (or G), the 5 play reversal is in effect.

THE HIGH-POST OPTION(S)

The ruled offense up to this point has been basically from the fly, which starts the offense in the low post. It is not difficult to change to a high-post set. Instead of simply flashing players to the high post, one player is generally there.

From the Fly

There are several ways to enter the high-post set from the fly. The basic way is for the big guard to simply come and down-screen for F to come to the high post. To go to a two-guard front, the point guard simply dribbles to the opposite side, as shown in diagram 8.34. The fly guard rotates back out to the weak-side guard position. If the ball is passed to the fly guard, the offense remains basically the same.

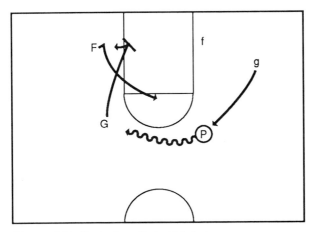

Diagram 8.34 Rotate from Fly to High Post

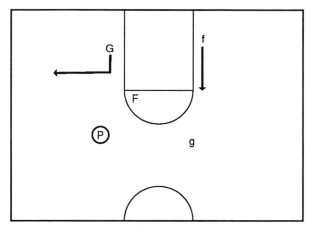

Diagram 8.35 G 2 Cuts – f Flashes for Entry

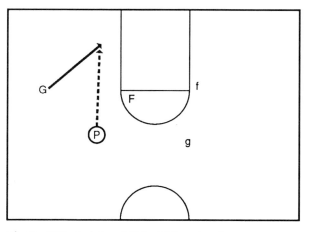

Diagram 8.36 Backdoor 2 Cut – G Overplayed

Entry

As P comes across, G should use a 2 cut to prepare for a 2 or 5 entry. Diagram 8.35 shows G using a forward 2 cut while f flashes. Now P may enter the offense with a pass to G, F, or f. If the defense overplays G on his initial 2 cut, G backdoors as shown in diagram 8.36. With f flashing, the backdoor has a better chance of success by taking out the help-side defense. Refer to Chapter 3 on Number 2.

P can enter the offense to F in the high post. Anytime the ball is passed to the high post, the forwards should post low.

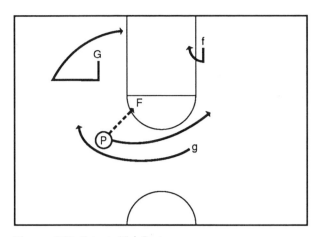

Diagram 8.37 Entry to High Post

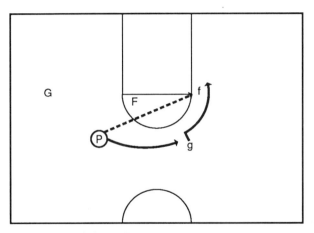

Diagram 8.38 Flash-Post Entry

The guards switch sides moving into the vision of F, who pivots and faces the forwards posting low. Diagram 8.37 shows the high-post entry.

P can also enter to the weak-side post, f. Diagram 8.38 shows this entry. The options are the same as flash post from the one-guard front.

If P passed to G, then we will have either a 2 or 5 cut. This must be called. Diagram 8.39 shows the 2 cut; diagram 8.40 shows the 5 cut. In both of these cases, we have cut a guard low. If he is open, obviously G passes the ball to him for a shot. All Number 2 or 5 options should follow here.

If P can't enter the ball, then P reverses the ball to g. Diagram 8.41 shows the player movement on the outside reversal before entry. In diagram 8.41, G has backdoored. As soon as P passes to g, G flashes to mirror the offense for entry by g.

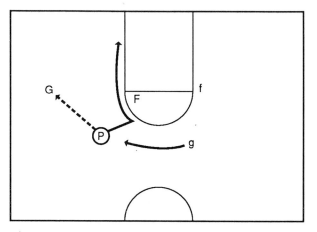

Diagram 8.39   Forward Entry — Number 2 from High Post

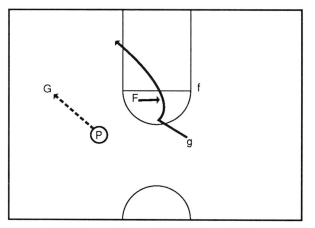

Diagram 8.40   Forward Entry — Number 5 From High Post

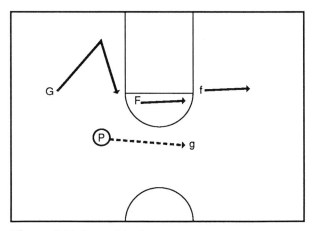

Diagram 8.41   Reversal for Entry

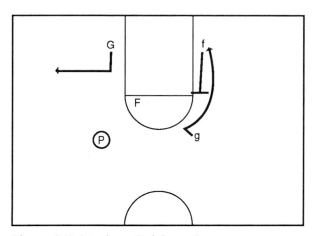

Diagram 8.42 Interchange Back-Screen 5

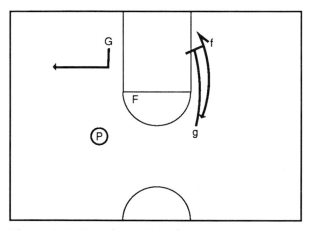

Diagram 8.43 Down-Screen 4 Interchange

Interchanges

Interchanges are basically the same after the entry. This is because there is a player in the corner, a player near the block, and a guard out front. The difference is that there is a player in the high post. This cuts down on the dribble penetration area, but creates another passing lane. In interchanges, there is also a possibility of a double screen in an interchange as well as a single screen.

Diagrams 8.42 and 8.43 are normal off-ball interchanges. Diagram 8.44 shows a Number 1 interchange with G rolling to the basket. Diagram 8.45 shows a Number 1 interchange with no roll. The guard-guard interchange simply sets up a reversal before entry.

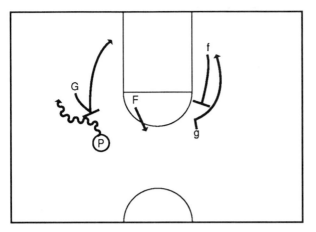

Diagram 8.44 Number 1 Before Reversal

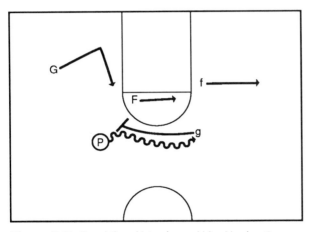

Diagram 8.45 Guard-Guard Interchange Using Number 1

Diagrams 8.46 and 8.47 show a pass-back to the high-post F before reversal. This simply interchanges P and G and also gets the ball into the high post. Anytime we can get the ball into the high post, we want the players in the forward positions to post for a high-low situation.

Diagrams 8.48, 8.49, and 8.50 show interchanges when G passes back to g. This gives an opportunity for a double screen. However, diagram 8.50 shows a double cross-screen 4 after g receives the pass.

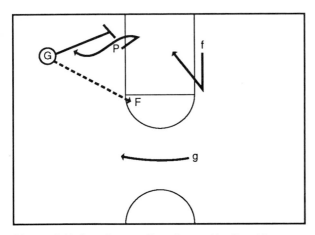

Diagram 8.46 Interchange – Cross-Screen 4 by G and P

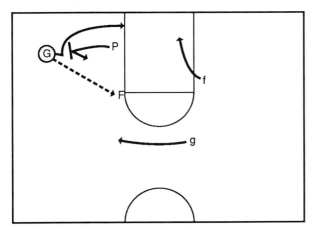

Diagram 8.47 Interchange – Back-Screen 5 by G and P

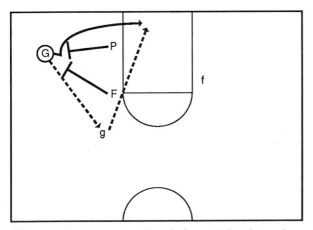

Diagram 8.48 Back-Screen 5 Double Screen Before Reversal

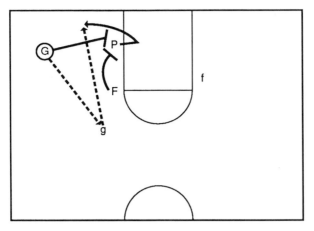

Diagram 8.49   Interchange of P and G — Use of Double Screen

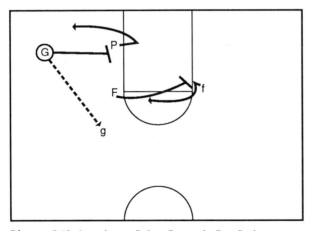

Diagram 8.50   Interchange Before Reversal — Pass-Back to g

Reversals

Number 1, 2, 3, or 5 can be used as reversals. Number 1 is shown with a double screen before the reversal in diagram 8.51. The weak side is cleared for the Number 1.

Diagram 8.52 shows a Number 2 reversal. If F and f interchange instead of F double screening, then g will rub his man off F as he 2 cuts.

Diagrams 8.53 and 8.54 depict a Number 3 reversal. If a single screen has been set to open P in the corner, as shown in diagram 8.53, then f should step out and receive a pass from g; f pivots and looks for the open man. Diagram

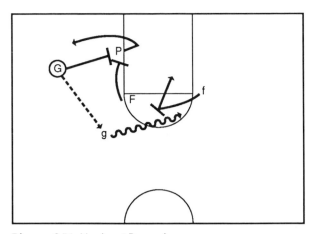

Diagram 8.51 Number 1 Reversal

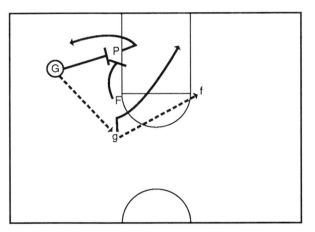

Diagram 8.52 Number 2 Reversal

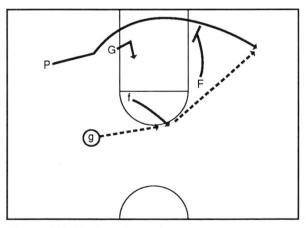

Diagram 8.53 Number 3 Reversal

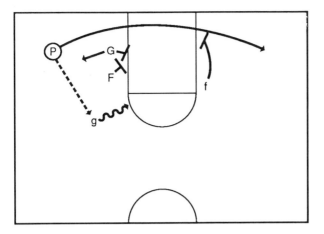

Diagram 8.54 Number 3 Reversal

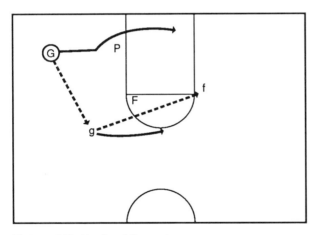

Diagram 8.55 Number 5 Reversal

8.54 shows P returning the pass to g after the double screen. Note that g penetrates to the middle. This causes f to go to the baseline and signals P to 3 cut across the baseline.

Diagram 8.55 shows the 5 cut reversal. This can be done before or after the interchange, obviously.

Dribble Penetration

Normally, the dribble penetration is not needed in the high post because of more passing lanes. However, defensive pressure may cause the guards to "put it on the floor." This can create some scoring situations. There are not as many gaps;

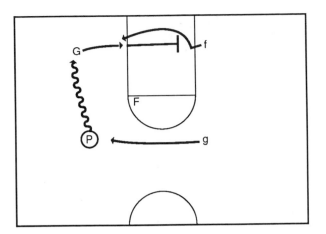

Diagram 8.56 Dribble-Down Penetration — G Posts Then Cross-Screens 4 for F

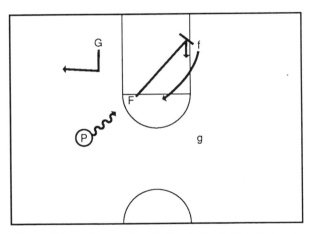

Diagram 8.57 Point (guard) Inside Penetration in High Post — Interchange of F and f

therefore, the opportunities arise from dribbling toward various teammates to create the offense. Diagram 8.56 shows a 4 play off the dribble-down toward G.

Diagram 8.57 depicts P penetrating toward the high post F with a corresponding interchange of F and f. Note G is breaking out for an entry if possible.

Diagram 8.58 shows P dribbling toward g; f back-screens 5 for g, then he can break out for a possible entry. As shown in diagram 8.59, g continues on through; G comes down and screens for g before flashing. Depending on the tightness of the defense, these dribble penetrations may provide some scores before entry.

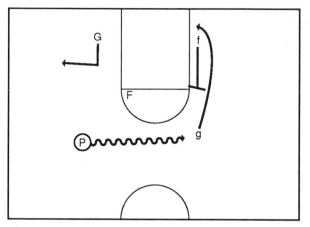

Diagram 8.58 Point (Guard) Dribbles toward Other Guard

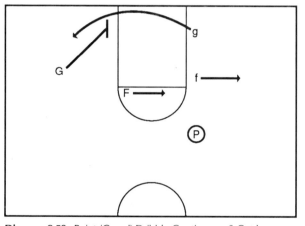

Diagram 8.59 Point (Guard) Dribble Continues — 3 Cut by g

SPECIAL RULES

Special rules need to be developed for specific talent. This is an advantage of the Fundamental Five. The flexibility lends itself to changes for special situations.

During the 1979-80 season at New Albany, we had unusual size for a high school team. We had 6'8" Richie Johnson, a high school All-American, at our big guard position on a low-post set. Richie went on to be an All-American at the University of Evansville and was drafted by the Detroit Pistons. Phil Benninger (Wright State University), at 6'8", was our post man. Jeff Stoops (Furman University), at 6'5", and 6'8" David Bennett, All-American at Kentucky Wesleyan, were the forwards. Mark Moody (Hardin-Simmons), at 6'0", and 5'10" Bob Bohannon (St. Ambrose College) were the point guards. All six of these players ended

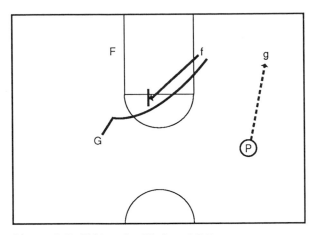

Diagram 8.60　Richie at G – f Flashes, G 5 Cuts

up on some All-State team their junior or senior year. Bohannon still holds the state finals records for assists (single game and tourney). They were backed up by 6'7" Mike Hunt (St. Bonaventure), 6'1" Herschel Barnett (Southeastern Illinois), 6'6" Tim Brandt (Purdue – on a track scholarship) and 6'3" Ken Booker. This was a super team. They were the first undefeated team in New Albany's rich basketball history. They were the Number 1 team in the State. They won 27 games in a row before being upset before 17,000 people in the State Championship Game in Market Square Arena. It took a good stall game and Richie Johnson's fouling out to do in one of Indiana's great high school teams.

We had some special rules for this team that emphasizes how rules must be made for the use of individual talents. Richie Johnson was a premier player. He is a 6'9" guard now. We naturally wanted Richie to have the ball in scoring position as much as possible. Therefore, we made the rule: the point guard would not cut. If the ball went to g, then Richie (G) would 5 cut, as shown in diagram 8.60. At 6'8", we liked to post him anyway. Diagrams 8.61 to 8.63 show the interchanges and ball reversals that keep a player like Richie keyed in the offense. Since the rest of the team were all Division One college players, opponents could not concentrate on Richie. If they did, a good shooter was left open for a shot. We ran Phil Benninger at low and high post. He could start either place.

David Bennett is one of the best 6'8" shooters I've ever seen. Jeff Stoops is also a pure shooter. When Richie would cut across, either 2 or 5, the defense usually helped by sagging on him. This left our corner players open for the shot. David, at F, and Jeff, at g, both hit well over 50 percent of their shots. This was a lot of our offense. Besides, we always had two good-sized rebounders on the offside of the ball. We ran this against zone and man-to-man. We back-screened 5 for Richie some also.

Some teams sagged their point guard down since our point guard didn't cut. This left four-time All-Sectional guard Mark Moody or two-time All-Sectional

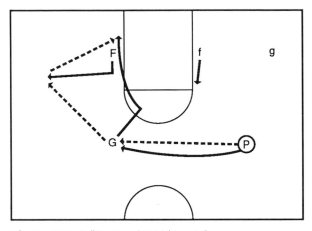

Diagram 8.61   Ball Reversed to Richie – 2 Cut

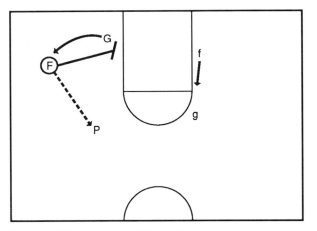

Diagram 8.62   Interchance Richie to Corner

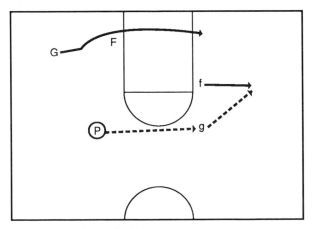

Diagram 8.63   Reversal – Richie at G

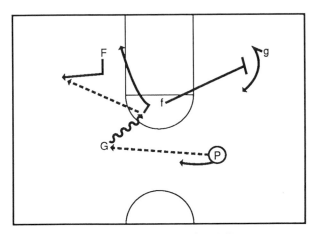

Diagram 8.64   Richie at G Penetrates Before 2 Cut

guard Bob Bohannon open, whichever we had at point guard. We did have everyone involved in the offense even though we decided on the 2 or 5 situation because of Richie Johnson. Many people wondered why we played a 6'8" guy at guard. After the first pass, he was under the basket. Richie could also penetrate very well for his size and would do this against man-to-man and zones before his 2 play developed, as shown in diagram 8.64.

In 1982, only 6'7" Bubby Mukes (University of Evansville) returned as a starter. He is Richie's cousin and became the single season scoring leader for New Albany that year. Jeff Hoback, 6'5" (St. Louis University), was also a good shooter. We needed role players to back up these players. They not only played their roles well, but went on to collegiate careers themselves. Troy Bensing, 6'5" (Western Kentucky, football) and Barry Howard, 6'5" (St. Joseph) were the forwards. Tony Duffy (Mount Marty) was the point guard.

Mukes was always at big guard G. Hoback always went to fly guard. Bensing always went to low-post f and Howard went opposite to F. Duffy always remained at point guard.

Troy Bensing was a big hard-nosed low-post player. He developed into a good passer. He went to the basket well, however he could always find Bubby Mukes or Jeff Hoback on the "ins and outs." We wanted Troy on the ball-side low post.

Barry Howard, as a junior, played good defense (set school record for blocked shots) and rebounded well. He didn't score much as a junior but in his senior year he led the team in scoring. If Troy and Barry would interchange on a cross-screen 4, Troy would always return low, as shown in diagrams 8.65 and 8.66.

We used a 3 cut reversal whenever Tony interchanged with either Jeff or Bubby. We also, because of Jeff's and Bubby's size and leaping ability, used back-screen 5 as shown in diagram 8.67. This was called from the bench, keyed by the fact that Tony had *not* interchanged.

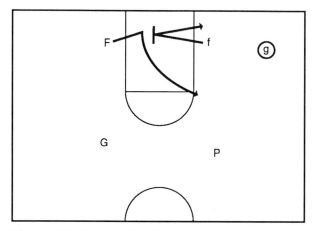

Diagram 8.65   Troy at f — Rolls Back Low

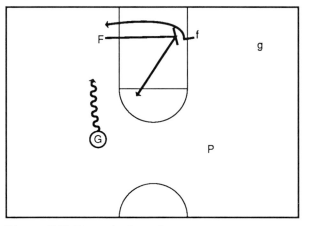

Diagram 8.66   Troy at f — Comes Low

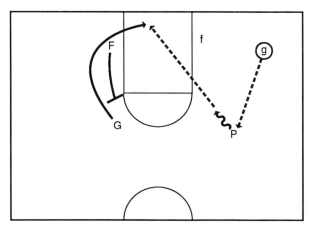

Diagram 8.67   Back-Screen 5 — P <u>Did Not</u> Interchange

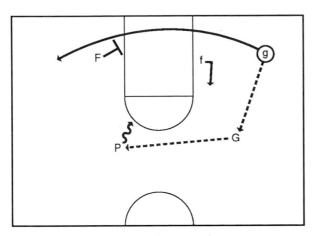

Diagram 8.68   3 Cut Reversal <u>After</u> P Interchanges

If Tony didn't interchange, we didn't use the 3 cut. We would interchange the other players by down-screen 4's and back-screen 5's. Number 1 could be used anytime Bubby or Jeff had the ball. When Tony interchanged with Bubby or Jeff, we ran the 3 cut reversal as shown in diagram 8.68. P had already interchanged with G after passing to g. We wanted Tony passing the basketball to the scorer. He always had defense.

The normal entries were used with the 3 cut as the reversal. It was basically a double low-post stack-set offense. It was simple, yet effective. We practiced the other parts of the Fundamental Five, but this was the offense that won the Hoosier Hills Conference.

These are just two examples of how rules are developed from the use of the Fundamental Five. If players are trained in the Fundamental Five, you can make adjustments to your ruled offense as well as your patterned offense.

Teaching the Ruled Offense

The ruled offense is difficult to teach. There is a great deal of ''savvy'' involved, more individuality can take place, and it is harder to scout, harder to coach and control.

Players have to be better able to judge shot selection. Pattern offense usually dictates the shots. Ruled offenses are closer to free-lance offenses where shots develop by player and ball movement. The coach has to designate shooters, places where certain individuals can shoot from, or be satisified with his players individual shot selection. Smart players will take good shots.

Sometimes when the ruled offense isn't going well, it's nice to be able to call a set play or pattern. The players who have been instructed in the Fundamental Five can do this. I have found it's like teaching in the classroom. You give the players more freedom as the year progresses and you don't lose discipline. If you need more discipline, you aren't too far away from obtaining it.

9

Attacking Zones with the Fundamental Five

The Fundamental Five can be used to attack zones. However, there are a few fundamental tactics that should be used before trying any play options.

Good fundamental basketball tactics tell you to look for the holes in a zone and attack them. I believe you should attack these holes in a zone first, then run your offensive plays as an "option." Alignment, overload dribble penetration, flash into the middle, spreading the gaps, ball reversal, ins and outs, and screening the zone are all ways to attack the zones. The Fundamental Five is involved in the ball reversal and screening the gaps.

Alignment

Alignment is very important in attacking zones. Most zones either match-up or change to a 2–3 zone after the first pass. The alignment can make the match-up harder for the defense.

If your offensive set-up places players in the holes or gaps of the zone to start with, the defense must make adjustments early. For example, if the defense has a one-man front, the offensive alignment should be a two-man front and vice versa. A good pass after penetrating can lead to a score without much player movement.

There are many alignments that do this. A team's personnel usually determines the alignment. Some examples of this are shown in diagrams 9.1 to 9.5. If you have a good corner shooter, diagrams 9.2, 9.4, and 9.5 show the placement of this shooter. The shooter is actually in an overload position.

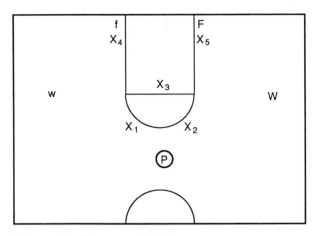

Diagram 9.1 Alignment vs. 2-1-2 Zone

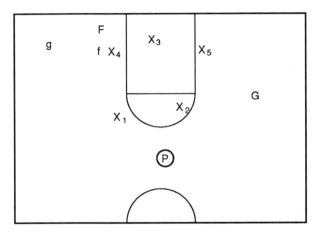

Diagram 9.2 Alignment vs. 2-2-1 Zone

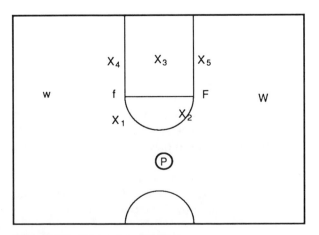

Diagram 9.3 Alignment vs. 2-3 Zone

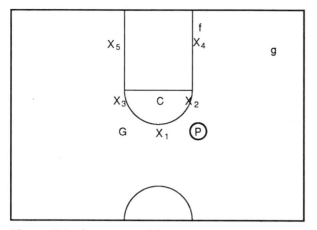

Diagram 9.4 Alignment vs. 1-2-2

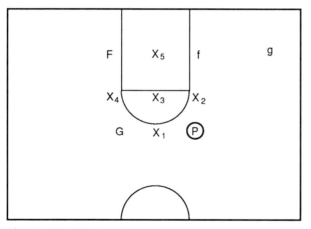

Diagram 9.5 Alignment vs. 1-3-1

Overload

This can actually be a part of alignment as was shown in diagrams 9.2, 9.4, 9.5. These diagrams show a player can be started overloading the zone.

Stack offenses can break players into overload position. Diagram 9.6 is an example of an overload from a stack offense. The stack should be aligned with the zone so that when the guard breaks out, both players in the stack will be in the gaps of the zone.

Another way to overload is through player movement. Number 3 by the pass-back rule is an excellent way to overload a zone. When the player cuts through to the opposite side, as shown in diagram 9.7, he overloads the opposite side.

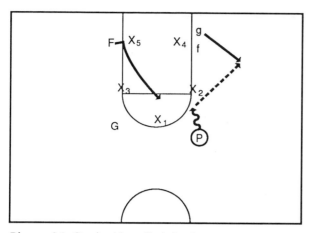

Diagram 9.6 Overload from Single Stack

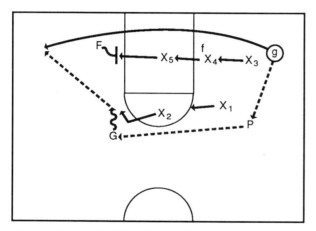

Diagram 9.7 Overload from Number 3

Dribble Penetration

Penetration is important. Against a two-man front, the point guard should penetrate the top of the key area as shown in diagram 9.8. The secret is how far. I do not want my small guard too far in the "land of the Giants." We want our point guard to follow the penetration rule.

RULE: The point guard should penetrate until one of the front defensive men moves toward him, then this wing is open.

The defense may do this far in front of the key area and the point must be willing to give up the ball well before the key area. This spreads the zone and

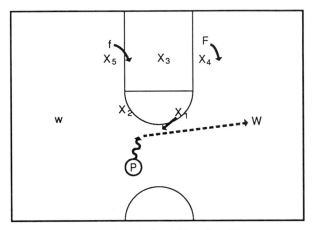

Diagram 9.8 Penetration of a 2-1-2 (Two-Guard Front)

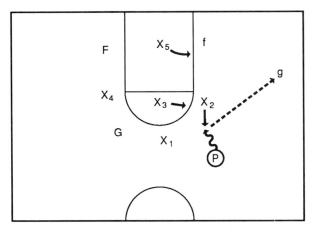

Diagram 9.9 Penetration of a 1-3-1 (One-Guard Front)

opens the gaps even farther. Since the defensive guard X_1 was moving toward P when he penetrated, X_1 will have a great deal of difficulty recovering to guard W. This causes the zone to make changes.

In a one-man front, the point guard should penetrate either the right or left side. Again, the point guard is trying to get one of two players to commit themselves. Actually, as shown in diagram 9.9, P is trying to get X_2 to commit to him. Then X_5 (or any corner player of a one-man front zone) must guard f or g. Again, the zone has to make adjustments to the offense.

There are two other dribble "penetrations." The angle dribble (not sideways) improves the passing lane as well as causing the zone to shift. Diagram 9.10 shows W penetrating to the corner causing X_3 to cover him. This improves W's passing lane to F. It also causes X_4 to cover F.

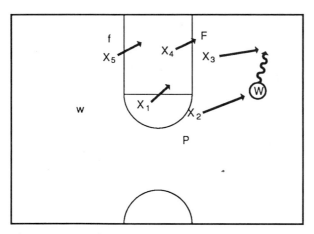

Diagram 9.10 Angle Penetration vs. 2-1-2

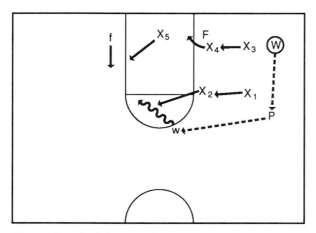

Diagram 9.11 Back-Side Dribble on Reverse

The other dribble is the back-side dribble. This occurs when the zone has sagged to protect the middle and middle penetration. Diagram 9.11 shows w using a back-side dribble to improve a passing lane to f. This dribble also reverses the ball.

Flash into Middle

The flash-pivot option can be used as the ball is penetrated. Forwards (baseline players) should start behind the zone and then flash into the gaps of the zone. Diagram 9.12 shows f flashing into the high post against a 2-1-2 zone. The type of zone doesn't matter if f flashes into a gap. If X_4 covers f flashing, then P throws a high pass to F. This alley-oop pass should be a two-hand overhead pass thrown

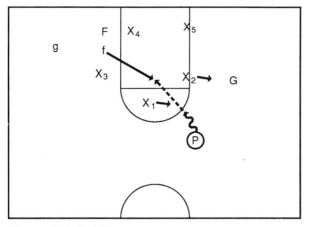

Diagram 9.12 Flash Pivot

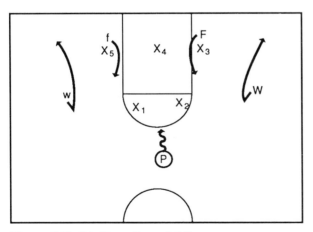

Diagram 9.13 "Up-Downs" vs. a 2-3 Zone

on a direct line to the edge of the backboard. Obviously if f is open, P should pass to him. Any zone has gaps in it. No matter what alignment you use, if the forwards are behind the zone, they can flash into the gaps.

Spread Gaps

With the forwards playing behind the zone and the threat of an alley-oop pass, the gaps in the zone are increased. Another method of spreading the gaps is the use of "up-downs, crosses, and switches."

The "up-down" is simply the forwards coming up into the gaps while the wings are going down. Diagram 9.13 shows this against a 2-3 zone. Diagram

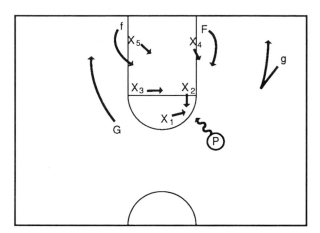

Diagram 9.14 "Up-Downs" vs. a 1-2-2 Zone

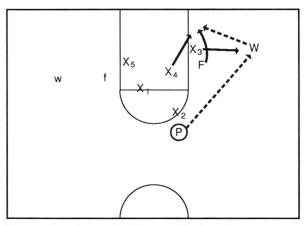

Diagram 9.15 Forward Roll-Down – "Up-Down"

9.14 shows "up-downs" versus 1-2-2 zone. In both cases the forwards put pressure on the defensive forwards to cover them. Therefore, the wings are open near the corner. Diagram 9.15 shows F rolling back down after W receives the ball. This roll-down should occur just after W receives the ball as the defense is trying to adjust.

The "cross" is a simple variation of the "up-down." Diagram 9.16 shows F and f crossing into the gaps of a 2–3 zone. This can be done with any zone. The roll-down is the same.

The "switch," shown in diagram 9.17, occurs before P penetrates. F and f switch positions just before P is ready to penetrate. Then they either cross or go up into the zone gaps. The player movement sometimes causes the gaps to widen in the zone.

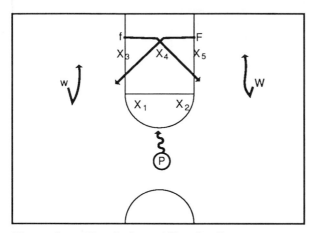

Diagram 9.16 "Cross" – Form of "Into Gaps"

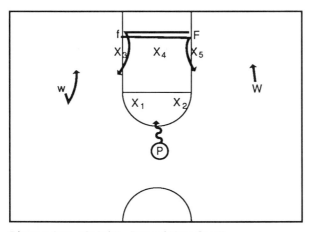

Diagram 9.17 "Switch" – Form of "Into Gaps"

The forwards make these verbal calls before the point penetration. They are generally side by side anyway. The point should hit the open man. If the defense tries to cover the wings early, one of the forwards should be open. Diagram 9.18 shows X_3 covering W early and receiving the ball. X_4 covers F. As soon as F receives the ball, f should roll low for a high-low situation. This forces X_5 to come from behind to cover f.

Sometimes the wings can flash into the gaps. If this happens, the wing looks for a high-low pass to the forward. In a 2–3 zone, there is more of a gap at the wing if the forwards post as the guards penetrate. Diagram 9.19 shows this. As P penetrates, F and f try to post up, forcing X_5 and X_3 to guard them. W and w

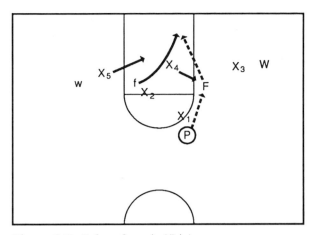

Diagram 9.18 Defense Spread — High-Low

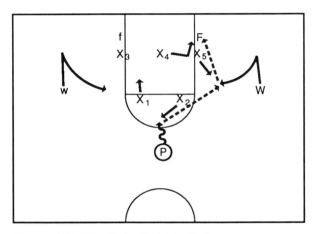

Diagram 9.19 Wing Flash — Back Into Gap

go down and come up the gaps. When W receives the pass, X_5 will shift to cover him. This is because of the penetration rule that P has forced X_2 to cover him. P passes to whichever wing side the guard (X_1 or X_2) has come to him. W looks for the high-low to F. X_4 must shift to cover F.

What normally occurs defensively on the wing flash is that X_5, as shown in diagram 9.20, covers W until X_2 recovers. X_5 tries to stay in the passing lane to F. P moves toward W to increase the gap or passing lane so that X_1 moves to cover him. If X_1 does move toward P, then w should flash into the gap left by X_1.

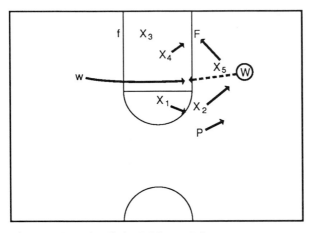

Diagram 9.20 Wing Flash — P "Creates" Gap

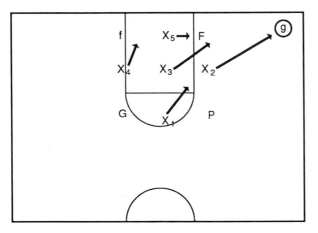

Diagram 9.21 1-3-1 Becomes "2-3"

Ball Reversal

Ball reversal gets a zone to shift and recover. If a defensive player fails to shift well, the zone weakens. Player movement, as well as ball movement, should be used in good ball reversal. This not only causes shifting problems recovering from ball movement, but defensive personnel assignments.

Ball reversal can be done with the use of Number 1, 2, 3, or 5. These provide both player and ball movement. Your personnel, the type of zone, and the opponent's personnel determine the type of ball reversal used. However, since all zones end up being basically 2-3 zones after the entry, ball reversal can be used from any of those previously listed. Change of reversal during the game obviously will cause the defense more adjustment problems. Diagrams 9.21, 9.22, and 9.23 show what I mean by the fact that all zones are 2-3 after entry.

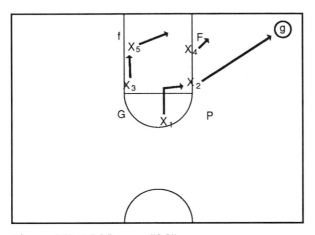

Diagram 9.22 1-2-2 Becomes "2-3"

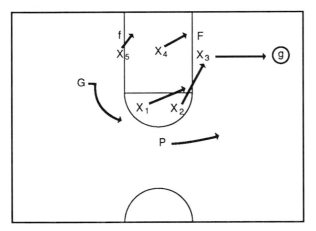

Diagram 9.23 "2-3" After First Pass

Number 1 is generally used in screening zones. However, it can be used as the ball reversal, especially if the team is matching up well. Number 1 is an excellent play against the match-up zone and will be discussed as a ball reversal against the match-up.

When the ball is reversed using a Number 2, the zone must react to a player cutting into the zone. Diagram 9.24 shows this cut. Obviously, G must be able to post well because the first option is to get the ball to him in the low-post area. The movement forces individual defense of X_5 on f and X_4 on G. X_4 has to work to deny a good cut by G.

Number 3 and Number 5 run players along the baseline. Diagram 9.25 shows a 3 cut using the pass-back rule described in the chapter on Number 3.

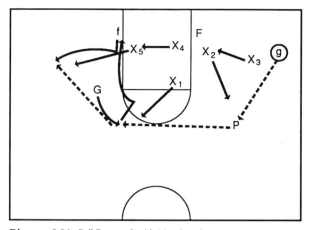

Diagram 9.24 Ball Reversal with Number 2

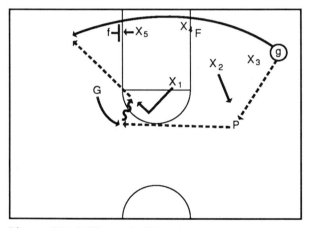

Diagram 9.25 Ball Reversal with Number 3

Diagram 9.26 shows Number 5 used as a ball reversal against a zone. If g can post well, as well as shoot from the corner, this is a good play. The Number 4 baseline screen that can follow all cuts and ball reversals will provide another opportunity for g to get the ball in the corner as shown in diagram 9.27.

"Ins and Outs"

The use of "ins and out" is discussed in Chapter 5 on Number 4. However, the zone defense that is collapsed, spread out, collapsed etc. is less effective. When the zone is packed in and the ball is inside, the zone will collapse even more. The ball goes quickly back out. Ins and outs work the best against zones and collapsing defense. This may be the single best way to beat the zone defense.

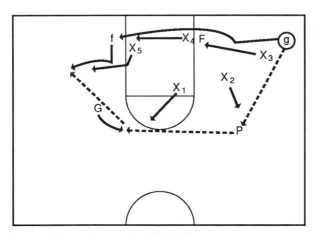

Diagram 9.26 Ball Reversal with Number 5

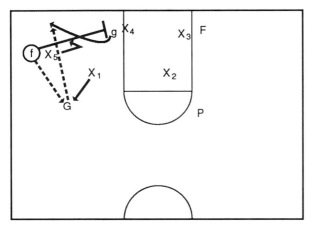

Diagram 9.27 Number 4 After Reversal

Number 5—"Alley-Oop"

An "alley-oop" or high, lob pass near the rim that ends in an easy basket is always a desired play. You need to have a good leaper to attempt this. It doesn't have to be a dunk shot, but it's good if the player can get up that high. Timing is extremely important on this play.

The number 5 alley-oop can be used on a ball reversal before the Number 2 play is attempted. It basically interchanges G and f, hoping G will be open for the high pass as shown in diagram 9.28. If P can't hit G, f pops out to the guard position. Then f can pass to G in the forward position and 2 cuts to the basket as shown in diagram 9.29.

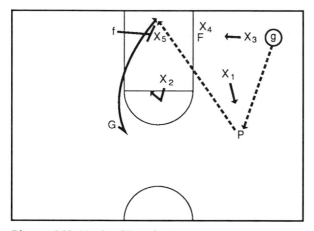

Diagram 9.28 Number 5 Interchange

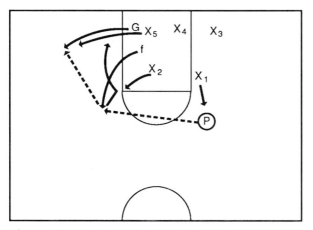

Diagram 9.29 Number 2 After 5 Interchange

If you are in the overloaded-stack offensive set like in diagram 9.30, the defense may play X_3 over the top to avoid being double-screened by F and f. When this occurs, F should screen X_4; f should pin X_3, then break to the goal for a high, two-hand overhead pass from P.

Another use of Number 5 alley-oop from the overloaded stack or any zone offense may be to free G for a high lob pass. Diagram 9.31 shows this play. The ball should start in G's hands. This shifts the defense to G before the ball is reversed. When G passes to P, F comes across for a back-screen 5 for G. P should fake to f or g before throwing the high, two-hand overhead pass to G. G must set up X_3 by rubbing him off F's screen.

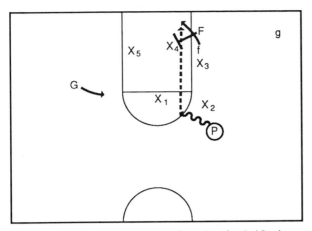

Diagram 9.30 Number 5 Alley Oop from Overloaded Stack

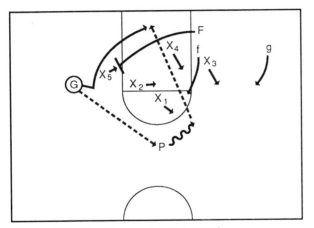

Diagram 9.31 Alley Oop for G After Reversal

Screening the Zone

When the zone is screened, it is not able to perform the necessary shifts to counteract ball or player movement. Number 3, of course, is used to prevent forward
movement. The screen hopes to open the good shooting cutter. Number 3 is
used by the offense to keep their post men near the blocks.

Number 4 can also be used to prevent defensive forward movement. Diagram 9.32 shows F screening X_4, the first defensive forward opposite him on the
zone. By screening X_4, X_3 must pick up f coming across the zone. Since many
teams have X_4 pick up any cutter flashing low, X_3 may relax for a second or go
help on the ball. This gives f just the necessary time to get open for the ball.

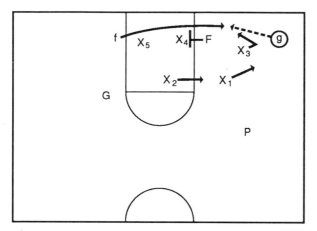

Diagram 9.32 Number 4 to Screen Zone

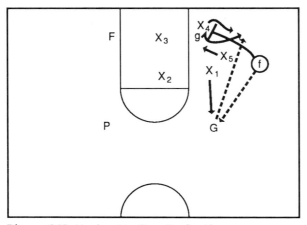

Diagram 9.33 Number 4 to Open Baseline Player

Diagram 9.33 shows Number 4 used to open a baseline player for a corner shot. If a player has made a 5 cut or 2 cut on a ball reversal, he is in the low-post position. If f is unable to hit g, he starts to reverse the ball to G. Then f screens X₄ for g and g cuts to the corner for a return pass from G. After a reverse pivot to keep X₄ at his back, f posts up for a return pass from g. If X₅ switches early to deny the pass to g, then G passes to f. In either a 2, 3, or 5 reversal, we end up in a low-post situation. At any time we could reverse again.

Number 1 can also be used against a zone. It's usually better to use the initial screen against a one-man front as an entry to keep the zone from shifting. Diagrams 9.34 and 9.35 show the use of Number 1 against 1-2-2 and 1-3-1 zones. Note that X₂ in both zones must cover P on the penetration. This opens

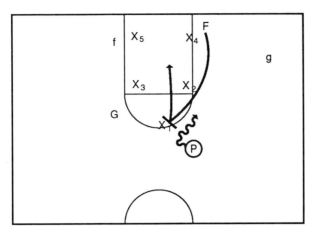

Diagram 9.34 Number 1 vs. 1-2-2 — Forces X_2 to Cover P

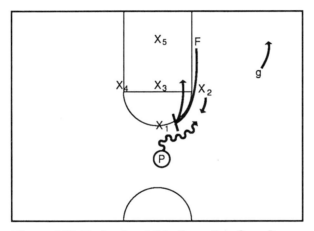

Diagram 9.35 Number 1 vs. 1-3-1 — Forces X_2 to Cover P

the corner for a pass to g or F on the roll-down. If X_4 (diagram 9.34) or X_5 (diagram 9.35) move out to defend g, then P hits F rolling down. If P passes to g, and then X_4 and X_5 move out to defend g, g looks for F posting low.

However, if the zone matches up extremely well on the ball as in a match-up zone, Number 1 can be used on a ball reversal. Man-to-man principles work well with the match-up.

THE MATCH-UP ZONE

The match-up zone is a ruled combination defense. It tries to combine the best of the zone defenses with man-to-man principles. In my opinion, every good zone has man-to-man principles, and conversely every good man-to-man has zone principles.

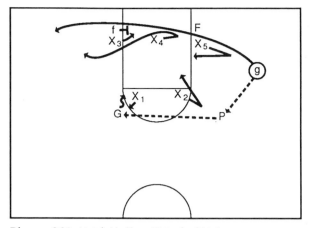

Diagram 9.36 Match-Up Zone "Matched Up"

The match-up tries to take away the attack-the-gap principle by adjusting players to match up to your offensive set-up. For example, if you have a one-man front, the match-up will shift to a one-man front zone. The defense will try to "switch men" as you send cutters through the zone.

Bill Green, of Marion, Indiana, now at University of Indianapolis, won five state championships with the match-up. He has written a book and lectured many times on the match-up zone. Against us, Madison-Grant, Marion started with a two-man front and followed our 3 play cutter g with their middle man X_4 (see diagram 9.36). When we prepared for Marion, we knew we had to have more than the 3 play or even 3 continuous.

The 3 play options (chapter on Number 3) worked well at times, because we screened their middle man who was picking up the cutter (diagram 9.36). However, they started overplaying the cut and switching well. This put them in a definite man-to-man situation early in the corner. They were adjusting to the early switch option (see Number 3). We had also been well scouted. Our corner shot was available, but on a rushed basis.

Since they were now in an overplaying man-to-man, we would reverse the ball after G had penetrated. We now had the floor cleared for a 1 play with P and F (diagram 9.37). Since Marion had overplayed the 3 play with defensive player X_2 and X_5 sagging heavily, they had difficulty recovering to P and F. In fact, P and F had a lot of room to maneuver their two-man Number 1 play. When we started scoring on this reversal Number 1 play, Marion's defense started breaking down. The X_2 and X_5 men started staying closer to P and F and the Number 3 play options worked better.

We practiced reversing the ball with a 2 cut, but the outside maneuver of Number 1 seemed to work better. If our point guard would have been a power big guard, this would have been better. We have used this with a degree of success.

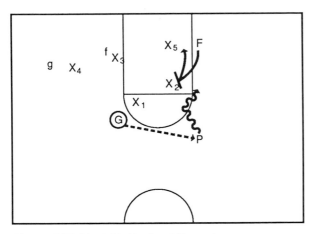

Diagram 9.37   Match-Up Number 1 Reversal

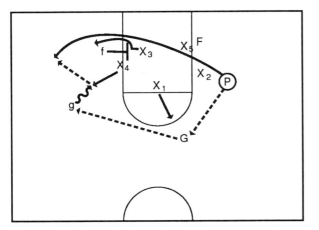

Diagram 9.38   Continuity Reversal — 3 Cut Forces Forward X_4 to Cover Wing

We had planned to use a 3–1 (3 play, 1 play) continuity. If the 1 play broke down by the pick being beaten, point losing his dribble, etc., we would use the continuity to keep the defense overshifted. Actually, we just applied the "pass-back" rule of Number 3 (diagram 9.38).

After P has cut through, G has become the new point guard. If the #3 cut doesn't work, then G and F can work a 1 play (diagram 9.39).

The "I" Set-Up

Another set up we used against Marion was the "I" set-up. This was used when we wanted to change our look of Number 3. Our point guard, Ron Small, was an excellent ball handler. He would bring the ball down and pass to one of the

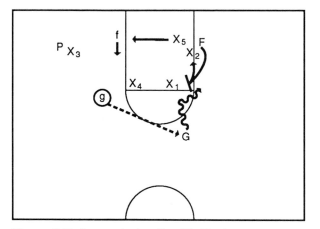

Diagram 9.39   Reverse Again — G and F — Number 1

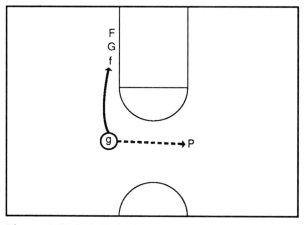

Diagram 9.40   Basic "I" Set-Up

other guards. g would return the pass to the point so his dribble would be remaining. The other three players would be in a triple stack (diagram 9.40). The wing, g, would go to the top of the stack to complete the "I" set-up.

g would signal "break" and the players in the "I" would break to their regular positions in the gaps of the zone (diagram 9.41). This made the match-up more difficult, even if the defense sagged into position.

We found the second pass to f rolling down worked well (diagram 9.42). After this, we ran a 31 play. If we got the shot before the 3 play, that was gravy. We hadn't changed our offense, only our look. This is the advantage the Fundamental Five gives.

If the defense actually matched up man-to-man with the "I," (diagram 9.43) we ran three different options before we started our 31 play. Our pass-back wing, g, could run a 3 play off the triple screen (diagram 9.44).

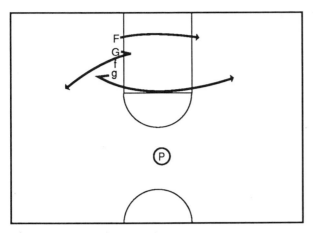

Diagram 9.41   "Break" to Regular Positions

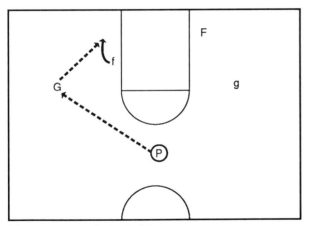

Diagram 9.42   "I" Set-Up Roll-Down

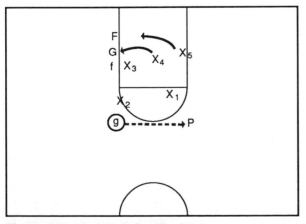

Diagram 9.43   Match-Up Before "Break"

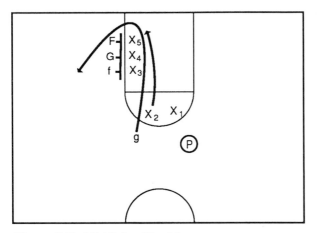

Diagram 9.44 3 Cut Before ''Break''

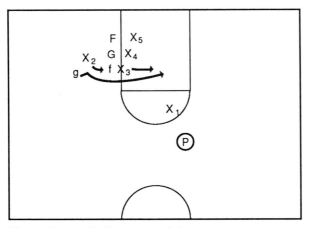

Diagram 9.45 3 Cut Continues as 5 Cut

If g is not open on the triple screen, he continues over the top. With X_2 trailing him, he can use a 5 cut off f and should be open in the middle as shown in diagram 9.45.

If X_2 can follow g or X_3 switches, W continues to the opposite side; then F comes over the top, trying to force another switch. F should be open in the same area W was as shown in diagram 9.46

If F isn't open, then f down-screens 4 for G coming to the wing position shown in diagram 9.47. Note that the players are now in position to run a normal 3 play. If G or g is passed to, the pass-back rule would be in effect if they returned the pass to P. The motion of this option really causes a match-up to switch a great deal.

Another option we used was a ''2 play.'' This was similar to our 2 endline out-of-bounds play. g would call ''2'' when he saw the man-to-man line up. He would go to his normal place in the ''I'' (diagram 9.48). The good shooting G

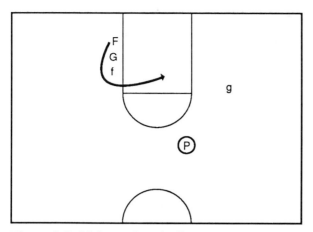

Diagram 9.46 F Follows g Over the Top

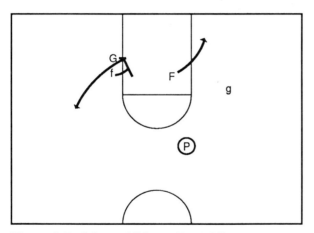

Diagram 9.47 G Comes Off Screen "Into" Offense

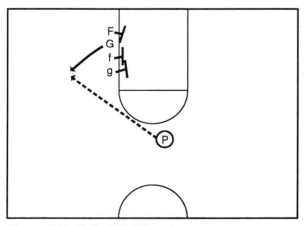

Diagram 9.48 "2 Play" Triple Screen

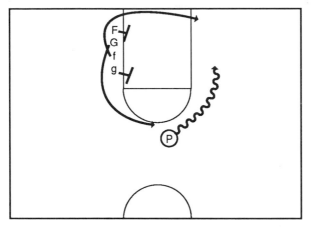

Diagram 9.49 One-on-One Option

would step out and the two forwards f and F would close the gap. This triple screen is not a normal 2 play, but is exactly like our endline play. This places G in his position on the floor for our regular offense. If the screen doesn't work, the players again break to their normal positions. You don't have much rebounding on this option, but if G is an excellent shooter you open him for a shot. We have used it against match-ups as a last-second shot play. It usually doesn't work more than once.

The third option was P going one-on-one. That's why we gave him the ball with the dribble. If we felt that g couldn't return the ball to P, we would use this option. If the defense was tight, P might get a basket.

However, the defense usually protected against this one on one move. Therefore, we ran a double 5 cut as shown in diagram 9.49. As P dribbled to the wing area, G came over the top to the point position. g screened for G; F screened for f. g headed out to the wing position after G came to the top. We were now in position to run a 3 cut, if P would pass back to G.

What we did against the match-up was basically make it play man-to-man more than it wanted. When they tried to go to their match-up rules, we tried to force them into one- and two-man plays. This hurt the zone principle.

Incidentally, we beat Marion by ten points. We were the only school to beat them in the Sectional in the seventies. In fact, no one has beaten them in the Sectional since. This was Madison-Grant's only Sectional Championship. Marion has about 3,000 pupils to Madison-Grant's 600.

Forward Number 3 vs. Match-up

In 1981, as was said before, we had 6'8" Indiana All-Star, David Bennett (All-American Kentucky Wesleyan) at one forward position. We ran some out of a two-guard front with this group. Either Bob Bohannon (St. Ambrose) or Mark

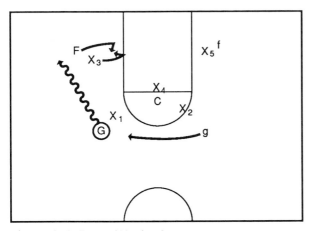

Diagram 9.50 Forward Number 3

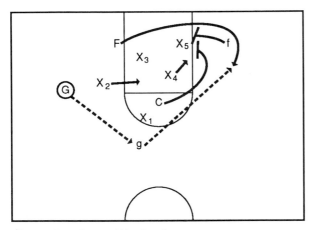

Diagram 9.51 Forward Number 3

Moody (Hardin-Simmons) would drive toward David's side, as shown in diagram 9.50. Dave would go to the low-post position. If we could hit him here, we would. Most teams would match up with us 2-1-2 and help well on the first option.

Bennett, at F, would then complete a 3 cut off a double screen from Bubby Mukes (Evansville) at f and Michael Hunt (St. Bonaventure) at C. This forced the match-up to switch. X_4 or X_5 had to take F coming across. If they got screened, David, at F, had a good shot, as shown in diagram 9.51. David Bennett, as was said before, was a tremendous outside shooter. Therefore, the defense usually switched.

If X_4 covered David as he came across, he simply circled around C and sometimes got a good shot coming toward g. Diagram 9.52 shows F coming to the ball. If F doesn't get the ball, he returns to the block he started from. This is a form of a 5 cut by F off C.

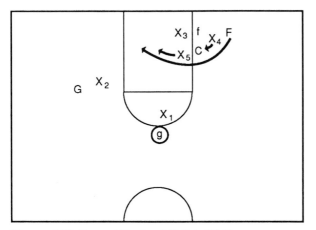

Diagram 9.52 Forward Number 3 (5 Cuts Off C)

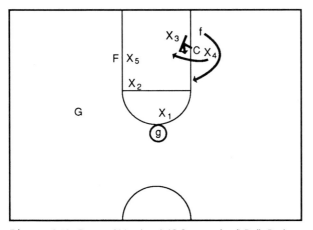

Diagram 9.53 Forward Number 3 (C Screens for f) Rolls Back

If X_5 covers F coming over the top early or X_4 is successful in covering F, the next option is a down-screen 4 by C for f; f follows F off C's screen, as shown in diagram 9.53. If f isn't open, C may be on the roll off the 4 play.

If X_2 is sagging to help in the middle too much, g can pass to G for a good medium-range corner shot as shown in diagram 9.54. G should be in range when he receives the ball. This worked well for us because both Bob and Mark were good shooters. This reversal back also had David returning to the low-post position with many times the defense spread out covering the other options.

This a good play option against both man-to-man and zone offenses. In fact, many man-to-man options will work against match-up zones. Screens are simply set on the man nearest the ball.

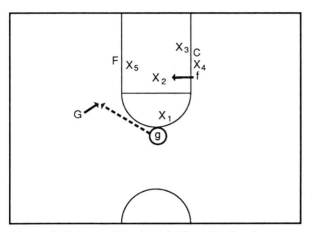

Diagram 9.54 Forward Number 3 (X_2 Sags, G Is Open)

These items have worked for me in attacking the match-up. It is simply easier to make adjustments when your team has all the fundamentals of the Fundamental Five.

10

Special Situations

Another advantage of the Fundamental Five is the continuity to special situations. You use the same five plays, coded the same way for out-of-bounds plays, press plays, last-second plays, box-and-one plays, and the delay game. You are not introducing new dialogue, more names for plays nor adding more confusion in stressful moments. Since these are only five offensive moves, the players are thinking of the five moves after the set-ups. The set-ups, like the other phases of the offense, can be changed, but the moves are the same. Therefore, our offense continues through special situations. If our scouting report shows weaknesses against any of the Fundamental Five, we want to exploit them in special situations as well as in half-court offense.

Out-of-Bounds Plays

Naturally, we have five. They are all very basic out-of-bounds plays; but they use the Fundamental Five. From the endline, the direct resemblance to the five plays are somewhat exaggerated. However, they are as close as possible so that the players are able to remember the plays better. The set-ups shown are basically the way we start to teach the out-of-bounds plays. They could be changed or options added. I will show some of the options that we have run, both end line, and sideline. The diagrams may be labeled with high-post players, ''fly'' situation, etc. It really is irrelative.

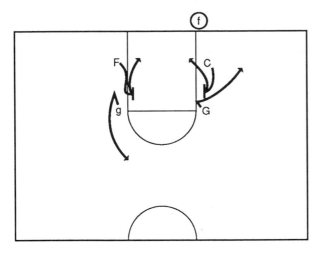

Diagram 10.1 Number 1 — End Line

End Line Out-of-Bounds Plays

Number 1

Number 1 is an exaggerated pick and roll. It's closer to a backscreen 5 play be-cause we are not really picking the ball, as shown in diagram 10.1. The play is one that I had used before the development of the Fundamental Five. Since the center C is picking for the best shooting guard G and then rolling to the basket, there is a strong relation to a pick and roll. The best big man should be C. He really becomes the primary target since the defense will know that you will try to get the ball to your best shooter (diagram 10.1).

F also screens for the other guard, g. However, g pops back out rather than using the screen. This gives an outside safety valve. It also occupies the off ball side of the play, since we are concentrating to get the ball into C or G. If the defense is not concentrating or sagging too much on C's roll-down, F sometimes is open.

The play can be used against man or zone defense. The screens are set on the outside of the top defensive guards of a zone defense.

This play gets our guards in our fly position of our corner break. Note that G is in the corner fly guard position (see "the Fly Fast Break," Chapter 7) and g is in the point guard position. Depending on the second option, f moves away from ball side to balance the floor.

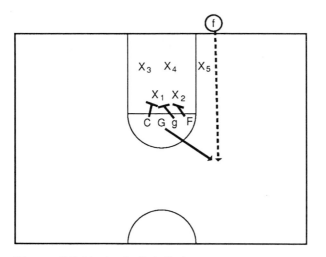

Diagram 10.2 Number 2 – Basic Option

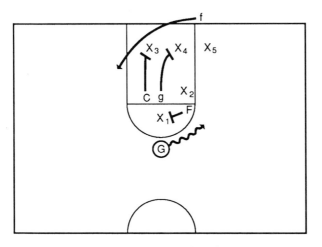

Diagram 10.3 Number 2 – X₁ Breaks Through

Number 2

Number 2 is the most exaggerated as far as a pass and cut play. The basic set-up is old, used before the concept of the Fundamental Five was developed. Diagram 10.2 shows the triple-screen option for the best shooter G to get open. The two inside players, C and g, step together and screen X_1. F screens any outside player, X_2, to his side from getting to G.

Naturally teams fight through or overplay. Diagram 10.3 shows X_1 through the defense before G can shoot. If this happens, F and G perform a Number 1. C and g screen for f to help clear the side for the 1 play.

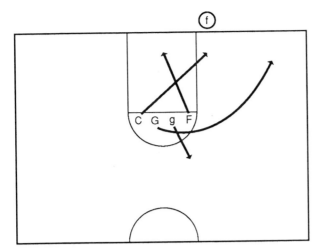

Diagram 10.4 Number 2 — "Break"

Number 2, with the "break," is called when the defense is overplaying the play enough that they may intercept f's pass to G. Diagram 10.4 shows this option. This is "an audible" called usually by G (point guard, etc.). The end players, C and F, cross and post near the blocks. G breaks to the ball-side corner. g steps back for safety valve. Note we are now in our fly fast break set-up that we can go into our ruled offense with. G is in the fly guard position, C is in the low post, F is on the weak-side block, g is out on the point guard, f, depending on the second option, will rotate to the weak side.

Number 3

Number 3 is another old play designed to hit the tallest player or best jumper with a lob pass. The first two players in line break in opposite directions while the third player steps up in the space left by the breaking players, as shown in diagram 10.5. The fourth player in line is a safety valve. If we can't get the ball to the third player or we pass to one of the breaking players, a Number 3 is run. The passer f cuts through to the opposite side. The ball is reversed and a Number 3 baseline screen is set by F. This, of course, works best against a zone defense.

Number 4

The end line play that most closely relates to the half-court offense is Number 4. The tall players are placed near the basket, and guards out front, as shown in diagram 10.6. The players closest to the passer f pick away from the ball. The center C rolls back after the switch. The guard G, who screens for g, rolls out for a safety valve. If the defense is a zone, the screens should be set on the defensive player nearest the ball.

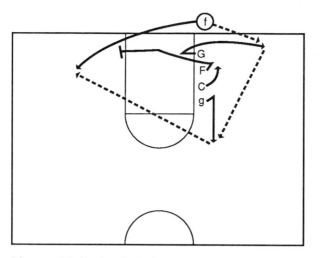

Diagram 10.5 Number 3 – Basic

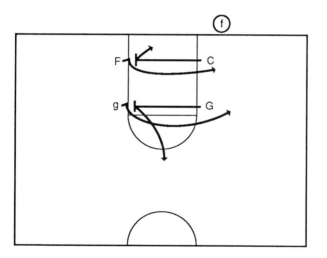

Diagram 10.6 Number 4

Number 5

Number 5 and Number 4 both have the "box look." Diagram 10.7 shows the first option of this play – when F fakes in and breaks out, G steps into the gap. If G is a good leaper, a high pass will sometimes get him a good shot. This maneuver will definitely make the defense collapse inside.

The "5 cut," somewhat exaggerated, occurs when f passes to F because the defense has collapsed on G; diagram 10.8 shows this. F reverses the ball to g, F and G screen the defensive forward on the baseline, and f shuffle cuts off the double screen.

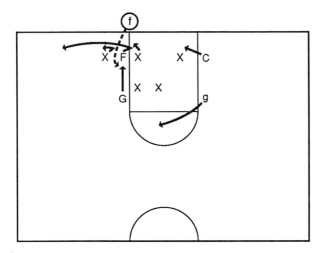

Diagram 10.7 Number 5 — High-Pass Option

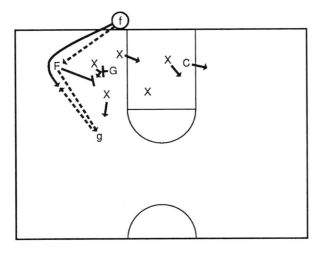

Diagram 10.8 Number 5 — Double-Screen 5 Option

If the defense overplays the double screen, then f can 5 cut off a screen set by C. If the defense overplays that much, a single screen easily frees f for a shot, as shown in diagram 10.9.

Options to End Line Out-of-Bounds Plays

Many times you will get the ball in on the initial phase, but not get a good shot. You have two options. The first is to go back out to your set offense. If you are in a ruled offense, your rules can now go into effect.

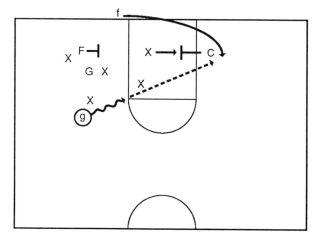

Diagram 10.9 Defense Overplays — Reverse 5

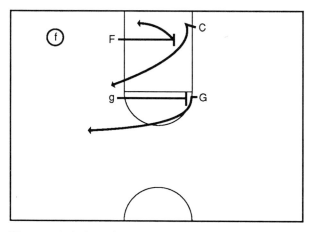

Diagram 10.10   34 End Line (4 Option)

The second option is to have a defined option for your out-of-bounds play. With the use of the Fundamental Five, you can insert various options to your out-of-bounds play, similar to your set offense. Diagram 10.10 shows f receiving the ball on a 3 out-of-bounds play. F isn't open to return the ball to him. Instead of going out to the guard to set up, F and C run a 4 play. This is designated in the week's practice previous to the game. We may run a 4 play as an option to all out-of-bounds plays before we go into offense.

Any play can be used as a second option to give your out-of-bounds plays a new look. The players are reminded by the two-digit number called by the forward f taking the ball out. In diagram 10.11, f has called "23." The coaching staff may have signaled the 2 play and planned previously to have 3 as the second

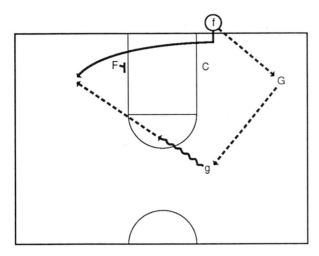

Diagram 10.11 23 End Line (3 Option)

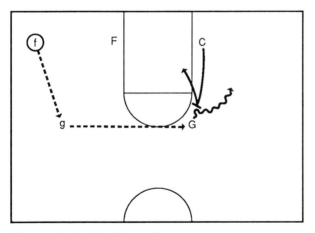

Diagram 10.12 31 End Line (1 Option)

option. f may notice that the 3 play will work and call out a "23" before the pass in. Diagram 10.11 shows a 2 play with a "break" with g receiving the ball on the pass in. If G doesn't get a shot, f steps for a return pass. G looks for C or f and then reverses the ball in a 3 play; f comes off the screen for a shot. The 3 play is used a great deal as an option since many teams zone out-of-bounds plays.

Another example of using other options is shown in diagram 10.12. This is a 31 play. After f has cut off the screen by F, the defense has matched up. Then a 1 option is run to the opposite side. When the ball can't be scored by f or passed to F, f reverses the ball, g passes to G, G anc C perform a 1 play. This option works well against teams who zone and match up quickly. All teams will match up on the ball when changing from zone to man-to-man. Number 1 works well because the defense comes from the sagging zone to man coverage.

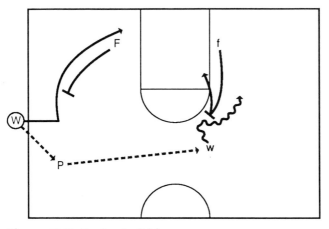

Diagram 10.13 Number 1 – Sideline

A good scouting report can designate the second option (or third). Knowledge and use of the Fundamental Five can help good teams make adjustments. Actually any of the five plays can be used as the second option. Personnel may also determine which option is best.

Sideline Out-of-Bounds Plays

We have taken some basic sideline plays along with the basic Fundamental Five to form our sideline out-of-bounds series. Actually we have started the ball in the hands of a wing, small forward or guard, depending upon where the ball is taken out and the set-up you use on half court. The diagrams 10.13 through 10.18 show a 3-2 set-up, with the same player, W, taking the ball out. In fact, we have the same player take the ball out on the end as well as the side. Coaches have to use their own philosophy whether they want the same player, guard, forward, etc. taking the ball out and adjust the offense accordingly.

Number 1

Number 1 from the sideline involves a back-screen 5 before the pick and roll as shown in diagram 10.13. Your personnel will determine how this play is run. If the defense is tight, W may be open for the alley-oop pass. This is especially true, if there isn't any switch. The timing of F's back screen is important to W being open. P can "freeze" the defense by faking to w and passing to W. When the defenses adjust to the alley-oop by sagging f's man to help, P rotates the ball quickly to w for a Number 1. The alley-oop attempt will help isolate w and f for Number 1. If there is a late adjustment and W is open when w gets the ball, we can still run the alley-oop. This is true if f's man comes back too early from help

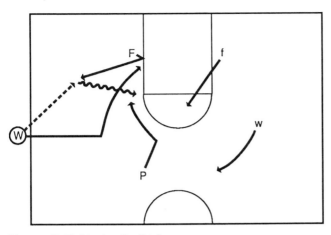

Diagram 10.14 Number 2 – Sideline

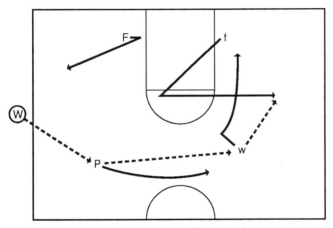

Diagram 10.15 Number 2 – F Denied, Ball Reversed

side. This can be run against man-to-man or zone; however, it is more adapted to man-to-man defense. The alley-oop option really gets the defense to sag to set up Number 1.

Number 2

Number 2 is started as if W was a wing in a 1-2-2 set-up, as shown in diagram 10.14. We don't run this play unless the ball is above the free-throw line extended. The forward F would not have any room to get open for the first pass. If F is denied, we rotate the ball through P and perform a Number 2 with w and f, as shown in diagram 10.15.

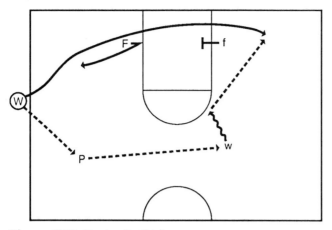

Diagram 10.16 Number 3 – Sideline

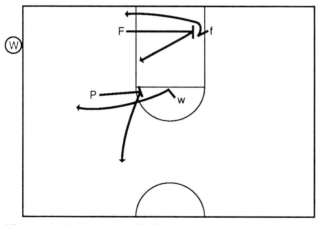

Diagram 10.17 Number 4 – Sideline

Number 3

Number 3 naturally is used most with zone defenses. Diagram 10.16 shows this play. It is just as if the wing started with the ball on the half-court offense. The ball is reversed to w; W cuts through and receives the ball.

Number 4

Number 4 is used more when the ball is below the foul line extended, as shown in diagram 10.17. It is also used when the defense is denying the ball into both guards and forwards. It is also the same as if we had performed a dribble-down to a forward position to execute a Number 4. If the defense is denying the pass, we sometimes use Number 4 before any play is started.

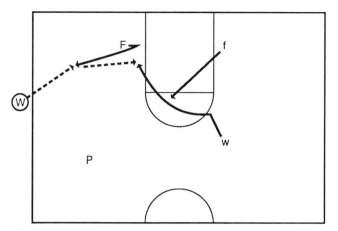

Diagram 10.18　Number 5 – Sideline

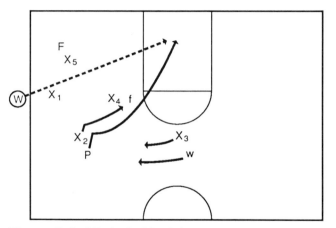

Diagram 10.19　5 Cut by P – F Denied

Number 5

Number 5 is exectued as if the ball was in the wing's hand. The 5 play is determined upon whom the ball is in-bounded to. The ball should be above the free-throw line extended for best execution. The forward F on ball side is looked for first, as shown in diagram 10.18. The opposite forward f moves to the high post to give the screen to w when f *receives* the ball; w 5 cuts off f for a pass from F.

If F is denied the pass, P then does a 5 cut off f. If f is being defended strongly, P should be open, as shown in diagram 10.19.

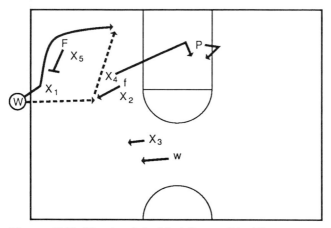

Diagram 10.20   f Receives Ball – F Back-Screens 5 for W

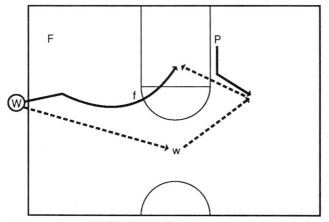

Diagram 10.21

If f's man switches on P, f should be open at the high post. Diagram 10.20 shows F back-screening 5 for W after W passes to f. P posts low to keep his man active or receive a pass from f. F is open for a good shot if F's man switches on W.

Diagram 10.21 shows that w is open if w's man sags to help on a pass to f. w then passes to P, who breaks back out to a forward position; W then 5 cuts off f or F; P passes to W for a good shot. This play is almost an offense in itself.

PRESS PLAYS

In 1973 at Madison-Grant, we had the best season in the school's history, won the Grant County Invitational and the school's only IHSAA Sectional over perennial winner, Marion. Though we were pressed many times that year, we simply gave the ball to our super guard, Ron Small, and he would get it down the floor. He could always get by two players and when they used three to stop him, we were 4 on 2. It was easy.

Many times, however, you need more than one press offense (you may not have a Ron Small) whether it be half court or full court. Again, the Fundamental Five can code your offenses so that your players can adjust to another offense quickly. Since the Fundamental Five gives five plays, it can give you five press plays. The basic movements are also similar. There are a number of press offenses. Some are better for certain defenses than others as is all the Fundamental Five.

Most teams rely on the one press offense that suits them best. We do the same, yet it certainly is good to have something in reserve or at least the knowledge that you can change easily if necessary.

What we are basically concerned with is getting the ball into play and scoring. The defense by pressing, is committing itself. The offense must try to score.

Press Philosophy

Before going into entry into the press, I feel it is necessary to explain my philosophy concerning the press. Obviously, the best way to beat pressure is to score. If the guards bring the ball up and pass to the forwards, they generally wait for the guards to come to the front court. Then the forwards give the ball to the guards and the half-court offense starts. Forwards generally don't handle the ball that well and therefore, don't take the ball to the basket when they receive the ball. If a guard gets the ball in the front court, he can take the ball to the basket and perhaps pass to a forward in scoring position. Too many times the guards are always trailing the offense because they've passed ahead to the forwards.

I, too, want the ball to be passed rather than dribbled. However, there are times that it may be necessary to put the ball on the floor — especially when the defense is matched up or in a straight man-to-man. When passing lanes are covered, the ball must be advanced by the dribble. I want my guards to do the dribbling. With some teams, I have ruled that my forwards do not put the ball on the floor except as a last resort to relieve pressure. Therefore, I need a guard in the front and back court on my press offenses. If one guard gets the ball in the back court, the other moves to the front court. Then when the ball is passed to the front court, a guard is there to move the ball to the basket.

I also feel that when you receive the ball you should face the basket. The basket is where we're trying to go. Too many times the defense "wins" when the offensive player pivots away from the basket because of the pressure. That doesn't mean you never pass to a trailer on the press. This, of course, reverses the ball while relieving the pressure. You want to face the basket so you can see a cutter going to the basket before reversing the ball.

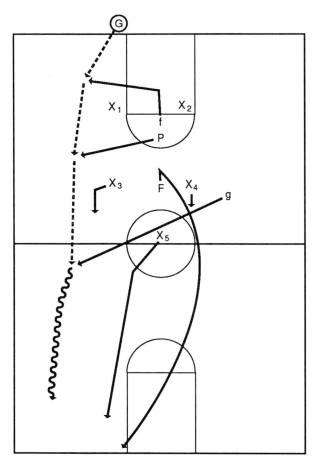

Diagram 10.22 Basic Press Offense

My press offense falls in line with my fast break theory (Chapter 7). When the first guard gets the ball, he looks for the other guard cutting diagonally across the floor. Forwards break to the middle and post. If a forward is passed to, the guards reverse their diagonals to the other side.

Diagram 10.22 shows the basic offense. You take what the defense gives you. The press shown is 2-2-1; this is without ball denial by the defense. The offense cuts into the gaps of the defense. G takes the ball out-of-bounds (similar to free-throw fast break), f breaks to the ball, P stays near the free-throw line. If the defense denies f the ball, P could also break to the ball. When f gets the ball, P cuts diagonally across the floor for the ball. F posts in the middle. P looks for g who also cuts diagonally across the floor; g drives to corner as in the "fly break." F (or f), the first forward downcourt goes to the ball-side free-throw block.

P can dribble to the middle for a middle break. P could hit g cutting across the middle for a middle break (see Chapter 7 on the Fly Fast Break).

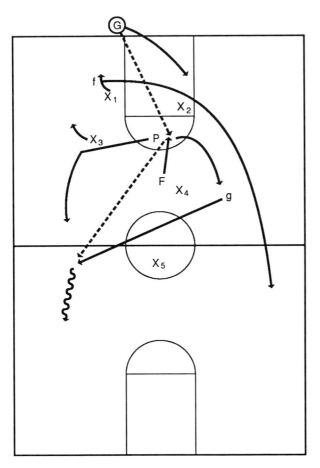

Diagram 10.23 Basic Press — Pass to F — f denied

If F is passed to in the post position, he pivots, faces the basket, and looks for g on his diagonal cut, as shown in diagram 10.23. If g is hit, the offense continues. F could hit f coming down the side and f and g could have a two-man break.

G is always back for a trailer. This is similar to our free-throw fast break offense.

If the defense is denying the pass in, it's a good idea to have two or three options to get the ball in. Obviously with the Fundamental Five, we have five. I don't necessarily use all of them, nor do I teach all of them at once. Just as you add things to your offense as the year progresses or as the opponents' force you to make changes, I add to the press offense. The longer your team is with the Fundamental Five, the easier new things are to teach.

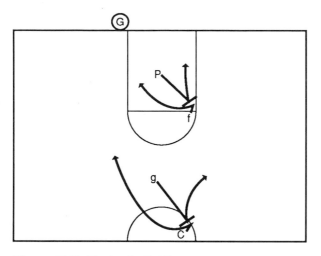

Diagram 10.24 Number 1 — End Line

Number 1 End Line

In Number 1, we place the players in a line (diagram 10.24). Again, since we are trying to score against the press with the fast break, we will diagram the plays as if we are in the fly fast break. Both guards pick for the forwards who are offset. The forwards come to the ball posting. The guards roll off the picks horizontally to ball side.

After the screen and rolls (Number 1), the players are in fly position. P is in the outlet position, g is in the fly, etc.

Obviously, if f or F is passed to, g and P run diagonal cuts as in our regular press offense. G remains as a trailer to reverse the basketball.

Number 1 Sideline

Diagram 10.25 shows the same principle involved in Number 1 end line. The forwards come to the ball in a posting manner. The guards screen and roll diagonally toward the ball. G passes the ball in and remains as trailer to reverse the basketball. A middle or corner (''fly'') break could occur after the pass in. This depends on the second pass. If the posting players are passed to, the guards may be forced to come back to the ball. Depending on where they receive the ball, the guards will basically determine a corner or middle break (see the fly fast break chapter). The forwards should look for the guards coming back or to reverse the ball back to G.

If the guards are passed to on the roll, they are moving to the basket. A two-on-one break could occur. However, depending on defensive adjustment, a corner or middle break could occur.

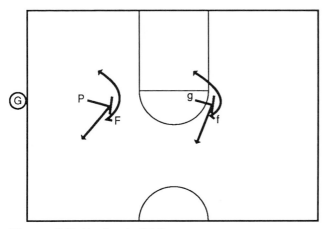

Diagram 10.25 Number 1 — Sideline

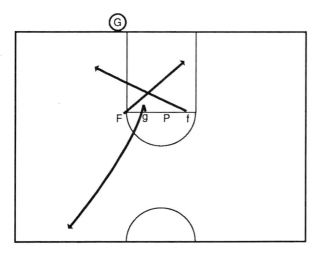

Diagram 10.26 Number 2 End Line — P Breaks to Outlet

Number 2 End Line

Number 2 is run like our Number 2 end out-of-bounds play, diagram 10.26. The players line up on the free-throw line. If the defense all face up to the offense, then G will be able to pass to g on the fly pattern. Normally this play is used just to get the ball in bounds with one or two seconds to go. G normally can run the baseline because the opponents have called time-out after a late score to come within one or two points. With three players breaking to the ball, usually one is open. The crossing of the players provide natural screens to open up the offense.

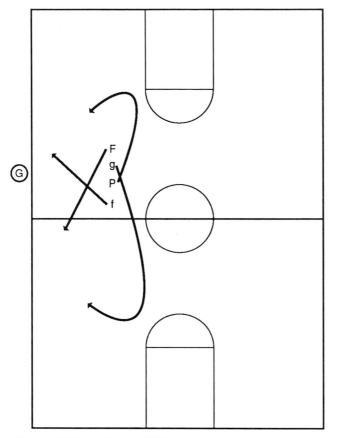

Diagram 10.27   Number 2 – Sideline

Obviously we are in a fly pattern with P moving to an outlet position and g in the fly guard position. This is not a bad change-of-pace entry. However, if used too often the defense can double up if prepared because of the number of players in the front court.

Number 2 Sideline

Number 2 from the sideline as shown in diagram 10.27, crosses both guards on the outside and both forwards inside. It is also like Number 2 end line with break. The guards g and P "button-hook" back to the ball. The defense doesn't know how far they will break before they "button-hook" back. The forwards, F and f, cross and post up. Since g is breaking toward the basket, he could be open on a fly pattern.

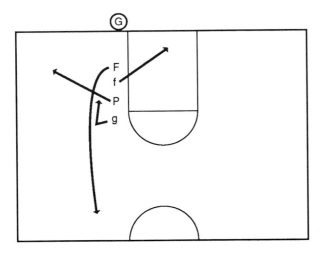

Diagram 10.28 Number 3 — End Line

Number 3 End Line

Number 3 is also similar to our end line play. The players line up in the same manner as the end line play as shown in diagram 10.28. This play works the best in extreme denial pressure. Instead of breaking to the ball, F reverses toward the offensive end, g steps out of the line and blocks F's man, F can be open for an easy basket. After F cuts, f and P cut diagonally to get open; g posts after screening for F.

If f or P gets the pass in, g cuts diagonally for the ball. We are now in the press offense as shown in diagram 10.29.

Number 3 Sideline

On sideline 3, one guard (fly guard) g lines up outside the line toward the defensive basket, as shown in diagram 10.30. As F goes around the line, g cuts between P and f, using them as natural screens. P rolls toward back court and f posts toward the ball, with g breaking as a fly guard. We are in the press offense.

Number 4 End Line Press

The 4 end line press is like the 4 sideline play. It is used to open the guards when man-to-man coverage is used. Diagram 10.31 shows the forwards F and f starting

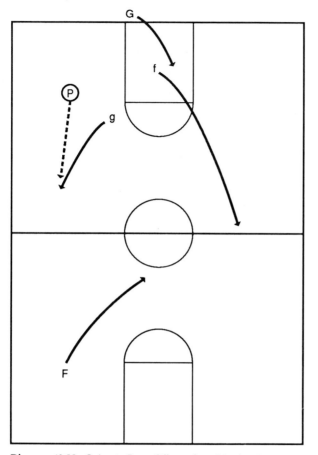

Diagram 10.29 Going to Press Offense from Number 3

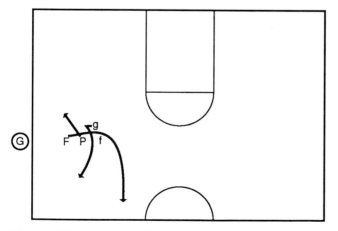

Diagram 10.30 Number 3 — Sideline

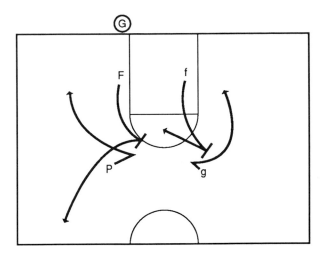

Diagram 10.31 Number 4 – End Line

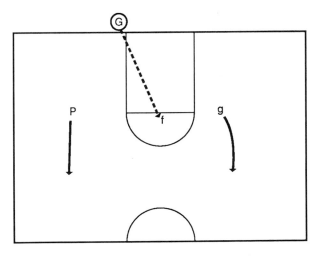

Diagram 10.32 Number 4 – Pass to f – Guards Break

near the baseline and then screening for g and P. If the forwards screen well, we are hoping the forwards' men switch. This puts a slower forward defending our guard one-on-one. Everyone clears for the guard when he gets it.

F rolls down for an easy basket if the defense doubles up on our play-making guard, P. This helps to keep the defense honest.

f rolls back to a post position after screening for g. If f is passed to, as shown in diagram 10.32, both g and P break up the sidelines for a pass from f. G is a safety valve for f.

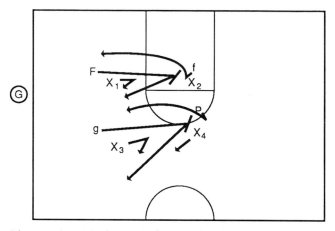

Diagram 10.33   Number 4 – Backcourt – Guards Against Defensive Forwards X₃ and X₄

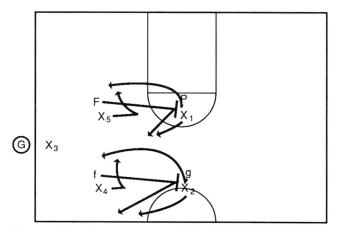

Diagram 10.34   Number 4 – Against Man-to-Man (Switch Forwards on Guards)

Number 4 Sideline Press

The placement of the players determines what this play will provide. The play is done exactly like the Number 4 sideline out-of-bounds play. If we want to get into the fly, the players should align themselves as in diagram 10.33. As P comes to the ball and g rolls to the basket, we are in the fly corner break. F and f are really safety valves until the ball is passed in, then they run the fly break. If the defense is in a guard-up match-up, 2-2-1, this align puts the offensive guards against the defensive forwards. The back man on the press will probably pick up anyone going long; therefore, whichever guard cuts down court must be at a sharp diagonal. The other guard must break to the ball.

   If the defense is straight man-to-man, the 4 play should be run like the end line press play. The guards are away from the ball as shown in diagram 10.34. The play rules are basically the same as the end line press play.

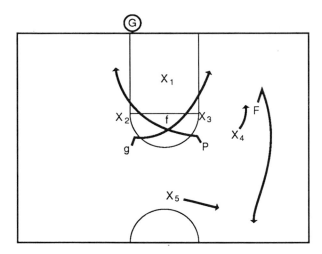

Diagram 10.35 Number 5 — Against a 1-2-1-1 Match-Up

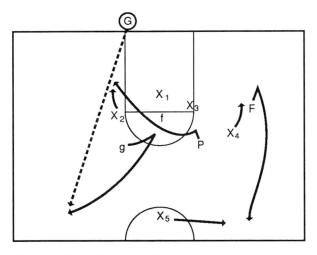

Diagram 10.36 g Fakes the 5 Cut as Defense Switches

Number 5 End Line Press

This play has similar principles to Number 4, i.e., that we want to get the ball into the hands of the guards. This is a good play against a 1-2-1-1 match-up. Diagram 10.35 shows the guards P and g using a 5 cut off forward f. Defensive player X_1 must match up with f or he is open. F, also, can force a match-up by coming to the ball before breaking downcourt to clear the area.

An option of this play to get into the fly quickly is a fake 5 cut by g. Diagram 10.36 shows P coming off the 5 cut to receive the ball; g fakes the split 5 cut and

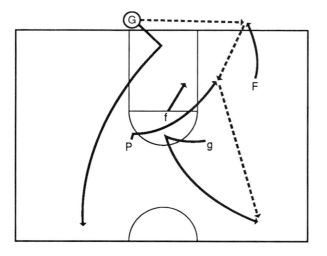

Diagram 10.37 F Steps Out-of-Bounds – P 5 Cuts

breaks to the fly position. F again comes up to the ball and then breaks down-court. Sometimes the denial is so strong that g and F "attack" the back man on the press for a long pass.

Another option of this play is to have F step out-of-bounds. Diagram 10.37 shows G passing to F out-of-bounds, P runs the 5 cut, g runs a fake 5 and breaks into the fly position, G breaks downcourt like F does on the normal 5 end line press play, f comes toward the ball after the 5 cut as a pressure valve and F assumes the role that G had after the pass in.

Number 5 Sideline Press Play

This is exactly like the end line play. Diagram 10.38 shows this play. The principles are basically the same; however, after the cut, P and g are in the fly positions. If the ball is inbound to P or g, then fly rules are in effect. The forwards go opposite ball side unless P or g run a middle break.

Development of the Box-and-One and Delay Game

Occasionally you get that super player that teams will use in a four-man zone and a chaser. The first really great individual I coached who was like that was 6'7" Craig Sullivan. Craig was at Madison-Grant High School. He later starred at the University of Richmond. Craig could shoot, handle the ball, and rebound. We really could have played him anywhere. However, it was more natural to put him in the middle of the floor. We would simply run our regular stuff around the high-post offense. We had a real "baby bull" in 6'5", 205 lb. Bob Starkey

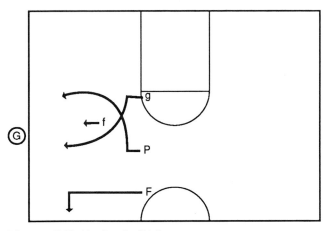

Diagram 10.38   Number 5 – Sideline

(William Penn) at one forward and 6'4'' Rick Robbins (Bemidji State) at the other forward. If the defense sagged in too much on Craig, the good-shooting guards, Ron Small and Rob Ricks, would be open. Of course, it opened up the underneath for two good-sized forwards in 1973. Talent has a way of beating any type of defense.

One of the reasons we ran the high post was that it kept Craig in rebounding position. Also, if the opponents were a little aggressive in guarding him, the officials were better able to see the fouls.

Two years later at Boonville High School, I was fortunate to have All-State guard Dan Labhart (All-American at Indiana State at Evansville). Dan was one of the best athletes I have had the fortune to coach. Boonville won the Holiday Tourney for only the third time in sixteen years, the first year I was there, beating a very good, very big Heritage Hills team. Dan had led us to the title. One year later we were again playing a very good, very big Heritage Hills team for the title. They decided Labhart was not going to beat them again.

Normally we would run a 3 play and try to free Danny for the ball in the corner. Danny not only was a good ball handler, but a very excellent shooter. If his man switched, Danny would feed inside (both against the man-to-man and zone), as shown in diagram 10.39. This is not a bad offense for a point guard box and one offense. However Heritage Hills collapsed as well we couldn't get the ball to Danny after he first passed the ball. They then manhandled him well in the corner after we reversed the ball (see diagram 10.40). The referees didn't see much after the ball reversed.

A couple of our other players, Joe Derr and Clint Greenlee were hitting somewhat to keep us in the ball game. We decided to put Danny in the middle just like Craig Sullivan of Madison-Grant. Danny was 6'1'' not 6'7''; however, he could play with his back to the basket. By being in the middle, the referees would see the handchecking and other items better.

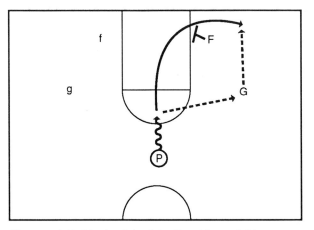

Diagram 10.39 Number 3 for Point Guard Danny Labhart

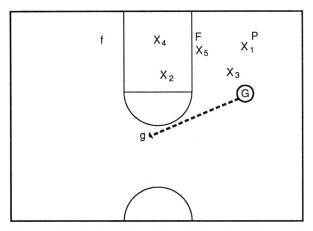

Diagram 10.40 Defense Sags — Corner ''Closed'' — Ball Reversed

Danny would move to get the ball, drive, or pass to our forwards Tony Baxton (Oakland City) and Brad Wilson. It was much the same as a regular four-corner offense. Diagrams 10.41, 10.42, and 10.43 show the ball being passed to P. P drives or passes off.

As soon as we got the lead, we decided to slow it down. They were much bigger than we were and somewhat slower. As soon as they saw we were slowing it down, they panicked somewhat and weren't sure what to do. Eventually, Danny would get the ball, and he would either penetrate, score, or drop it off.

We scored over 80 points in the ''delay'' game and won rather handily. This was the start of our use of the delay game which eventually took us to the Sweet Sixteen that year. The more teams concentrated on Danny, the more our other players scored.

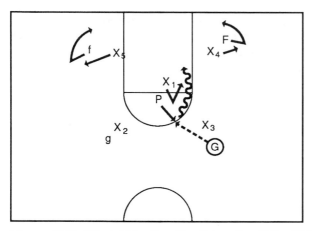

Diagram 10.41 P Posts High — Drop-Step Drive — F and f "Look" for Ball

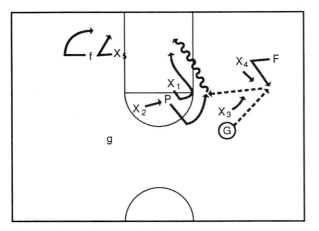

Diagram 10.42 F Passes to P — Drive

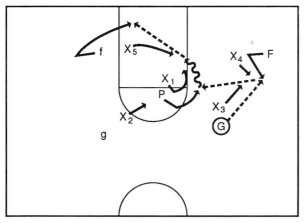

Diagram 10.43 F Passes to P — X₅ Helps — f Is Open

The box-and-one offense became our delay or controlled offensive game. Our philosophy was and still is that you want your best player to have the ball or at least concentrate your offense around your best player when you want to score. If you are delaying and can get the ball to your best player, the pressure really is put on the defense. First of all, they know the clock could be against them. Secondly, with the ball in your best player's hands, you have a better opportunity to score. Finally, the defense will put more pressure on your best players leaving others open to score.

During a delay situation, if the ball is not in the hands of your best player, it should be in the hands of good free-throw shooters. The Boonville team with Dan Labhart shot 76 percent as a team and the starting five shot over 80 percent. They made 21 to 22 free throws in the Championship game of the Regional. The best things in life are free throws.

In 1972, at Lowell High School, we had started the season running. After all, running had converted a 64 game losing streak into not only winning seasons, but championships. This 1972 team, however, was not a running team. Rensselaer beat us 85-50 the first game of the season. It was obvious who was doing the best running. It wasn't long before we knew we had to slow it down, if we were going to win. We couldn't hit from the outside, but we could shoot free throws and score from the power area.

Nelson Schoon, 6'5" (Wabash) and Chuck Shuttz, 6'3" (Lake City) were two good scorers inside. They, along with 6'0" Steve Carter, (Harvard) were good free-throw shooters.

Nelson's brother, 6'7" Rodney Schoon (University of Pittsburgh), was an excellent shooter and a member of the original group of the Fundamental Five in 1968. This group, the first Sectional winner in Lowell's history in 1968, had, overall, much better talent. Along with Shoon, there were Dave Roberts (Indiana University), John McLellan (Houston Baptist), Dan Van Deurson (Wabash), Tom Keithley (Brevard), Tom Hoffman (Harvard), Tom Johnson (Wayland Baptist), and Terry Padgett (Tri-State) — a lot of future college basketball talent. They were beaten in the State Tourney by a very strong State Championship team of Gary Roosevelt High School of Gary, Indiana. They were ahead 8-0 and should have gone to a delay game after getting the early lead. This projected the thought of using the Fundamental Five in a delay basis and having two styles of games if necessary to win the big ones. I have always felt that if we would have worked and played a delay game during the year we would have gone to the State Finals and maybe won it with that 1968 group.

In 1972, though we didn't have the talent, we *did* have the desire. We struggled with a delay or control basis using our defense. We found that with this group we wanted the ball in Steve Carter's hands so he could get it to Chuck Shuttz and Nelson Schoon inside, as in diagram 10.44. If I had the same array of talent today, I would try the same thing. No one beat us man-to-man with this play option. Teams had to switch to zone to beat us. Remember, we couldn't shoot from the outside. We ran out of a stack situation, diagrams 44 through 46.

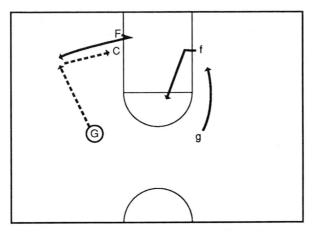

Diagram 10.44 Lowell High School ``Bread and Butter''

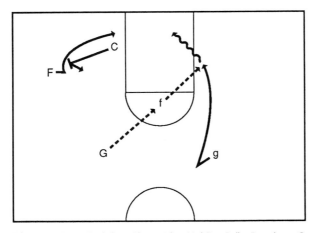

Diagram 10.45 Backdoor Play — After Holding Ball — Pass from G

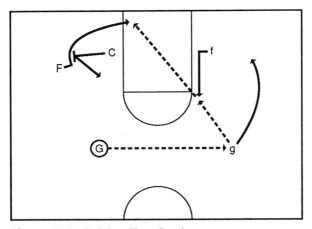

Diagram 10.46 Backdoor Play — Pass from g

Chuck Shuttz was F, Nelson Schoon, C, and Steve Carter, G. The other two players remained offside and worked the boards and were open when the defense sagged too much. As is shown in the diagrams, we were basically a one-guard front, because the other guard would break to the basket if C got the ball. However, we always tried to walk the ball down the floor. Steve Carter would hold the ball out front with an occasional pass to the other guard, 6'1" Flint Alm. Dave Cassman, a big, slow, 6'6" forward might break to the key for a backdoor 5 play (diagrams 10.45 and 10.46), but basically the ball was in Carter's hands. Steve always looked for the "bread and butter" option. He might penetrate similar to a four-corner. Rensselaer was a man-to-man team. They never switched to a zone. In the Championship game of the Sectional, even though behind much of the game, we still worked for a good shot. Steve Carter made eight free throws in the last minute of play to insure a 47-42 upset over the team that had beaten us 35 points in the opening game of the season. We would not have won without the delay game and the ability to shoot free throws.

If you can't shoot free throws, I don't think you should be in a delay game. If you look back at games that were lost in delay situations, the team that lost couldn't hit their free throws in most situations. If you can't shoot free throws, you're better off getting a good shot right away and taking it. Otherwise, the opponents are going to foul you as you are delaying. The rebounded, missed free throw, however, is just like a turnover.

The 1975-76 Boonville team didn't have the inside players the 1972 Lowell team had. As was said, we found the high-post set-up was working. However, as we approached the opportunity to go to the Sweet Sixteen, we knew we needed more than a pass to Danny Labhart and a "wheel and deal" move.

We found that many teams really went to a good man-to-man against us, denying Dan Labhart the ball in the middle. The 5 play was one that we'd always relied upon against tight man-to-man defense. Labhart would still move in and out of the post to receive the ball. However, when the ball would go to the forwards, instead of rolling Labhart to the ball as we did with Craig Sullivan, we would 5 cut the opposite guard. He would be open many times because Labhart's guard would be guarding Danny so hard that it was easy to 5 cut. The player that was guarding Danny wanted to keep him from scoring so badly he would fail to help his teammate through. The result was an easy basket as shown in diagram 10.47.

To have continuity and help eliminate help-side defense, we rotated the forward f up to replace g, as in diagram 10.48. We also found some forwards weren't used to defending the 5 cut. By having f at g's position, f could score on the 5 play as shown in diagram 10.49.

This 5 play, continuity spread offense was used for the rest of the year as end-of-game offense. By Sectional time, we had defeated every team in the Sectonal and some twice. However, before the Sectional we weren't convincing enough to the writers, because we weren't predicted to win the Sectional. Boonville hadn't won a Sectional Championship in over ten years. After the Championship, the writers still weren't convinced. One newspaper came out with the

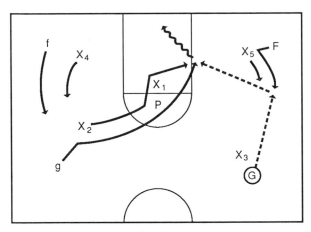

Diagram 10.47 Spread Number 5

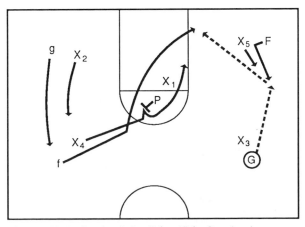

Diagram 10.48 g Not Open – Rotate

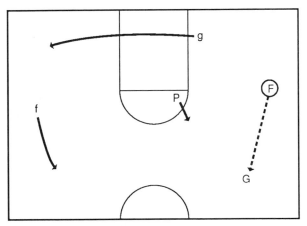

Diagram 10.49 f Makes 5 Cut (Fakes High, Goes Low)

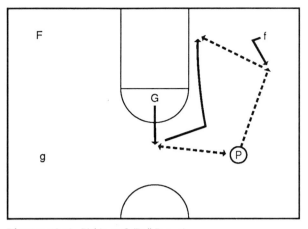

Diagram 10.50   Richie at G (Roll-Down)

statement, "Evansville Bosse will perform open-heart surgery on Boonville." This might have been true if we had let the tempo get out of hand. Boonville beat the State's third-ranked team, Boose, in the afternoon and fifth-ranked Princeton at night to advance to the Sweet Sixteen, Boonville's very first trip. The 5 spread offense gave numerous lay-ups and the title, "A Pioneer Virtuoso" by the Evansville *Courier.*

In 1980, at New Albany High School, we were fortunate to have 6'8" High School All-American Richie Johnson (University of Evansville). We ran the delay slightly differently. If Richie would come from the high post out to point (normal 4-corner set-up) and return the ball to a guard, Richie would roll down the lane after the guard passed to the forward, as in diagram 10.50. Being 6'8" and very mobile, the defense had a difficult time stopping a high pass to him. Also, Richie was an excellent passer, penetrated well and could dump the ball off to open men via the regular four-corner. Richie played guard on our regular offense.

Richie would occasionally use a 4 play for either 6'8" Dave Bennett (All-American Kentucky Wesleyan) or 6'8" Phil Benninger (Wright State), and they could break to the middle for an open shot. This worked well once the defense was spread, as in diagram 10.51. The same philosophy of the defense guarding the star worked on 4 play as it did with the 5 play. This time we went to our strengths inside rather than quickness. All five starters ended up scoring in double figures.

In 1981, Richie was gone, and no one could play the middle like he did. However, Bob Bohannon (St. Ambrose) showed the poise and control of a true 4-corner point guard. Bob could operate with the grace of the traditional four-corner. One of the reasons this worked well was the ability and the penetration of Bohannon and the scoring ability of 6'8" Dave Bennett and 6'7" Mike Hunt (St. Bonaventure) who played the forwards. Also, if Bohannon was ever in foul trouble, Mark Moody (Hardin-Simmons) could easily fill in as he played the point guard his junior year.

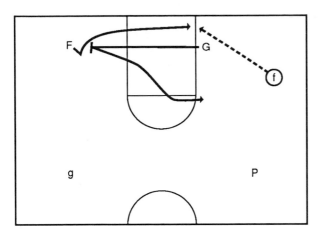

Diagram 10.51 G Cross-Screens 4 for F

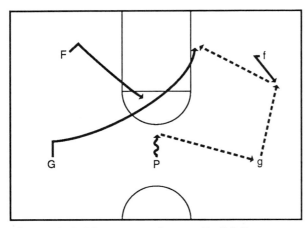

Diagram 10.52 P Penetrates — g Passes to F — G 5 Cuts

Since we played without a post man, we still felt the 5 option would work especially if Indiana All-Star Dave Bennett would flash the middle. However, we still wanted David to shoot, if he got an open fifteen-footer. After all, that was like a lay-up for him. We found that a backdoor 5 option really opened things up when our forwards would flash, as shown in diagrams 10.52 and 10.53. If we went to the post then we backdoored the same side wing and the opposite forward. If the post man shot, the wing and forward would be in position for a rebound.

If we hit the ball-side forward, the opposite wing would 5 cut, as shown in diagram 10.52. The key for either forward breaking up was the pass from P to either G or g. David Bennett wasn't quick, but he could really shoot. The threat of him getting the ball was just as effective as Richie or Danny.

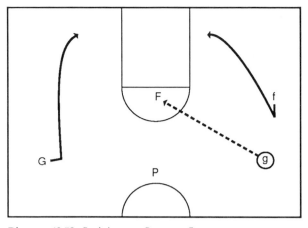

Diagram 10.53 Backdoor – g Passes to F

In 1981-82, we had a pair of All-State swing players, 6′7″ Bubby Mukes (University of Evansville) and 6′5″ Jeff Hoback (St. Louis). Mukes set the single season scoring record for New Albany by averaging 26 points a game. Jeff Hoback was quite capable at 17 points a game. They were the number one and five scorers in the area. We not only ran into the box-and-one, but triangle-and-two. Our center was a beefy, 6′5″ All-Conference football and basketball player, Troy Bensing (Western Kentucky). Our point guard, 6′0″ Tony Duffy (Mount Marty) played his role well. At the other forward was a junior 6′5″ forward, Barry Howard (St. Joseph).

Bubby Mukes scored over 30 points in his first three games his senior year. He had many of the offensive attributes of his cousin, Richie Johnson. Therefore, we put Bubby at high post. However, Bubby was a much better high school shooter than Richie. When a box-and-one was employed by the defense, we used a roll-down 5 play. Bubby, at G, would roll to low post when G would pass to F, as shown in diagram 10.54. If we could pass to Bubby in the high post, we generally had a score.

The defense would generally collapse to prevent the low-post option. We then would have F pass back to G and screen for Bubby (G), as shown in diagram 10.55. Bubby (G) could take the shot or return the pass to the forward in the low post. This is an "ins and outs" procedure.

What the defense did with their guards determined where we played Jeff Hoback, our other good shooter. If the ball-side guard sagged to help on the low post, then we played Jeff at g, as shown in diagram 10.56. When defensive guard X_1 collapsed to help, Jeff was open for the jump shot.

Most of the time we played Jeff at g. If the defense collapsed completely, as shown in diagram 10.57, then the ball would be rotated to Jeff for a medium-range jumper. Jeff was instructed to step in when the defense sagged, so he would get a better shot.

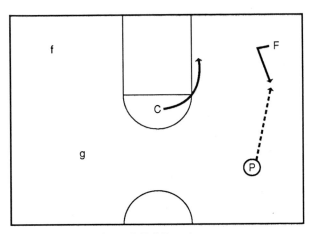

Diagram 10.54 Bubby at G (Roll-Down)

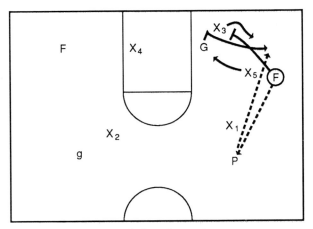

Diagram 10.55 F Pass-Back Cross-Screen 4

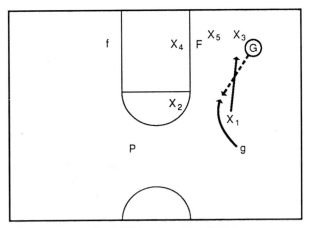

Diagram 10.56 Jeff — Ball Side — Steps in as X_1 Helps

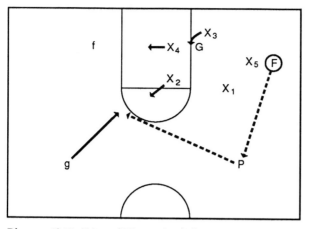

Diagram 10.57 ''Normal'' Reversal to Jeff

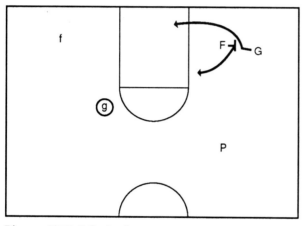

Diagram 10.58 5 Cut by G

At the same time the ball was reversed to Jeff at g, Bubby (G) would 5 cut off F back to the post area, as shown in diagram 10.58. Even if Jeff shot, Bubby was moving to the basket for the offensive rebound. This put Bubby back in the middle and we were ready to start the offense again. Bubby had the option of going backdoor or over the top.

Triangle-and-Two Options

If the defense played a triangle-and-two, we still started the offense with the box-and-one sequence. Since the defense is not sagging on Jeff, the middle is open for the opposite forward to flash, as shown in diagram 10.59. When f received

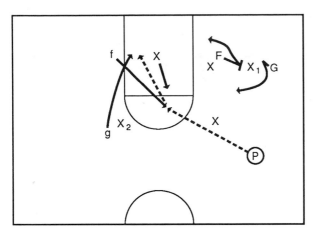

Diagram 10.59 Triangle-and-Two z — Backdoor g or F

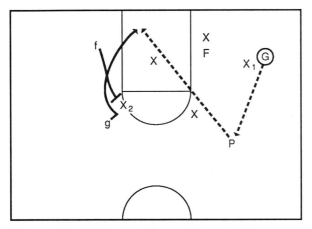

Diagram 10.60 Back-Screen 5 Against Triangle-and-Two

the ball, Jeff (g) would backdoor for the basket. Since X_2, the player guarding Jeff in the triangle-and-two, was usually trying to deny Jeff the ball, the play worked even better. If the defense overreacted to Jeff's backdoor cut, Bubby, coming off F's screen, was more likely to be open. This option got Troy Bensing, F, some easy baskets as the defense overreacted to Jeff's and Bubby's cuts.

Another option that worked well was the backdoor-screen 5, as shown in diagram 10.60. The sagging to Bubby's side, especially when he had the ball in the corner, helped this play work.

If the defense was sagging, but recovering to Jeff when the ball was reversed, Number 1 was used as an option to get Jeff a good shot. The defense wasn't denying Jeff the ball. Therefore, we could reverse it to him. Then the

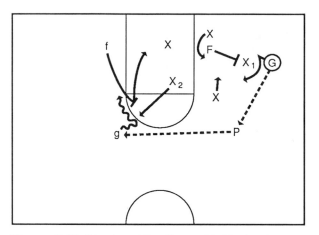

Diagram 10.61 Triangle-and-Two Reversed to Number 1

defense was on him. Barry Howard, at f, would come up to Number 1 with Jeff, as shown in diagram 10.61. Note that Bubby, at G, comes over the top to the middle to occupy the now weak-side defense.

By keeping the two best players on opposite sides of the floor, the defense has difficulty helping. When the defense has helped by sagging on one side, the other side gives the offense room to operate.

The development of delay, box-and-one, and triangle-and-two offenses must be done with the best of your personnel. Your regular offense may be able to get the job done. However, sometimes adjustments need to be made. The teams trained in the Fundamental Five will be better able to make these adjustments. There are many offensive set-ups, but they should be designed for your personnel. As was shown, a certain set-up was chosen to put big, tall stars like Craig Sullivan or Richie Johnson in position for them to receive the ball. A good, slick guard can be used in the four corners if you have him. When you make adjustments, the Fundamental Five comes into play.

Index